D1713188

Partiality and Impartiality

Partiality and Impartiality

Morality, Special Relationships, and the Wider World

BJ
1533
F2 P37
2010
WEB

Edited by

Brian Feltham and John Cottingham

OXFORD
UNIVERSITY PRESS

OXFORD
UNIVERSITY PRESS

Great Clarendon Street, Oxford OX2 6DP

Oxford University Press is a department of the University of Oxford.
It furthers the University's objective of excellence in research, scholarship,
and education by publishing worldwide in

Oxford New York

Auckland Cape Town Dar es Salaam Hong Kong Karachi
Kuala Lumpur Madrid Melbourne Mexico City Nairobi
New Delhi Shanghai Taipei Toronto

With offices in

Argentina Austria Brazil Chile Czech Republic France Greece
Guatemala Hungary Italy Japan Poland Portugal Singapore
South Korea Switzerland Thailand Turkey Ukraine Vietnam

Oxford is a registered trade mark of Oxford University Press
in the UK and in certain other countries

Published in the United States
by Oxford University Press Inc., New York

© the several contributors 2010

The moral rights of the author have been asserted
Database right Oxford University Press (maker)

First published 2010

All rights reserved. No part of this publication may be reproduced,
stored in a retrieval system, or transmitted, in any form or by any means,
without the prior permission in writing of Oxford University Press,
or as expressly permitted by law, or under terms agreed with the appropriate
reprographics rights organization. Enquiries concerning reproduction
outside the scope of the above should be sent to the Rights Department,
Oxford University Press, at the address above

You must not circulate this book in any other binding or cover
and you must impose the same condition on any acquirer

British Library Cataloguing in Publication Data

Data available

Library of Congress Cataloging in Publication Data

Data available

Typeset by Laserwords Private Limited, Chennai, India
Printed in Great Britain
on acid-free paper by
MPG Books Group, Bodmin and King's Lynn

ISBN 978-0-19-957995-2

1 3 5 7 9 10 8 6 4 2

Contents

Acknowledgments

All these papers are published for the first time in this collection,[1] and all of them were presented as part of a three-year research project on 'Impartiality and Partiality in Ethics', which ran from 2005 to 2008 at the University of Reading and was sponsored by the United Kingdom's Arts and Humanities Research Council. The thanks of the editors go to everyone who participated in this project, whether presenting a paper or attending one of the three annual conferences or the series of seminars spread over the three years. Thirty-six papers were presented in all, and they were impressive not only for their quality but also for the great variety of questions addressed and approaches explored. (For reasons of space, it has been possible to include only a selection of the papers here, but a second volume covering other aspects of the subject is in preparation.) The project committee comprised John Cottingham (Director), Jonathan Dancy, Brian Feltham (Co-ordinator and Post-Doctoral Fellow), Brad Hooker, David Oderberg, Philip Stratton-Lake (Assistant Director), and (for the first year) Andrew Williams. Also associated with the project as Doctoral Assistant was Ian Folland, to whom special gratitude is due for all his assistance in the coordination of the project. Special thanks are also owed to the graduate students of the Department of Philosophy at the University of Reading during those three years. Their sustained and imaginative engagement with the issues explored greatly enhanced the work of the project.

[1] Samuel Scheffler's paper is also being simultaneously published in a collection of his own papers, *Equality and Tradition* (New York: Oxford University Press, 2010); it is printed here by agreement with the publisher.

Notes on Contributors

John Cottingham is Professor Emeritus of Philosophy at the University of Reading, Professorial Research Fellow at Heythrop College, University of London, and an honorary fellow of St John's College, Oxford. His books include *Philosophy and the Good Life* (1998), *On the Meaning of Life* (2003), *The Spiritual Dimension* (2005), *Cartesian Reflections* (2008), and *Why Believe?* (2009). *The Moral Life*, a Festschrift on his work in ethics, moral psychology, and philosophy of religion, appeared in 2008. He is co-translator of *The Philosophical Writings of Descartes* and his edited collections include *Western Philosophy* 2nd edn, 2007). He is Editor of the journal *Ratio*.

Stephen Darwall is the Andrew Downey Orrick Professor of Philosophy at Yale University. He has written broadly on the history and foundations of ethics, and his books include: *Impartial Reason, The British Moralists and the Internal 'Ought': 1640–1740, Philosophical Ethics, Welfare and Rational Care,* and, most recently, *The Second-Person Standpoint: Morality, Respect, and Accountability.* He has edited a number of anthologies in normative and metaethics and is, with David Velleman, a founding editor of *Philosophers' Imprint.*

David Estlund is Lombardo Family Professor of Humanities, in the departments of Philosophy and Political Science at Brown University, where he has been teaching since 1991. He taught previously at University of California, Irvine, and held fellowships at Harvard University and Australian National University. He is the recipient of fellowship support from the American Council of Learned Societies, and the National Endowment for the Humanities. He edited the collections, *Sex, Preference and Family* (with Martha Nussbaum, Oxford University Press 1997), *Democracy* (Blackwell Publishing 2001), and is the author of *Democratic Authority: A Philosophical Framework* (Princeton University Press 2008).

Brian Feltham lectures in political theory at the School of Politics and International Relations of the University of Reading. His principle areas of research are the scope for and significance of political consensus, partiality and impartiality, practical reason and value theory. His publications include the edited volume *Justice, Equality and Constructivism: Essays on G. A. Cohen's Rescuing Justice and Equality* (Wiley Blackwell, 2009).

Gerald F. Gaus is James E. Rogers Professor of Philosophy at the University of Arizona. His essay 'On Justifying the Moral Rights of the Moderns' won the 2009 American Philosophical Association's Kavka award. Among his books are *On Philosophy, Politics and Economics* (Wadsworth-Thomson, 2008), *Justificatory Liberalism* (Oxford, 1996), and *Value and Justification* (Cambridge, 1990). His most recent book is *The Order of Public Reason: A Theory of Freedom and Morality in a Diverse and Bounded World* (Cambridge, 2010) and, with Julian Lamont, *Economic Justice* (Blackwell, forthcoming). With Fred D'Agostino, he is currently editing the *Routledge Companion to Social and Political Philosophy*.

Maximilian de Gaynesford is Professor of Philosophy at the University of Reading; he was formerly Fellow and Tutor in Philosophy at Lincoln College Oxford. He is the author of 'I: The Meaning of the First Person Term' (OUP, 2006), 'Hilary Putnam' (2006), 'John McDowell' (2004), and of a number of papers, mainly in the philosophy of mind and language.

Brad Hooker is Professor of Philosophy at the University of Reading and is author of *Ideal Code, Real World* (OUP, 2000) and many articles on normative ethics. He is currently working on a book on fairness.

Niko Kolodny is Associate Professor of Philosophy at the University of California, Berkeley. He has held positions at Harvard University and the Research School of Social Sciences at the Australian National University. His main interests are in moral and political philosophy.

Michael Ridge is Professor of Moral Philosophy at the University of Edinburgh. His main research interests presently are in meta-ethics, and in that context he is developing and defending a new form of expressivism which he calls 'Ecumenical Expressivism.'

Samuel Scheffler is University Professor in the Department of Philosophy at New York University. He is the author of *The Rejection of Conse-quentialism, Human Morality, Boundaries and Allegiances*, and *Equality and Tradition*.

Sarah Stroud is Associate Professor of Philosophy at McGill University in Montreal, Canada. Her work ranges widely across foundational issues in moral philosophy and moral psychology. She has published articles in *Ethics, Philosophy & Public Affairs, Philosophy and Phenomenological Research, Philosophical*

Studies, and the *Stanford Encyclopedia of Philosophy*, and she was Co-editor of *Weakness of Will and Practical Irrationality* (Clarendon Press, 2003). She is currently an executive editor of the *Canadian Journal of Philosophy* and one of two associate editors of the *International Encyclopedia of Ethics*, to appear in 2012.

Introduction: Partiality and Impartiality in Ethics*

BRIAN FELTHAM

'When I was alive and had a human heart,' answered the statue, 'I did not know what tears were, for I lived in the Palace of Sans-Souci, where sorrow is not allowed to enter. . . . And now that I am dead they have set me up here so high that I can see all the ugliness and all the misery of my city, and though my heart is made of lead yet I cannot chose but weep.'

. . . Then they melted the statue in a furnace, and the Mayor held a meeting of the corporation to decide what was to be done with the metal. 'We must have another statue, of course,' he said, 'and it shall be a statue of myself.'

'Of myself,' said each of the Town Councillors, and they quarrelled. When I last heard of them, they were quarrelling still.

Oscar Wilde, *The Happy Prince*

1. Demandingness, Partiality, and Impartiality

What is owed to others that I may not keep for myself? What may I keep for myself, even when others are in need? What might be owed to myself that I may not give to others? May I lavish expensive gifts of time, money, and trinkets upon my friends while a stranger goes without a roof or a meal? These transparently moral questions may immediately invite knee-jerk moralistic answers. Any attempt to treat myself with special preference seems shabby to say the least. To whom do I matter more than a stranger? To myself and my

---

* Special thanks to John Cottingham, co-editor of this volume, for his substantial advice on the content and style of this Introduction.

friends perhaps. But I could hardly use this special concern when pleading with a third party for special privileges. And morality, it may be thought, makes us all third parties to our own interests. In other words, morality is by its nature impartial, so that when I consider the question of what morally I ought to do, there can be no special place and precedence for myself and my loved ones, my projects and my preferences.

This is a natural enough first reaction when considering the issue in the abstract, but it quickly comes into conflict with our ordinary moral convictions and practices. Take a person with noble moral ambitions. This person is a reasonably affluent Westerner, aware of the great disparities of wealth and well-being in the world. We might say to her: 'You can spare a little money, can't you, to help those in great need?' And she will agree. 'Oh, but just a little more—and you would still be better off than nearly everyone else on the planet.' And so she pays a little more. 'But, still, you couldn't really describe yourself as needy, even now, could you? How about giving a little more?' And so on, until she is no better off than the very worst-off person in the world.[1] This would be to give more than nearly all of us would seriously countenance in our own lives. If we can't live up to a demanding view of morality, then either we must face our own hypocrisy, or revise our moral judgements.

This is the problem of demandingness. It is a problem we all face in our ordinary moral lives; and it is one that comes to us prior to intellectual reflection and categorization, not because of them. I feel the pull of the interests of people I meet, or hear about, and I feel the importance of pursuing my own projects and relationships. These inclinations are felt independently of any neat division of interests into 'Mine' and 'Other' columns. And there are many other ways of categorising these practical concerns—crucially, the problem of demandingness may not be a contest between self-interest and altruism.[2] Imagine a parent who consistently favours the world's most needy over the relatively less urgent concerns of his own children. Imagine also that this favouring is shown not just in financial contributions but also in time

---

[1] Shelly Kagan and Peter Singer present demanding accounts of morality along these lines. See Peter Singer, 'Famine, Affluence and Morality', *Philosophy & Public Affairs* 1 (Spring 1972), pp. 229–43; and Shelly Kagan, *The Limits of Morality* (New York: Oxford University Press, 1989). These demands might not seem so bad if everyone freely redistributed their wealth until a point of equality was reached that was of a level high enough to leave no one badly off. But since not everyone will comply, this leaves the conscientious person with a heavy burden. Mike Ridge addresses this issue in his contribution to the present volume (Chapter 9).

[2] Or egoism versus universal moral concern. This kind of theoretical division is exemplified strongly in Henry Sidgwick, *The Methods of Ethics*, 7th edn [1907] (Chicago, IL: University of Chicago Press, 1962)—see esp. the 'Concluding Chapter'; and more recently in Thomas Nagel, *The Possibility of Altruism* (Princeton, NJ: Princeton University Press, 1978).

and emotional engagement. Those children might very reasonably resent this ordering of their parent's priorities.[3] Rather than being a conflict of morality and prudence (narrowly construed), this can be seen as a problem of morality on all sides—what is owed to one's children may be special, different, and *greater* than what is owed to humanity in general. If the paradigmatic puzzle is that impartial morality can seem too demanding, the deeper question may well be how we are to understand and delineate the moral demands that are partial.

With social and political morality in mind, Thomas Nagel writes:

> My belief is not just that all social and political arrangements so far devised are unsatisfactory. That might be due to the failure of all actual systems to realize an ideal that we should all recognize as correct. But there is a deeper problem—not merely practical, but theoretical: We do not yet possess an acceptable political ideal, for reasons which belong to moral and political philosophy.[4]

Nagel goes on to propose his own line of investigation, which will start from a 'conviction that ethics, and ethical bases of political theory, have to be understood as arising from a division in each individual between two standpoints, the personal and impersonal'.[5] These different standpoints are said to yield (or reveal) different reasons for action, 'agent-relative' and 'agent-neutral'.[6] These labels, whether applied to reasons, principles, values, or relationships, are often used as co-extensive, if not synonymous, with 'partial' and 'impartial', respectively. Whether or not this practice is sound, or useful, it is worth remarking that there is no single agreed definition of these technical terms. Very roughly, though, the underlying idea is something like this: I have an agent-relative reason for action if my having that reason depends on something's being mine; while reasons that don't depend on such a relationship are agent-neutral. For example, I might have an agent-relative reason to care for the baby because she is *my* daughter; and no doubt I would also have an agent-neutral reason to care for her because she is an infant in need (and I can supply that need). But it is the former, agent-relative, reason that would typically be seen as settling the question of whether I or some competent stranger should care for her.

---

[3] As happens in the case of Mrs Jellyby in Charles Dickens's *Bleak House* [1852–3], although Mrs Jellyby might be better described not as impartial, but as partial to the plight of distant strangers. Nevertheless, her case is instructive when thinking of impartiality as a virtue; a universal love of humankind might be unnerving rather than redeeming in a person who can't feel any more personal affection for others.

[4] Thomas Nagel, *Equality and Partiality* (New York: Oxford University Press, 1991), p. 3.

[5] *Ibid.* In this collection, Sarah Stroud (Chapter 6) explicitly addresses the difficulties of working out the significance of granting the importance of the personal point of view.

[6] Thomas Nagel, *The View from Nowhere* (New York: Oxford University Press, 1986), esp. pp. 152–3; Nagel's phrasing of the distinction is owed to Derek Parfit, *Reasons and Persons* (Oxford: Oxford University Press, 1984), p. 143.

It is important to notice that we started with a moral problem of demandingness. This is not a theoretical problem in any usual sense—it is a practical
question, framed in terms of what to do. Nagel suggests that we cannot solve
this practical problem without engaging in some ethical theory. That is true to
some extent: theory and practice must overlap in refining the question (What
should/ought/must I do? What would be good to do?) and in ordering the
considerations that bear upon it. Various subsidiary questions will arise; an
example important for Nagel is the division of responsibility between the state
and its citizens. Who should feed the starving? I, acting independently, or my
government as my moral representative?[7] And it is not unreasonable to suppose
that the deeper our reflections go, the more philosophical they will become.
And so, whether professional philosophers or simply reflective moral agents,
we begin to engage in a theoretical enterprise.[8]

Demandingness is by no means the only route into reflections on impartiality
and partiality. For example, we might start with the perennial question of
ancient ethics: How may I live well?[9] This can lead to a concern with
the role of personal attachments in a good life, and so with theoretical
questions regarding the nature of partiality. Is it the value of the thing (project,
relationship, person) that I am partial to that gives it special practical importance
for me, or is it the value of my special attachment that gives distinctive value
to that thing for me? Is value, in some sense, partial? This is not quite the
same as asking whether it is subjective—since I may subjectively care about
impersonal matters, such as the position of the stars, and impartial matters,
such as the condition of the distant poor (and these could also, but needn't, be
matters within the domain of my own partialistic concern—as they might be
if I were an astronomer, or an aid worker). Impartiality begins to figure when
I consider how I should respond to the good of others to whom I have no
close affiliation.[10]

---

[7] David Estlund's contribution to this volume (Chapter 10) explores a way in which we can,
potentially through the state, affect the personal moral demands faced by others by offering to match
any contribution they make to help the needy, thus increasing the overall good that would be done.

[8] Samuel Scheffler's contribution in this collection (Chapter 5) presents such a theoretical perspective. He argues that a moral view that takes proper account of human valuing will leave space for
certain kinds of 'reasons of partiality' in the face of impartial moral demands. He goes on to explore the
prospect that these impartial demands might themselves be understood in terms of the same normative
structure that gives rise to partial reasons.

[9] See Julia Annas, The Morality of Happiness (Oxford: Oxford University Press, 1993), p. 27. Annas
offers a variety of related questions, such as 'What should my life be like?', to indicate the typical
starting point for ethical reflection in the ancient world.

[10] The Stoics understood something like this move to impartiality in terms of increasing the circle of
me and mine outwards from oneself and one's loved ones, to one's city, one's country, and so on until
it includes everyone (as described by M. M. McCabe in her 'The Stoic Sage in the Original Position',
typescript).

The topic of impartiality and partiality is made up of very different kinds of questions, and one can take an interest in some but not in others. In this collection, Brad Hooker and John Cottingham are in approximate agreement about the priority we should give to the interests of strangers. But Hooker is concerned to outline the idea of an impartial moral theory that sets all personal deliberations against a background of assessment of conduct in general, while Cottingham's approach is to trace how a concern for others arises out of the moral life of each individual. Or again, R. M. de Gaynesford's contribution focuses on understanding the role of the first person in moral deliberation, investigating in particular the role that something's being mine has to play. These reflections could serve as a shared point of reference for those who disagree more substantively. The problem of demandingness, then, is not identical to the topic of impartiality and partiality. But it is the paradigmatic route into meditations on impartiality and partiality and, even more so, it is the paradigmatic moral/ethical/practical question that gives that theoretical topic its great interest for us.[11]

2. Plato, Aristotle, and Aquinas

In order to get a better picture of the topic, and the range of positions adopted, it will help to consider a number of key thinkers who have helped shape the discussion in the Western tradition. This task will occupy most of the remainder of this Introduction.

To begin somewhere near the beginning, Plato and Aristotle each offered views that are often regarded as paradigmatic of their kind, with Plato's approach being impartial in structure, while Aristotle's seems to allow more space for partiality and self-preference. It is no accident that in Plato's vision of the ideal society the use of words like 'my' and 'mine', inasmuch as they mark the separateness of individuals with distinct interests, is as far as possible to be eliminated;[12] Aristotle, by contrast, devotes a great deal of his ethics to the phenomenon of personal friendship, where a certain (necessarily limited) number of people are the objects of my special concern.[13]

---

[11] For more on demandingness specifically, see Tim Chappell (ed.), *The Problem of Moral Demandingness* (Basingstoke: Palgrave Macmillan, 2009).

[12] *Republic* [375 BC], 462. References for Plato are given by page numbers of the Stephanus edition of his complete works (Geneva, 1578), which are standardly used in all editions and translations.

[13] *Nicomachean Ethics* [c. 325 BC], bk VIII. But see Stephen Darwall's contribution to this volume (Chapter 7) for a defence of the view that, in order to make sense of ethical partial relations (such as friendships), we must draw on the idea that individuals have an impartial, equal, ethical standing.

At a more abstract level, the ethical systems of Plato and Aristotle have certain common features, both focusing on well-being (or *eudaimonia*), and being concerned to outline the nature of a well-lived life. To this extent, moreover, they share a teleological approach, with the goal of a good life being a focal point of their ethical reflections. However, there are also major differences. Plato's ethics is impartial to the extent that it begins outside of the individual person, asking what is good, what is just, as such. Value descends, as it were, from above; and we must make our lives fit its precepts if we are to live well. Aristotle, by contrast, can be seen as working from below, beginning with the individual human being: I take stock of the kind of being that I am (rational and social) and the circumstances in which I find myself (a certain kind of political society, or *polis*), before uncovering the personality traits and external goods (leisure, wealth, friendship, and freedom)[14] that make for a life I can think well of. Certainly, this contrast can be overdrawn. For Plato, I should live in a way that is good for me, given the kind of being that I am—and this is not so different from Aristotle's concern with human nature. And for Aristotle, the person best able to judge what would be a good life is a good person; what makes my life go well is not settled by any old set of priorities and attachments that I may happen to have. Nevertheless, there is a clear difference of focus. Aristotle is more concerned to begin with what we are, and Plato to focus on what is independently good. A little more detail will make the contrast clearer.

For Plato, the ordinary world of sense perception is uncertain and approximate. It is, to be sure, the world in which we make our lives and interact with other people. But, in order to make any sense of it, we have to appeal to certain set types, or forms. A round table is understood to be round because it partakes of the form of roundness. And while the table is round only approximately and variably (it may be chipped, it may warp, and at the molecular level it is far from regular), the form of roundness is perfect and invariable.[15] This form exists eternally and independently of the existence of any particular

---

Niko Kolodny's contribution (Chapter 8), by contrast, seeks to understand which partial relationships, including friendships, are important without resorting to more basic impartial reasons.

[14] For components of the good life other than virtue, see Aristotle, *Nicomachean Ethics*: 1099a–b (external good generally), 1153b (physical advantages and good fortune), 1177b5ff (leisure); and in general on the life of contemplation, see 1178b–1179a. (Note: references to Aristotle are given by 'Bekker numbers', which are standardly used in all editions and translations—these are the pages, columns (a or b), and sometimes line numbers also, of Immanuel Bekker (ed.), *Aristotelis Opera* (Berlin, 1831).)

[15] For a general outline of Plato's theory of forms and his account of value, see his discussion of the comparison of the sun to the form of the good, the 'divided line' that illustrates kinds of reality and what can be known, and the simile of the cave. *Republic*, bks VI and VII up to 521b.

round objects. The same is true, also, of values and virtues. There is a form of courage, of honesty, and so on. And all of these are integrated into the form of justice—the just person has all the virtues. Indeed, for Plato, virtue is simply the knowledge of these forms. There is also a special form, the form of the good, by which all things may be judged according their kinds. To judge that a particular object is a human being, we must ask ourselves whether it partakes of the form of 'human being' in general, and this involves asking to what extent it approximates the perfection of that form. In other words, to be a human being is to approximate the form of 'human being' well. And likewise, to live well is to approximate the form of justice well.[16] Thus the form of the good is the measure of all things.[17] The nature of value is, in this way, set independently and prior to any particular goals, projects, relationships or interests that a person might have. To put it in terms of practical reasoning, this is to say that reason itself is impartial: how a person should live, and what she should aim at, is set externally to the particular agent.[18]

Plato's view is impartial not only in its formal structure but also in its substantive content. A person wise enough to know what is just will love philosophical contemplation, but is expected to take their turn running society for the benefit of everyone. They are also to be limited in respect of personal attachments and property, as such things may be distracting.[19] These people make up the rulers, or guardians, of the city (although there is also a subdivision, the auxiliaries, who do not issue orders so much as implement them); there is also a class of ordinary people, the producers of goods, led more by their appetites than by anything nobler, and these people are to be ruled over and controlled in the interests of society as a whole.[20] An individual person is to be deemed just when they are internally well ordered, with their appetites and high spirits controlled by their knowledge of the good. That is to say, the wise and virtuous are ruled by what is impartially good. A society, too, is just

[16] Perfection is too much to be asked of anyone, but it is by approximation to the ideal case that we judge someone to be just. See Plato, *Republic*, 472b–c. Compare G. A. Cohen's more recent arguments along similar lines: that an account of justice stands outside of pragmatism and other compromise. See Cohen, *Rescuing Justice and Equality* (Cambridge, MA: Harvard University Press, 2008).

[17] By contrast, Protagoras suggested that 'Man is the measure of all things' (H. A. Diels, ed., revised Walther Kranz, *Die Fragmente der Vorsokratiker* (Berlin, 1952), 80B1 DK), and see also Plato's *Theaetetus*, 152a. For Plato, human beings at best can come to know what is already and independently true, good, beautiful.

[18] For a key discussion of the internality and externality of reason (and reasons), albeit with a Humean focus, see Bernard Williams, 'Internal and external reasons', in Ross Harrison (ed.), *Rational Action* (Cambridge: Cambridge University Press, 1980), reprinted in Williams, *Moral Luck* (Cambridge: Cambridge University Press, 1981), pp. 101–13.

[19] *Republic*, 416d–417b.

[20] *Republic*, 412b–415d. For a concise description of the relations of these different classes, see Julia Annas, *An Introduction to Plato's Republic* (Oxford: Oxford University Press, 1981), pp. 172–4.

when it is well ordered—ruled by the wise, controlled by the spirited, with those driven by baser appetites constrained within the system. This society, so ordered, will be a good one. But the question at this point is not, is it good for me, or us, or every each individual; but whether it partakes of the eternal form of justice. A good society is good for those in it—Plato is clear on this; but there is not a prior and separate question of what is good for us independent of facts about what is good and just. And these are matters that are independent of the projects and commitments of any individual or group.

To some extent this outline risks caricature. There is certainly some space in Plato for individuals to pursue their own interests, and a just life is understood to be a good life for the person who lives it.[21] The philosopher rulers get to spend time doing what they love—namely, philosophy. And the ordinary citizens get to trade, to pursue wealth and property (indeed, they are the only ones to be permitted private wealth and property), albeit within the broader structure of the state. And these 'producers' have only a limited direct concern with pursuing justice, since they aren't equal to the task.[22] But this is a poor sort of acknowledgement of the value and place of partiality and self-preference: only those incapable of anything better can be self-interested, and only to the extent that their rulers allow; and while those who know the impartial good get to do precisely what they want (to contemplate and pursue the good), this is strictly in accordance with the demands of impartial justice.[23] Plato's morality is certainly very demanding. But more importantly, it is paradigmatically impartial; and any partiality must be justified in line with the model of society deemed to be just by impartial standards.

Like Plato, Aristotle is concerned with the society a person finds themselves in, and asks how this should be organised. Unlike Plato, Aristotle can be seen as moving up from the nature of a good life for individuals, asking what kind of society will service the interests of such individuals in common. Man, for Aristotle, is 'by nature a social being', and so our happiness is bound up with the lives of others; thus too our own self-sufficiency includes what is sufficient for our 'parents, wife and children, friends and fellow-citizens'.[24] Nevertheless, the individual good life is measured in relation to the liver of that life.[25] We can differentiate between good and bad ways of life for a person simply by taking a more comprehensive perspective on that person's whole life. We can ask: Do this person's character traits and habits conduce to a

---

[21] See Annas, *Introduction to Plato's Republic.*, ch. 12.

[22] In fact, by the time Plato returns to the question of justice in the individual, the focus is heavily upon the rulers, so we learn little about the virtue of ordinary citizens.

[23] *Republic*, 540b.   [24] *Nicomachean Ethics*, 1097b10–11.

[25] See Aristotle's discussion and rejection of Plato's approach in *Nicomachean Ethics*, 1096b–1097a.

harmonious and satisfying life, or do they thwart that person's own aims (as where laziness thwarts avarice)?[26] Since the good life is to be measured across an entire lifetime, not just at a moment, it is not enough that one's present desires be satisfied in order for one to count as living well.[27] Rather, one must develop dispositions, make commitments, and adopt goals that could make for a good life taken as a whole. These elements taken together—particularly the appreciation of our social nature—make the importance and desirability of a virtuous life intelligible to us; and they do so from a partialistic perspective, with the individual agent focusing on how their own life can be lived in such a way as to develop their capacities and talents to the full. For example, despite the potential rewards of betraying a friend on this or that occasion, I am able to recognize how, for social creatures such as myself, a life of fidelity to one's friends would be a better life overall.[28]

None of this implies an endorsement of crude self-interest. Practical reasoning has a partialistic orientation for Aristotle, as it begins with the agent's own overall aim to live well and moves from there to aim at the detailed elements that will make up such a life.[29] But if I am truly virtuous, I don't take account of the concerns of others simply because, and inasmuch as, it is good for me to do so: many of the virtues involve a direct concern with the needs and interests of others. The partiality in this picture is found in the underlying vindication of a virtuous life—that it is, after all, a good life for the person who lives it. Nevertheless, the substantive picture we get in this way is also, albeit qualifiedly, partialistic. Certainly, the good life will not be egoistically self-interested; a person with such a character would thwart their own aspirations to live well. But neither will the virtuous person slip into the excess of giving too much of themselves for others. True, they would not run from a noble self-sacrifice, since to do otherwise would be to live the unsatisfactory life of a cowardly

---

[26] Indeed, one might argue that avarice thwarts satisfaction all by itself, since it never achieves satiation. The avarice/laziness example is not Aristotle's but is added for illustration.

[27] *Nicomachean Ethics*, 1098a19–22.

[28] And in general, a person who has perfected the art of achieving their own ends will also select the right ends—that is, the happiness they pursue will be the happiness of a virtuous person. Aristotle explains this by saying that the (perfectly) prudent person is also virtuous. *Ibid.*, 1144b–1145a. It is also worth noting a potential implication of Aristotle's definition of pleasure as unimpeded activity (*ibid.*, 1154a1–2; cf. also 1174b14–1175a10); a vicious pursuit of pleasure would be self-defeating inasmuch as the particular activities will not harmonise as do virtuous activities, and so at least some impediment is inevitable.

[29] However, cf. Aristotle's remark that 'while it is desirable to secure what is good in the case of an individual, to do so in the case of a people or a state is something finer and more sublime. Such, then, is the aim of our investigation . . .'. *Ibid.*, 1094b9–10; trans. J. A. K. Thomson, with revisions by Hugh Tredennick and Jonathan Barnes (London: Penguin Books, 2004), pp. 4–5. I take these remarks to foreshadow the importance of harmonizing the well-being of everyone in a community, rather than as an indication that social good should be prioritized over individual well-being.

failure.[30] But their central concern is to live a fulfilled and fulfilling human life, for which a virtuous character is indispensable.

Plato and Aristotle, so drawn, mark out paradigms for what is to come after them in relation to this topic. Very often, impartiality and partiality are not discussed explicitly, but they are key to understanding the shape of moral theories, to understanding their approach to practical deliberation, value, and well-being, and to characterizing the basic nature of morality/ethics. Greek philosophy could be said to enter into the Christian European tradition through St Paul, but Plato and Aristotle also had a great deal of direct influence on the philosophy and theology of Western Europe. Key examples are St Augustine, who was heavily influenced by Plato, and St Thomas Aquinas, whose work is greatly indebted to Aristotle. It is to Aquinas that we turn now, as a seminal exponent of the natural-law tradition.

Developing an idea of Aristotle's, Aquinas writes of a natural law governing the choices we make over our particular social and political practices. Natural law applies where the choice of the practice we adopt has independent importance, and not just any convention will do.[31] For Aristotle, even natural law is changeable, and he offers the example of how our right hand might be stronger than our left, but that practice could make us ambidextrous.[32] But Aquinas inclines instead to the view that the natural law is an eternal immutable moral standard by which conduct, and positive law, can and should be judged.[33] It is not merely a matter of recognizing the relevance of natural facts in evaluating and selecting possible conventions, but of applying unvarying moral standards, accessible to reason, that set out what our practice should be. So understood, despite its debts to Aristotle, natural law in Aquinas has much in common with Plato's impartial value. Practical reason reveals the standards by which we learn what we are to do, just as we look to the form of justice to learn

---

[30] *Ibid.* 1169a25. Gerald J. Hughes claims that for Aristotle we should 'see the fulfilled life not just as satisfying but as fine and noble'. See his *Aristotle on Ethics* (New York: Routledge, 2001), p. 179. Although, on the reading of Aristotle I have offered here, it is also the case that no virtuous person could be satisfied with an ignoble life, and no vicious person could be perfectly satisfied.

[31] Aristotle, *Nicomachean Ethics*, 1134b18–1135a14. Aristotle contrasts this natural law with purely conventional law. A modern example of conventional law would be regulations about which side of the road we should drive on—it doesn't matter which side, so long as we all follow the same convention on the same roads.

[32] As Aristotle puts it, 'among the Gods, indeed, justice presumably never changes at all; but in our world, although there is such a thing as natural law, everything is subject to change'. *Ibid.*

[33] See Bernard Yack, *The Problems of a Political Animal—Community, Justice, and Conflict in Aristotelian Political Thought* (Berkeley, CA: University of California Press, 1993), pp. 140–49. As he notes, Aquinas read Aristotle as being closer to his own natural-law ethics than may be warranted. For Aquinas's statement on variability of the natural law see *Summa Theologiae* [1265–1274] I–II, Q. 94, A. 4–5 (that is, the first part of the second part (*prima secundae partis*), question 94, articles 4 and 5), and also I–II, Q. 95, A. 2 and as regards the importance of custom and circumstances see I–II, Q. 97, A. 1.

what a just person or society is like. This is unlike the Aristotelian partialistic approach that starts from individual well-being, and asks how we are to live given the conditions obtaining in the world in which we find ourselves.[34] To be sure, both these ways of conceptualizing our approach to ethical standards make reference to standards for good human lives. But, crucially, if there is an absolute standard of the kind envisaged by Aquinas, it will be binding upon us independently of our particular circumstances and personal commitments. For Aquinas, the natural law dictates that we are subject to certain obligations and prohibitions that remain incumbent upon us, in a way that is not a function of our personal fulfilment or individual well-being.[35]

This greater impartiality is underwritten by another respect in which Aquinas presents a more impartialist version of Aristotelian ideas. Aristotle claims that ethics is a study of 'the good for man'—that is, the good for human beings quite generally.[36] He also claims that the prudent person, who has practical wisdom, will aim at the good—and that this too can be the good for people in general (although it might be their own good, or the good of their household or state).[37] So, too, Aquinas takes us to be concerned with human good quite generally. He argues that, fundamental to moral law, and to sound practical reasoning, is the idea 'that we should do and seek good and shun evil'.[38] As Aquinas puts it, 'good is the first thing that falls within practical reasoning'.[39] But despite the level of agreement here, there is difference too. As we have seen, Aristotle presents a partialistic vindication of the virtuous concern for the good of others, one that is presented in terms of individual well-being. Ethics may study human good quite generally, but we are each connected to the good of others through our own ends, including the personal overall goal to lead a flourishing life. For Aquinas, our concern with human good in general is as fundamental to our practical reasoning as avoiding self-contradiction is to our theoretical reason. The thought here is that to see the aim of practical reasoning as the pursuit and performance of what is evil—the opposite of good—is every bit as fundamentally absurd as to assert a manifest contradiction. Just as it makes no sense to assert both X and not-X, so too it makes no sense to knowingly

---

[34] Aristotle, *Nicomachean Ethics*, 1134b25–30.

[35] A standard variant along these lines is found in the natural-rights tradition, whereby there are strict limits on the treatment of others, no matter what benefits might be achieved by violating these rights. Two key figures in this tradition are John Locke and Robert Nozick. See Locke, *Two Treatises of Government* [1690], ed. W. S. Carpenter (London: Everyman's Library, 1924), bk II; Nozick, *Anarchy, State, and Utopia* (New York: Basic Books, 1974).

[36] Aristotle, *Nicomachean Ethics*, 1094a6–7.   [37] See *ibid.*, bk VI, 1140a25–1140b30.

[38] *Summa Theologiae* I–II, Q. 94, A. 2. Aquinas, trans. Richard J. Regan, ed. William P. Baumgarth and Richard J. Regan, *On Law, Morality, and Politics*, 2nd edn (Indianapolis, IN: Hackett, 2002), p. 43.

[39] *Ibid.*

pursue what one takes to be bad.[40] But this good, which we are to pursue and which it would be absurd to shun, is entirely unindexed—it is human good generally, not this or that person's good. Thus, as John Finnis describes it in the course of expounding Aquinas's view, 'the principles [of practical reason] contain no proper names, no restrictions such as "for me" '.[41] So, if I am to avoid pain and privation as evils, so far as that goes it will not matter if they are my own or a stranger's. A stranger's evil is still evil, and a stranger's good is still good; and since a virtuous person seeks to promote the good quite generally, that stranger's good will figure among the outcomes that are to be desired by me.

Aquinas, then, takes the Aristotelian picture and gives it its most impartialist interpretation. We still work from the ground up, moving from our own practical reasoning and the question of what is good for beings like us. But we end up with a more generalized concern with the good. My concern with the good of others is not merely grounded in the way such sociability is good for me. Rather, it is built into the fundamental structure of practical reasoning. Thus our own faculty of reason puts us in touch with the unvarying standards of the natural law, which law applies to us independently of our own goals, and directs us to a concern for the good of others.[42]

3. The Early Modern Period

If we now move forward to the early modern period, Hobbes can also be read as working within the natural-law tradition, although he certainly brings something very different to it. The idea of a social contract goes back a long way—it is present in Plato's *Crito*, for example—but Hobbes's work on the

---

[40] See Ralph McInerny, 'Ethics', in Norman Kretzmann and Eleonore Stump (eds), *The Cambridge Companion to Aquinas* (Cambridge: Cambridge University Press, 1993), pp. 210–11. The idea that reason is oriented to the good, and the avoidance of the bad, can be found in Plato as well as in Aristotle. See esp. Plato, *Protagoras* [380 BC].

[41] See John Finnis, *Aquinas—Moral, Political, and Legal Theory* (Oxford: Oxford University Press, 1998), p. 111. However, Don Adams argues that Aquinas's picture here is better described as a kind of communal egoism, where morality requires us to do what is in the group's interests. See Don Adams, 'Aquinas and Modern Consequentialism', *International Journal of Philosophical Studies* 12 (2004), pp. 395–417.

[42] See Martin Rhonheimer, trans. Frederick G. Lawrence, 'Sins Against Justice (IIa IIae, qq. 59–78)' in Stephen J. Pope (ed.), *The Ethics of Aquinas* (Georgetown, Washington, DC: Georgetown University Press, 2002), pp. 287–303. Rhonheimer explains how, for Aquinas, justice (that is, virtue directed towards others) has the structure of beneficence, which is the virtue of acting for the good of others. More particularly, 'every act injurious to justice also transgresses love for one's fellows' (p. 288). This illustrates the marked Christian character of Aquinas's ethics.

scope for social agreement provides us with a new way of thinking about impartiality in relation to partiality. Given European turmoil over religious and other disagreements, Hobbes's concern with stability and security is readily understandable. But what is interesting is that he wished to anchor this stability not in the enforcement of one true view over the others. Rather, he looks to what is common to all of us, whatever our particular views. Hobbes's contention is that, whatever else we may take ourselves to have reason to do, we have reason to preserve our own lives. Hobbes writes of a 'precept, or general rule, found out by reason, by which a man is forbidden to do, that, which is destructive of his life'.[43] Even liberty is secondary to survival, since life is required for the enjoyment of any other privileges; and thus the preservation of life provides not only a point of agreement, but a point that is fundamental relative to our other interests. Hobbes's idea is that a more fundamental agreement can be used to resolve conflicts at a less fundamental level. I may favour ice cream, while you favour fruit. In this way, our pictures of value may differ. If we must shop together, and can afford only one dessert, we face the potential for conflict. If we wish to preserve our relationship, we must find some way of resolving our differences. We might, for example, find that we share a concern for good nutrition—we might find that this concern dominates—and so I might agree to purchase the fruit after all. Or we might decide that preserving our friendship is more important than dessert, and so will simply fail to attach enough importance to the matter for it to cause a major rift between us. Hobbes's reflections take a similar path, albeit addressing somewhat weightier matters. Where conflict may threaten our lives, Hobbes refers to the first fundamental law of human nature: 'that every man, ought to endeavour Peace, as far as he has hope of obtaining it'.[44] He concludes that no one could reasonably deny that a strong state, which protects and preserves us, is a good and desirable thing.

Hobbes's starting point is the several distinct reasons of different people. These arise out of their own desires and goals: these may be self-interested in nature,[45] or they may simply express people's differing and often conflicting values (including religious affiliations).[46] Individually, we might rationally pursue goals that would place us in conflict; but given the reason each of

[43] Thomas Hobbes, *Leviathan* [1651], ed. Richard Tuck (Cambridge: Cambridge University Press, 1991), pt 1, ch. 14, para. 3, p. 91. I have modernized the spelling in the quotation.

[44] *Ibid.*, para. 4.

[45] For a careful working out of the view in terms of self-interested reasons, see David Gauthier, *The Logic of Leviathan* (Oxford: Oxford University Press, 1969).

[46] As emphasized by Bernard Gert, 'Hobbes's Psychology', in Tom Sorrell (ed.), *The Cambridge Companion to Hobbes* (Cambridge: Cambridge University Press, 1996).

us has to preserve our lives, we have reason to find a way of avoiding that conflict—to prioritize the achievement and maintenance of peace over every other goal. As Gauthier puts the point: 'Subjective prudence fails as a guide to action. . . . Thus Hobbes claims to erect an objective morality from the ruins of subjective prudence.'[47]

In this appeal to common reason, Hobbes in effect gives us a variety of impartial reason. But this impartial reason proceeds not by appeal to eternal immutable forms, but simply by appeal to what no one can fail to recognize as worthwhile. In effect, it is the point of agreement between every individual's partial perspective, and is grounded in every individual's own self-interest. Such an approach can be applied to the justification of both political and moral authority; and, in the form of various laws of human nature, it can also help to reveal the life-preserving substantive content of ethics. Gerald Gaus's contribution in this collection (Chapter 2) reflects on the extent to which impartial reason of this kind may underdetermine the precise content of morality.

A key, and not unrelated, development in the century following Hobbes was Hume's understanding of justice as an artificial virtue.[48] Hume shared with Aristotle an interest in virtue as being conducive to a good life; but he judged virtues in terms of their pleasantness to people generally, rather than centring on their value to the possessor.[49] (In this generalized concern with pleasantness, Hume anticipates utilitarianism, and so yet another form of impartiality, which will be discussed below.)[50] But Hume reasoned that, in circumstances of limited want, it would not be enough to leave our interactions with each other to be governed by beneficence. Our beneficence would be limited by our self-concern, and so conflict might arise in the settling of disputes. Instead, we would need justice to settle what was owed to one another.[51] In calling justice an artificial virtue, Hume was not claiming that it is merely conventional, but that it arises in the particular circumstances of potential dispute—it is a virtue of which there would be no need if there were no want, and which could gain no purchase on our motivations if there were too few resources to go around (we would not find it pleasant to be bound by regulations that threaten our

[47] Gauthier, *The Logic of Leviathan*, p. 90.
[48] David Hume, *A Treatise of Human Nature* [1739–40], ed. David Fate Norton and Mary J. Norton (Oxford: Oxford University Press, 2000), bk 3, pt 2, section 1.
[49] *Ibid.*, bk 3, pt 1, section 2.
[50] In fact, the term 'utility' is used widely and frequently by Hume by the time of the *Enquiries*. David Hume, *Enquiries concerning Human Understanding and the Principles of Morals* [1751], ed. L. A. Selby-Bigge with revisions by P. H. Nidditch (Oxford: Oxford University Press, 1975); see especially section V of the *Enquiry concerning the Principles of Morals*.
[51] *Ibid.*, section III, pt 1; esp. pp. 183–4.

survival). This standard of justice, as with Aristotle's version of natural law, may not be fixed in every particular, but it is important that our conventional practices and laws match up to some standard of appropriateness. Justice, then, provides an impartial standard; and so, too, those who live up to this standard are deemed pleasant by their fellows. We have here a dense interweaving of the partial and the impartial. My pursuit of my own interests is limited not merely for my own advantage; but I am held to such a standard only because the circumstances of justice obtain and so every one of us has an interest in just conduct in general.

A further development from this period is explicitly expressed in terms of impartiality by Hume's friend Adam Smith. This is the idea of the impartial spectator, an imaginary point of view that one can adopt in order to reach judgements of conscience—that is, in order to take the moral point of view itself. In assessing ourselves morally, '[w]e endeavour to examine our own conduct as we imagine any other fair and impartial spectator would examine it'.[52] The importance of considering the perspective of spectators was not entirely new. Hutcheson appealed to the disinterested (impartial) approval of disinterested benevolence, and regarded this as the moral sense.[53] Hume also wrote of the 'judicious spectator'[54] who departed 'from his private and particular situation, and must choose some universal principle of the human frame, and touch a string, to which all mankind have sympathy'.[55] According to Hume, benevolence is founded on human sympathy. Hume held that our sympathetic nature means that we feel some measure of the same emotions as our fellows—be it pleasure or suffering—and so each person's well-being is to some degree bound up with that of those around them. But this would remain a partialistic concern if the extent of my interest in the well-being of others were limited by the extent to which their concerns bear upon my own. (It need not be egoistic in any straightforward way, however. If the pain of a stranger moves me because it pains me, it need not be that I act to stop my own pain. It would be only a mere shadow of benevolence to act solely for that reason. But his pain may gain effective purchase on my motivations through the sympathetic pain it gives rise to in me.) Impartiality enters the picture in the idea of an impartial, disinterested, spectator who has no direct

[52] Adam Smith, *The Theory of Moral Sentiments*, 6th edn [1790], ed. D. D. Raphael and A. L. MacFie (Oxford: Oxford University Press, 1976), pt III, ch. I, para. 2, p. 110.

[53] Francis Hutcheson, *An Inquiry into the Original of Our Ideas of Beauty and Virtue*, 4th edn [1737] (London: Elibron Classics, Adamant Media, 2005), treatise II, section I. On Hutcheson's contribution to the idea of the impartial spectator, see D. D. Raphael, *The Impartial Spectator: Adam Smith's Moral Philosophy* (Oxford: Oxford University Press, 2007), p. 28.

[54] Hume, *Treatise*, bk 3, pt 3, section 1, para. 14; p. 371.

[55] Hume, *Enquiry concerning the Principles of Morals*, section IX, pt I, para. 6; p. 262.

connection with those involved in the case, and who is entirely uninvolved in any action. If I help someone in need, I face a cost to myself in doing so. The sympathy I feel for the other person's suffering may be, then, tempered by my more intimate concern with my own interests. However, when an impartial spectator observes me and the suffering stranger, she faces no costs of her own. If she sees me walk away, and disapproves, this is because she feels that the cost of helping was proportionate to the need. If she sees me helping and admires me, then she provides a standard by which my action can be judged virtuous. In short, the impartial spectator is not biased, and so reacts to gains and losses directly, in abstraction of who should happen to suffer them.

Our interest in the impartial spectator arises because of the prior idea that, morally speaking, albeit at an abstract level, everyone counts equally. If I am to take up this moral point of view, I must surrender all the natural bias I feel towards myself and my personal attachments. Morality does not care who wins a football match, no matter how passionately I may prefer the victory to go to Reading.[56] This impartial point of view is often associated with a 'God's eye' view, and Smith refers to it not only as an 'abstract man, the representative of all mankind', but also as a 'substitute for the Deity'.[57] However, the impartial spectator is a recognizably human figure, a person who merely happens to be uninvolved in the case that she is observing. This makes her perspective somewhat easier to imagine.

As mentioned at the beginning of this Introduction, the idea that morality is truly impartial is quite natural to us. But it is important to recognise how, in the case of the impartial observer, it requires a peculiar leap beyond and outside of ourselves. What reason have I to care about the reactions of an imaginary impartial judge? For Hume, in fact, this step to impartiality had nothing to do with reason at all.[58] In this way, the notion of the impartial spectator paved the way for a radical schism: one that was only incipient in Hume and Smith, but that takes clearer form in later thinkers, particularly Sidgwick and Nagel. In Aristotle, Plato, and Aquinas, the pursuit of the good is the primary principle of all practical reasoning. For Plato and Aquinas, to be biased towards my own interests is to make a simple mistake about my own fundamental end.

[56] That is, leaving aside desert; if only one side cheats, perhaps an impartial spectator would favour the victory of the innocent.
[57] Adam Smith, *The Theory of Moral Sentiments*, p. 129 n. (the quote is actually from the 2nd edn, pt III, ch. II, but is included as a footnote in the cited version of the 6th edn). Elsewhere the impartial spectator is more modestly described as a 'demigod'; *ibid.*, pt VI, ch. III, para. 25, p. 247.
[58] David Hume, *Treatise*, bk 4, pt 1, section 1, p. 295: 'Reason is wholly inactive, and can never be the source of so active a principle as conscience, or a sense of morals.'

In Aristotle, while my own interests take centre stage, it would nevertheless be a mistake to think that ignoble actions further my own well-being. But if instead the moral point of view is wholly separate from the normal course of my personal practical reasoning, then we are left with a puzzle. A motivational puzzle and a puzzle of rationality, certainly, but also a conceptual one. How do we integrate, or move between, the perspectives? Which is to take priority should morality and prudence conflict?

4. Kant

In Kant, we find this impartial perspective within ourselves, not without. In typical means–end reasoning, my starting place is what I want to achieve; I then aim to discover how I might best achieve this end. Where a particular means (say, buying a ticket) is necessary to a particular end (say, watching *Giselle*), Kant says that there is a hypothetical imperative. It is, we might say, imperative that I buy a ticket, granting the hypothesis that I want to see the ballet. But, of course, I may not want to see the ballet. Or perhaps I want to see the ballet, and I want to visit a sick friend, but I can't do both. Hypothetical imperatives won't help settle the question of a choice between ends unless we can appeal to a more basic end, an end that, relative to these options, is unrevisable and takes precedence. When discussing Hobbes, we observed that such a step could resolve conflicts between people. In Kant, the initial problem is to find a framework for the choice, between ends, of a single individual. For Kant, this framework is provided by the agent's own free will. A will that is not in thrall to any particular ends can select ends based upon universal principles. If I am not being driven by any particular desire, I have only the structure of my will to shape my deliberations. This gives us one of Kant's formulations of the categorical imperative: 'Act as if the maxim of your action were to become through your will a universal law of nature.'[59] Given that my own particularity, in the form of my desires, is set aside, the principle I turn to applies categorically—which is to say, it does not depend on any particular desire that I might have, but applies to me whatever my desires may happen to be. The maxim, or principle, that I am to assess, then, is to stand independent of particularity. Thus it also applies quite generally; it is to be a maxim for every agent—just as if it were a universal law of nature. Since

---

[59] Immanuel Kant, *Groundwork of the Metaphysic of Morals* [*Grundlegung zur Metaphysik der Sitten*, 1785], trans. H. J. Paton (London: Hutchinson, 1948), Ak. 421. (The 'Ak.' page references are to Royal Prussian Academy (eds), *Kant's Gesammelte Schriften* (Berlin: Georg Reimer, 1900–).)

it applies independently of particular desires/ends, this categorical imperative gives us the means of adjudicating between possible ends. If an end (or the maxim, or principle, that selects the end) is one that could be adopted by everyone, then it passes this test. If it is one that I could be driven to only by my own misaligned passions, and in the hope that others do not act likewise, then it fails this test. Thus, for example, all forms of deceit fail the test since, while I may want to deceive others, I wouldn't want to be deceived in turn.[60] Kant offer various formulations of the categorical imperative, but the unifying idea is that pure practical reason, unenslaved by the fickle passions, wills only ends that harmonize with each other. For Aristotle, harmony makes a good life possible for the agent; but for Kant, harmony is laid down as a principle by the very possibility of free agency. And so, too, it applies to every free agent; and harmonizes the ends and actions of every person.

Of course, I may get swept along by my desires instead; and these desires may be selfish. But in such cases, I am, for Kant, acting 'heteronymously', in thrall to my desire, and so am not acting with true freedom, which is to say 'autonomously'. When I am 'swept along' by my desires I am in effect ruled by them, and at any rate I fail to rule myself. Inasmuch as I choose freely, inasmuch as I deliberate rationally about what to do, I place myself under the moral law. Yet this moral law is given by the structure of a free will; it is not an independent standard, whether understood in terms of the eternal form of justice (Plato) or by the conditions of human flourishing (e.g. Aquinas). The moral law is internal to my own agency and yet is genuinely impartial in that, having stripped away the contingencies of desire, it addresses every agent in common. And this impartiality between agents gave Kant another formulation of the categorical imperative, one that is perhaps of greater rhetorical appeal: 'Act in such a way that you always treat humanity, whether in your own person or in the person of any other, never simply as a means, but always at the same time as an end.'[61]

Hobbes found a point of impartiality in the agreement of the partialistic reasons of different agents; but for Kant pure practical reason is perfectly impartial. And so it is not surprising that Kant's moral theory is also, in one respect at least, very demanding. Every action I perform must be in accordance with my moral duty (that is, with the categorical imperative). But in another way, it may not be so demanding. For example, a principle that requires every

---

[60] More precisely, in discussing false promises, Kant argues that if everyone made lying promises it would defeat the purpose in making a lying promise. The thought is that if everyone lied whenever it suited them, no one would be believed. See *ibid.*, Ak. 402–3. See also his later remarks about treating the deceived as mere means, at Ak. 429–30.

[61] *Ibid.*, Ak. 66–7.

person to put others before themselves may not pass the universalizability test. Perhaps if we all put others before ourselves, we would refuse the help that we offer to others, who in their turn would refuse it in their attempts to be of service to us. Kant's system does not obviously lead to moral demands for great self-sacrifice; it insists only that every one of our aims should pass an impartial eligibility test.

5. Utilitarianism

The utilitarian tradition owes much to the work of Hume and Smith; yet it also varies greatly. This is particularly clear in the argument John Stuart Mill offers in favour of utilitarianism (not a deductive proof, which he took to be unachievable). First, Mill argues for hedonism, that happiness-as-pleasure is the sole good; everything else that is good is so as a part of someone's happiness. Thus Mill comments that 'each person's happiness is a good to that person'.[62] This much makes sense, since how could my happiness be good at all but for being good for me?[63] The next move is 'the general happiness, therefore, [is] a good to the aggregate of all persons'.[64] This is very much like the perspective of the impartial spectator. If I act to help another person, the impartial observer takes account of my sacrifice (unhappiness) and my beneficiary's gain (happiness). If the exchange excites the approbation of the impartial observer, then the action is good and right. The gains and losses are measured without bias, without the distortions of personal interest. Similarly, for a utilitarian, each person's good figures only for its impartial worth, measured on a fair scale and summed with the rest. Indeed, Mill writes that the utilitarian principle would be 'a mere form of words without rational signification, unless one person's happiness . . . is counted for exactly as much as another's'.[65] What is added to the picture of the impartial observer

---

[62] John Stuart Mill, *Utilitarianism* [1861], in Mary Warnock (ed.), *Utilitarianism* (London: Fontana Press, 1962), ch. IV, para. 3, pp. 288–9.

[63] However, this is called into question by G. E. Moore. He argued that what is good is so not for this or that person but, so to speak, 'good absolutely'. See Moore's *Principia Ethica* (Cambridge: Cambridge University Press, 1903), esp. section 59, at p. 99.

[64] Mill, *Utilitarianism*, ch. IV, para. 3, p. 289. In his letter to Henry Jones, dated 1868, Mill explains that in this passage he 'did not mean that every human being's happiness is a good to every other human being', but that, if each person's happiness is a good, then 'the sum of all these goods must be a good' (*Collected Works* XVI, ed. Francis E. Minkea and Dwight N. Lindley; series ed. John M. Robson (London: Routledge, 1972), p. 1414). But whose good? Either the good of the aggregate, or else, perhaps, the good absolutely, unqualified as to possession.

[65] Mill, *Utilitarianism*, ch. V, para. 36, p. 319.

is the notion of interpersonal aggregation, of summing the total happiness. My assistance is right if the sum of my beneficiary's happiness, less my unhappiness, is greater than the sum of happiness that would result from my refusing help: that is, my happiness at not making the sacrifice, less the unhappiness of the person going without help. Thus we get the 'Greatest Happiness Principle', which, in Mill's formulation, 'holds that actions are right in proportion as they tend to promote happiness, wrong as they tend to produce the reverse of happiness'.[66]

This contrasts with the Smith/Hume approach, where the impartial observer may be concerned with gains and losses, but these don't automatically determine her reaction.[67] Consider someone, a stranger, who asks for money for a luxury item, such as a video games console, which they want but can't afford. I may make the sacrifice, and give them the money. Additionally, this may make them very happy indeed while hardly putting a dent in my happiness (I might be very wealthy, and they might really enjoy video games). But the impartial observer may watch this and deem me to be a soft touch, and so disapprove of my action. Impartially speaking, it might be better for people to go without video games than to get them by begging from strangers. This is not a matter of rejecting Mill's hedonism; Hume, too, is concerned with what is pleasant. Nor is it a lapse in impartiality: the impartial observer accords me no special preference over the video games fan. But there is nothing in the impartial-observer story to suggest that right actions can be determined simply by the total sum of happiness; nor anything to suggest that the sum of the good of every each individual is a good for all individuals in aggregate. And so the utilitarian innovation is to be found in this view of the possibility and importance of interpersonal aggregation.

Utilitarianism needn't be hedonistic, nor need it aim simply at the sum total of good; it might prioritize a particular distribution of goods (perhaps according to desert, perhaps in line with equality). But its conception of impartiality is aggregative. In the moral accounting book, each person counts for one, and no one more than one. And in order to act morally, a person

[66] Mill, *Utilitarianism*, ch. II, para. 2, p. 257.

[67] Hutcheson is a little closer to the utilitarians on this point. He originated the basic formula for utilitarianism: 'That action is best, which procures the greatest happiness for the greatest number' (*Inquiry*, treatise II, section III, sub-section viii). But there is a variety of complicating factors in interpreting his position, chief among which is the fact that Hutcheson used this formula to explain approval and disapproval rather than recommending it as a principle for selecting actions directly. See J. B. Schneewind's explanation of this feature in his (ed.) *Moral Philosophy from Montaigne to Kant* (Cambridge: Cambridge University Press, 2003), p. 505.

must act as directed by the outcome of these impartial calculations. Thus, at some level, we are each to give no special role to our own good. There are two main steps from the pursuit of my own good to the pursuit of the utilitarian impartial good. The first step is a simple process of abstraction. If our concern is with the good, unindexed to particular people, then there is no ground for distinguishing my good from anyone else's. (There are echoes here of the unindexed good in Aquinas's picture of practical reason.) The second, and distinctively utilitarian, step is to think that goodness can be summed, and that more rather than less good is always to be preferred (albeit perhaps with some distributive structure to be applied to this). Although it can be used more widely, the term 'consequentialism' is often applied to those moral theories that share these steps, whatever other differences they may have.[68] They may, for example, apply this calculus to the selection of moral principles or virtues, rather than being directly applied to the consequences of particular actions.[69] More generally, the term 'consequentialism' might be applied to any theory that determines right conduct by appealing to a ranking of consequences, preferring the better to the worse consequences.[70] But these views share utilitarianism's basic conception of impartiality. The ultimate moral measure is the merit of the overall circumstances; this is calculated by combining all the separate good and bad elements of those circumstances, without preference to any particular people affected.

6. Taking Stock

This is, of course, only the briefest of tours through the history of the topic of partiality and impartiality. But it may serve to bring out the main issues. There is the substantive matter of what morality demands of us, of what a virtuous

[68] The use of this term in this context is owed to G. E. M. Anscombe, 'Modern Moral Philosophy', *Philosophy* 33 (1958); also in her *Ethics, Religion, and Politics* (Oxford: Basil Blackwell, 1981), see especially p. 36.

[69] Sometimes the term is used to exclude theories that include the merits of actions as part of the consequences to be assessed. See Brad Hooker, *Ideal Code, Real World: A Rule-consequentialist Theory of Morality* (Oxford: Oxford University Press, 2000), p. 33 n. 2, and Samuel Scheffler, *The Rejection of Consequentialism* (Oxford: Oxford University Press, 1982), pp. 1–2, n. 2. Hooker and Scheffler are both inclined to be inclusive in their definition.

[70] However, this does raise the danger that the term could be applied to theories that have very little in common. See Bernard Williams's contribution to Williams and J. J. C. Smart, *Utilitarianism For and Against* (Cambridge: Cambridge University Press, 1973), pp. 82–93. Cf. Scheffler's remarks on the impartiality of any consequentialist theory; *The Rejection of Consequentialism*, p. 1.

person will do for others. And there are the more abstract questions, about the nature of value and practical reasoning. Am I to understand value solely in terms of my own engagement with it? Or is value something that can be understood in more generalised terms, with its immediate practical significance for me depending only on what value I am presently in a position to realise? We can also see something of the diversity of ways in which we might conceptualize impartiality and partiality in moral theory. There are many ways of understanding impartiality: for example, the hedonistic utilitarians, building their argument from observing the importance of pleasure in our lives, would have little sympathy for the idealism of Plato's form of the good. And so, too, the Kantian concern to strip away our contingent differences has little to do with maximizing the sum of aggregate goods.[71] Partiality, too, is not a simple matter. As we have seen with Aristotle and Hobbes, it is not simply narrow self-interest; and as we have seen with Hume and Smith, it can be any kind of priority or preference that a truly disinterested spectator would lack. It can be understood as a matter of deliberating from one's own perspective—not necessarily an inappropriate bias, but rather a matter of according practical priority in one's own personal decision-making to one's own personal concerns, priorities and commitments.

Many of the positions adopted today in moral theory can be categorized, with varying precision, as being impartialist in either a consequentialist or a Kantian way, or else of being partialist in the Aristotelian tradition of virtue ethics. There is also a strong continuing tradition of natural law.[72] Hobbes too has left his mark,[73] albeit sometimes filtered through a Kantian lens. Rawlsian contractualism, for example, aims to achieve an impartial perspective by imagining what codes of conduct people would agree to, were they to set aside biasing information or inclination. Rawls argues that, given the wide range of disagreements people might have about the nature of a good life, people suitably situated would agree to an equitable division of the all-purpose means of pursuing any kind of good life.[74] But perhaps the

[71] Although see Derek Parfit, *On What Matters* (Oxford: Oxford University Press, forthcoming). If a version of consequentialism were independently true, then we might well expect people who set aside their contingent desires and biases to agree to abide by it. (This is notably reminiscent of, but different from, Sidgwick's reconciliation between 'the Intuitional and Utilitarian methods' in *The Methods of Ethics*, 'Concluding Chapter', p. 496.) On this, see Hooker, this volume, pp. 40–1. For the attempt to present Kantian contractualism as an alternative to utilitarianism, see John Rawls, *A Theory of Justice* (Cambridge, MA: Belknap Division of Harvard University Press, 1971).

[72] Such as John Finnis, *Natural Law and Natural Rights* (Oxford: Oxford University Press, 1980).

[73] See especially David Gauthier, *Morals by Agreement* (Oxford: Oxford University Press, 1986).

[74] Although he allows for some forms of inequality, provided only they are to the benefit of the worst off. John Rawls, *A Theory of Justice*; see especially section 46 for the summary of his proposal.

dominant position is a hybrid version of consequentialism, where the pursuit of good consequences is constrained by rights and/or other principles and prerogatives.[75]

At a substantive level, as with the figures discussed here, we find traces of both partiality and impartiality. In particular, it is common to think that an agent may show at least a little preference for themselves and their attachments. One key dimension of the exploration of this idea is the attempt to understand the practical importance of our commitments to other people, and the proper role of such personal relationships in our moral thinking.[76] More generally, one of the main theoretical problems remains the need to make sense of the scope for partiality, and to try to delineate its nature and its limits. There remains also considerable interest in the nature of value and reason, and in general the theoretical modelling of impartiality. The essays in this collection present a survey of some of the central issues being addressed in the ongoing work on the topic of impartiality and partiality in ethics. They all have some concern with the substantive requirements of morality, while drawing on a range of traditions of moral theorizing.

In the first chapter, Hooker argues that while impartial benevolence may not always be appropriate in our ordinary lives, nevertheless, other things being equal, we should prefer a moral theory that offers an impartial way of picking out and justifying moral rules. In the next chapter, Gaus examines the apparent conflict between the idea that morality is both universal and ahistorical (and so based on wholly impartial reason) and the fact that its content is informed by actual historical processes and social circumstances (so that we cannot determine its content outside of a particular context). Cottingham's chapter then argues that we should approach ethics from the perspective of an individual's own life, which necessarily implies a privileged sphere for self-development; but that since the good so pursued is part of the necessarily linked good of an essentially social species, the better we come to understand it, the more our self-concern will necessarily be implicated in a

---

More generally, contractualists often seek to understand morality in terms of what can be justified to others; in Scanlon's version, we look to what it would be unreasonable for anyone to reject. See especially, T. M. Scanlon, *What We Owe to Each Other* (London/Cambridge, MA: Belknap Division of Harvard University Press, 1998).

[75] More often than not, this is assumed in practice rather than defended explicitly; see Ronald Dworkin, 'Rights as Trumps', in Jeremy Waldron (ed.), *Theories of Rights* (Oxford: Oxford University Press, 1984), pp. 153–67, at p. 153. Dworkin himself sees the concern for collective goods (the consequentialist aspect of the hybrid view) as resting in a fundamental right to 'concern and respect', see his *Taking Rights Seriously* (London: Duckworth, 1977), p. xv.

[76] There hasn't been space to discuss it here, but Aristotle's work on friendship in his *Nicomachean Ethics* remains a key focus of study on this topic.

wider concern for other humans. De Gaynesford's chapter takes up some of these themes by arguing for the importance of the first-person perspective, via an examination of the work of William Godwin, famous for his challenge 'What magic is there in the pronoun "my". . . ?'.[77] De Gaynesford argues that even impartialists have to recognize that there is some significance to the first-person perspective, while partialists would be mistaken to see it as the whole of the moral story. There follows a chapter by Scheffler, which develops his view that we are permitted to show some preference for ourselves, our projects, and our loved ones, but that we are not permitted to give infinite weight to partial matters in the face of impartial moral demands. Stroud's chapter complements and contrasts with Scheffler's by arguing that special permissions may be best understood not in terms of partiality to self, but in terms of constitutive elements of joint projects. Next, Darwall argues that all interpersonal relationships, however partial they may be, presuppose an equal, impartial second-person authority to make demands on one another. Kolodny's chapter focuses on partial reasons concerning people to whom we are specially related, and argues that, without reducing these reasons to wholly impartial moral concerns, we can still distinguish between those special relationships that are and those that are not morally important. Next, Ridge addresses the question of the extent to which we are morally required to take up the slack when others fail to do what they should to help those in need. He argues that while we should do more than what would be our share of the moral labour if everyone did as they should, nevertheless we are not required to take up all of the moral slack, but only a portion of it, thus leaving us moral permission to devote the rest of our energies to our personal concerns—even when there are still people in dire need. Finally, Estlund explores the way incentives can be used to turn unrequired beneficence into morally required beneficence. While you are permitted to refrain from benefiting others when the benefit would only be up to a certain amount, this impartial beneficence may be morally required when the benefit would be greater. Considering cases such as 'if you give £10, the state will match your donation', Estlund argues that social institutions might be designed so that permissions could be turned into requirements by topping up the amount of good that would be done.

   While none of these essays constitutes a final, definitive statement on the topic as whole, they each make a contribution to the ongoing debate, to the task of understanding partiality and impartiality, their interrelationship and

---

[77] William Godwin, *Enquiry concerning political justice and its influence on modern morals and happiness* [1798], 3rd edn, ed. I. Kramnick (London: Penguin, 1985), p. 170.

practical implications. As this Introduction has aimed to show, the contrast between partiality and impartiality is not only encountered in our day-to-day decisions about how we should act. It also plays a key structural role in the development of philosophical frameworks for understanding the human moral predicament and the nature of ethical reasoning.

1

When Is Impartiality Morally Appropriate?

BRAD HOOKER

With respect to morality, the term 'impartiality' is used to refer to quite different things. My chapter will focus on three:

1. Impartial application of good (first-order) moral rules
2. Impartial benevolence as *the* direct guide to decisions about what to do
3. Impartial assessment of (first-order) moral rules

What are the relations among these three? Suppose there was just one good (first-order) moral rule, namely, that one should choose whatever one thinks will maximize aggregate good. If there were just this one moral rule, then impartial application of that one rule might be compatible with impartial benevolence as *the* direct guide to decisions about what to do.

But now suppose there are other good moral rules, such as ones that prohibit certain kinds of act, ones that permit some degree of preferential concern for oneself, and ones that require some degree of preference for one's friends and family in one's decisions about how to allocate one's time, attention, and other resources. If there are these other good rules, then at least sometimes impartially applying and complying with them will conflict with letting impartial benevolence dictate what to do. More importantly, we can reject impartial benevolence as *the* direct guide to decisions about what to do while endorsing impartial application of good (first-order) moral rules.

Likewise, rejecting impartial benevolence as *the* direct guide to decisions about what to do does not entail rejecting impartial assessment of (first-order) moral rules.

Section 1 of this chapter argues that impartiality in the application of good moral rules is always appropriate. Section 2 argues that impartial benevolence as a direct guide to decisions about what to do is appropriate only sometimes. Section 3 argues that impartiality in the assessment of rules is or is not appropriate—depending on how plausible the impartially selected rules are.

1. Impartial Application of Rules

Many people closely associate morality and impartiality. I think a large part of the reason for this is that the impartial application of good moral rules is virtually always appropriate. If some rules really are good ones, and if these rules are being applied, then they should be applied impartially.

I am not saying that the impartial application of *bad* rules is appropriate. Indeed, with respect to *terrible* rules, *no* application of them is appropriate. And their impartial application might be, on balance, worse than their partial application.[1]

Of course, there can be enormous uncertainty and debate about which possible moral rules are good ones, and about what makes them good. There are different plausible views about these things, especially about what makes rules good. I shall come back to these issues later when I discuss impartial assessment of (first-order) moral rules. At the moment, however, I want merely to make the point that the impartial application of good moral rules, whatever such rules turn out to be, is virtually always appropriate.

I should also acknowledge that some philosophers might reject the idea that there are good moral rules because they think that *rules* cannot help but be too coarse-grained to be good. I hope that such philosophers have something instead of rules—e.g. defeasible generalizations, default reasons, or hedged principles—the substitution of which will allow to go through much of what I argue below.

Now what does impartially applying a rule involve? Bernard Gert puts forward an account of *impartial treatment*:

A is impartial in respect R with regard to group G if and only if A's actions in respect R are not influenced at all by which member(s) of G are benefited or harmed by these actions.[2]

I take it that A's treatment of members of group G must be either random or patterned. If it is intentionally patterned, then it is probably guided by a rule. If it is guided by a rule, then when is the rule being impartially applied? Gert's account suggests an answer: a rule is being impartially applied with regard to a group if and only if its application is not influenced by which members of the group are benefited or harmed.

---

[1] This is a point Joel Feinberg makes: see his *Social Philosophy* (Englewood Cliffs, NJ: Prentice-Hall, 1973), pp. 106–7.

[2] Bernard Gert, *Morality* (New York: Oxford University Press, 1998), p. 132. I have discussed Gert's view of impartiality before. See my *Ideal Code, Real World: A Rule-consequentialist Theory of Morality* (Oxford: Oxford University Press, 2000), pp. 23–4. There I criticized Gert for not building consistency into impartiality. I advance different criticisms in this chapter.

With respect to many rules, this account of impartial application is attractive. The rules I have in mind are ones that, because of vagueness or complexity, do not always have clear implications. In effect, applying such rules requires lots of judgement, and leaves some degree of 'wiggle room'. An example might be the rule 'The product of a collective enterprise should be divided in proportion to people's contributions to the enterprise'. There is room for reasonable dispute about what makes one contribution greater than another.

To illustrate, suppose that Ivan applies the rule 'reward people in proportion to their contribution', and his allocations of reward are within the band of reasonable interpretations of 'contribution'. But suppose his interpretation ranks contributions of strength over contributions of planning and innovation. And suppose he does this because he likes the strong more than the intelligent. In this case, when Ivan applies the rule 'reward people in proportion to their contribution', he is not doing so impartially.

Gert's own list of moral rules comprises prohibitions on how we treat others.[3] His first five rules prohibit us to cause any of five kinds of harm to others: death, pain, disability, loss of freedom, and loss of pleasure. His other five rules prohibit deceiving, cheating, breaking our promises, disobeying the law, and failing to do our conventionally determined duty. He insists that to comply with these prohibitions is to act impartially with respect to these rules. For example, if you never break your promises to anyone, then you have impartially complied with the rule against breaking promises. I accept that this is an example of impartially applying a moral rule.

What I cannot accept, however, is that impartially applying rules must involve not being influenced by which people are benefited or harmed. Consider the rule:

> When you could devote your own time, attention, or other resources either to benefiting your friends and family or to benefiting people to whom you have no special connection, and when the benefit given would be about the same size, you should choose to benefit your friends or family.

In other words,

> Given that you are selecting from the group of people who would benefit a fixed amount if you devoted your own time, attention, or other resources to them, you should choose your friends or family as the beneficiaries.

Rules such as this tell you to be influenced by which members of the relevant group will benefit from your action. There are many such rules. Another

---

[3] Gert, *Morality*, chs 5, 7, 8.

example is one mentioned earlier: 'The product of a collective enterprise should be divided in proportion to people's contributions to the enterprise'. Such rules can be applied impartially.

Gert seems to have two possible responses to this line of thought. One possible response is to stick with the idea that to treat members of a group impartially is to treat them according to a rule that takes as irrelevant who benefits and who is harmed. If we stick with that idea, then we must say that you cannot treat members of a group impartially if you are following a rule specifying which members of the group qualify for benefits or harms, or for *more* benefit or harm. If you donate your own time and energy to helping your friends rather than to helping strangers, you have not treated your friends and the strangers impartially. But you may have impartially applied the rule 'donate your own time and energy to helping your friends rather than to helping strangers'.

Gert's other possible response is to give up the idea that to treat members of a group impartially is necessarily to treat them without regard to who benefits and who is harmed. If we give up that idea, then we can say that treating members of a group impartially is not incompatible with following a rule specifying which members of the group qualify for benefits or harms, or for *more* benefit or harm.

I favour allowing that impartial treatment of a group *can* be compatible with treating members of that group in accordance with a rule specifying which members of the group are so qualified. For example, acting impartially towards the company's workers with respect to rewarding productivity requires making decisions that give greater benefits to those of the company's workers who have been more productive. What impartial treatment of the company's workers requires is being guided by their past productivity rather than by other things, such as how much you like them.

How then should we characterize the impartial application of rules? Impartial application of a rule consists in being guided solely by the distinctions identified as relevant by the rule. Some rules make the issue of who is benefited or harmed irrelevant. This is true of rules against lying, stealing, and breaking the law. But other rules distinguish between others by picking out who qualifies for benefits or harms, or for *more* benefit or harm. Examples are rules about benefiting friends and family members over others when one is allocating one's own resources and the size of the benefits (by 'benefits' I mean positive contributions to welfare or personal good, not merely material goods) would be the same, and rules about rewarding productivity.

I turn now to a different aspect of Gert's account of impartial treatment of rules. Gert holds that someone can be morally impartial either in obeying rules or in violating them. He thinks there are cases where violation of a rule is justified, e.g. lying to the murderer at the door. And he offers us a criterion for determining whether the rule was violated, either, on the one hand, impartially or, on the other hand, in order to make an exception for oneself or someone else. His view is that moral impartiality is satisfied as long as whoever violates a moral rule is willing for everyone to know that this kind of action is 'publicly allowed'.[4] Gert's suggestion is that impartial violations of a moral rule entail the proposal of a *new, more specific* public moral rule indicating that in such circumstances violations of the older, less specific rule are permissible.

However, impartially applying and complying with a public rule might not yet be enough for moral impartiality. To be sure, the idea that the same rules apply publicly to everyone is associated with impartiality. However, advocating a single set of rules for public application to everyone hardly qualifies the advocate as impartial. Suppose Stephan wills and advocates public acceptance of a certain code of rules, but does so because he and his sub-group will be advantaged by public acceptance of this code. Stephan may apply these rules completely impartially. If he does, then he impartially applies rules that he sincerely wants to be publicly accepted. Still, to impartially apply rules that one sincerely wants to be publicly accepted is compatible with being very partial at the level of assessing rules.

Admittedly, publicly advocating rules that one publicly acknowledges to be particularly favourable to a group of which one is a member will often be pointless or even alienating. But publicly advocating rules that one publicly acknowledges to be particularly favourable to a group of which one is a member can be successful. Suppose you are hardworking and publicly advocate rules that are particularly favourable to the hardworking. These rules might well be accepted, and partly on the basis of your advocating them. Nevertheless, if you endorse these rules at least partly because you benefit from them, your endorsement of such rules is hardly unbiased. And other people's endorsement of these rules might also spring from partiality toward the hardworking.

2. Impartial Benevolence as the Direct Guide to Decisions about What To Do

By impartial benevolence as a direct guide to decisions about what to do, I mean impartial benevolence as the direct and sole determiner of everyday

---

[4] Gert, *Morality*, pp. 151–2, ch. 9.

practical decisions. By impartial benevolence, I mean an equal concern for the good of each. And by equal concern for the good of each, I mean treating a benefit or harm to any one individual as having the same moral importance as the same-size benefit or harm to any other individual.

What would it be to have impartial benevolence as the direct determiner of your everyday decisions? Benefits to anyone else would count in your reasoning for no less than the same-size benefits to you. Benefits to strangers would count in your reasoning for no less than the same-size benefits to your partner, child, or mother. So, if you recognized that donating most of your wealth to Oxfam would benefit the starving more than keeping it for yourself would benefit you, you would donate it. Indeed, you would go on giving your money, time, and effort to others as long as you thought the benefits others were getting were at least a little more than the benefits you were losing.

You might know more about how to benefit your family and friends than you know how to benefit strangers. Thus you might attend to your family and friends more than to others—but not because you have greater concern for your family and friends. On the contrary, whenever you were sure that doing something for a stranger would benefit the stranger at least a little more than doing the same thing for yourself or your family member or friend, you would benefit the stranger. If you could save three lives by giving to one person one of your kidneys, to the second person the other of your kidneys, and to the third person your heart, you would do so.

So far, I have been referring to what you do with your own money, time, effort, body parts, and other resources. But, if impartial benevolence really did determine *all* your everyday decisions, then presumably you would also be disposed to direct other people's resources in whatever way would maximize aggregate net benefit. If you could get away with channelling some of your employer's money to Oxfam, you would. If you could get away with channelling some of your friend's money to Oxfam, you would. If you could save two children by arranging for your child's kidney to go to one and her heart to the other, you would.

Absurd? Yes. Unfamiliar as an ethical ideal? Well, notoriously, we have William Godwin calling for the sacrifice of his mother to save the important do-gooder Archbishop Fénelon.[5] And act-utilitarianism is routinely ridiculed for supposedly requiring agents to be prepared to do whatever it takes to maximize aggregate net benefit, impartially calculated.

---

[5] Godwin, *An Enquiry concerning Political Justice, and its Influence on General Virtue and Happiness*, 2 vols (London: G. G. & J. Robinson, 1793).

W. D. Ross was right that act-utilitarianism ignores the 'personal character of duty'.[6] Ross was referring to the special relations each stands in to only some other people. The moral relations between friend and friend, or family member and family member, are, in many contexts, relevantly different from the moral relations between people with no special connection, and not just because we typically know more about our family members and friends than others. Even where we know equally well what would benefit a stranger and what would benefit a friend or family member, common moral opinion requires us to favour to some extent our own friends and family in the allocation of our own resources such as our time, energy, and material goods.

As John Cottingham has stressed, the duty of partiality pertains to the allocation of the agent's *own* resources. There is no implication that the agent is permitted, much less required, to commandeer *someone else's* resources for the benefit of the agent's child. As John Cottingham puts it,

What *is* wrong with the Pope giving the Red Hat to his nephew, the judge deciding a case in favour of her cousin, the civil servant giving a contract to his pal, the admissions officer reserving a place for her friend's daughter, is that such acts involve disrespect for the resources or rights of others. If I am working for the Church, or the Courts, or the Government, or the University, then the goods in question are not *mine*, to assign at will: I control the relevant good in trust for the institution that employs me, and I am no more justified in bestowing them on my favourites than I am justified in dishing out someone else's cream to my cat, or 'giving' someone else's bicycle to my child.[7]

In short, aiming to benefit oneself or one's family, friends, or other associates is often off limits.

Indeed, *constrained* impartial benevolence as the determiner of practical decisions is absolutely mandatory in certain contexts. The person running CARE or the UN's world food programme is charged to consider the welfare of everyone, considered impartially. For someone in such a role, the welfare of people of one religion, race, or region matter just as much as the people of any other religion, race, or region. And even in more restricted contexts, say a country or a county, various kinds of officials are charged to have the best interests of all their constituents equally at heart.

Nevertheless, *unconstrained* impartial benevolence would be inappropriate even in such roles. Even if you occupy such a role, you are *not* charged to do just *whatever* would maximize aggregate welfare. Some possible actions

---

[6] W. D. Ross, *The Right and the Good* (Oxford: Clarendon Press, 1930), p. 19.

[7] Cottingham, 'The Ethical Credentials of Partiality', *Proceedings of the Aristotelian Society* 98 (1998), pp. 1–21, at p. 11.

are ruled out by deontological prohibitions on, for example, murder, torture, robbery, fraud, etc. However, when you occupy one of various official roles and are choosing among possible actions none of which is ruled out by deontological prohibitions, then impartial benevolence should determine what you choose.

In contrast, where the resources you are allocating are your own, some degree of partiality is permitted or required. Yet, even here, the amount of permissible partiality is not *infinite*. You should give a benefit to your child or friend even when you could instead give a stranger a *somewhat* greater benefit. But, if you could either give to your mother an additional *minute* of happy life or give to someone with whom you have no connection an additional *decade* of happy life, you would be wrong to choose the tiny benefit for your mother rather than the very large benefit for the stranger.

Where exactly is the line dividing permissible from impermissible degrees of favouritism? A large grey area looms. On the one side, there are cases where the gap in the size of benefits is small enough to make it clear that you should favour those with whom you have special relations. On the other side, there are cases where the gap is big enough to make it clear that you shouldn't choose the smaller benefit for your friend or family member over the larger benefit for the other person. Between these two sets of cases is a large grey area, which itself has grey borders.

Complexities about patterns of decisions are also relevant. There are over a billion people in the world living in terrible poverty, with the usual concomitants—hunger, disease, low life expectancy, high infant morality, etc. Imagine that, on every occasion when I could spend some time with my friends or instead devote that time to raising money for the worst off, I chose to raise money for the worst off. In doing this, I might on each occasion be helping to produce a vastly greater good than I would produce by using the occasion to spend time with my friends. But I would probably be starving my friendships of the sustenance they must have in order to survive. Surely morality wouldn't typically require of people a pattern of decisions that effectively deprives them of friendships.

Most humans have an immediate and intense special concern for themselves, their family, and their friends. Such partiality is widespread in the animal kingdom, and the theory of evolution easily explains this. Since humans evolved from animals, it is hardly surprising that a fairly high degree of partiality is instinctual in humans. Furthermore, as Cottingham comments, while such partiality might be flawed, it 'certainly is not self-evidently so'.[8]

---

[8] Cottingham, 'The Ethics of Self-Concern', *Ethics* 101 (1991), pp. 798–817, at p. 814.

Another point of Cottingham's that I accept is that personal relationships, including family ones, are one of the central elements of the good life.[9] He focuses on the sense of fulfilment that people get from their personal relationships. While hardly rejecting that sense of fulfilment, I think personal relationships also have non-hedonic value as an element of personal good. The value of personal relationships provides some grounds for concluding that, if impartial benevolence as a guide to everyday decisions is incompatible with personal relationships, so much the worse for impartial benevolence as a guide to everyday decisions.

Even if there were not such high value in personal relationships, natural human partiality might be so deep in our genes that there is little point in claiming that we ought to be impartial. And even if natural human partiality can be suppressed to the point of elimination, how much effort and energy and stress would be involved in this suppression? And how often would the effort and energy and stress recur? Absent genetic engineering, the costs of stamping out partiality in any generation would be high. Whatever the education and habituation of one generation, the next generation would come out of the womb pretty much the same as previous generations have—that is, with a very strong predisposition to partiality. So partiality would have to be stamped out in each new generation (unless it was eliminated by genetic engineering).

In this section, I noted (a) that common-sense morality endorses constrained partiality, (b) that, very plausibly, personal relationships, which are hugely valuable, wouldn't be possible without partiality, and (c) that partiality would anyway be costly to stamp out.

3. Impartial Assessment of (First-order) Moral Rules

As I indicated in the first section, almost everyone believes that morality requires impartiality in the application of good moral rules. And those who reject the idea that morality requires impartiality in the application of good moral rules reject this idea because they reject the idea of good moral rules, not because they reject the requirement to apply good moral rules impartially if there are any good moral rules.

We have also seen that impartiality construed as impartial benevolence is required if one is occupying certain official roles. And yet, again, impartial

[9] 'Ethical Credentials of Partiality', p. 10; 'Ethics of Self-Concern', p. 816; 'Partiality and the Virtues', in R. Crisp (ed.), *How Should One Live?* (Oxford: Oxford University Press, 1996), pp. 57–76, at pp. 63–4.

benevolence as the determiner of *all* practical decisions is incompatible with people's intense special concern for themselves, their family, and their friends. Intense special concern for family and friends certainly seems permissible and even obligatory. Intense special concern for oneself certainly is natural and seems permissible, even if not obligatory. So, is impartial concern appropriate only when one occupies certain official roles?

Consider the two-level approach to impartial concern. What I mean by this is the idea that we might find that impartial assessment of (first-order) moral rules ends up favouring rules that give very considerable scope to partiality.

I contended earlier that impartial application of a rule consists in being guided solely by the distinctions and relations identified in the rule. And I pointed out that rules often direct that greater benefits go to some (e.g. the productive) than to others (e.g. the unproductive). But why are some rules the right ones? Why are the distinctions made by such and such rules the right distinctions to make? Here impartiality returns. The right distinctions, the right rules, are the ones that are impartially defensible.

What is it for a rule to be impartially defensible?

One idea is that for a rule to be impartially defensible is for it to be defensible from an agent-neutral point of view. If this idea is right, then your evaluating rules impartially is your evaluating them apart from any special attachments of yours. In your assessment of rules, you would not give extra weight to benefits that the rules produce for you, for your friends, for your family, etc.

In the assessment of rules, agent-neutrality does seem much more appealing that agent-relativity. The agent-relative assessment 'Everyone's accepting these rules is good because this maximizes benefits for me' is utterly unconvincing. So is 'everyone's accepting these rules is good because this maximizes benefits for my group'. Agent-neutral assessment effectively eliminates bias towards oneself, one's group, and indeed anyone with whom one has some special connection. The elimination of such bias at the level of fundamental assessment of possible moral rules certainly seems desirable.

One objection to the thesis that rules are impartially justified as long as they are selected by agent-neutral assessment is that there is very little prospect that the requirement that rules be evaluated agent-neutrally will by itself lead to convergence between us. Why is this an objection? One of the appealing prospects of impartial evaluation of rules is that, unlike agent-relative evaluation of rules, impartial evaluation of rules might, at least if we are all equally well apprised of the expected consequences, produce convergence among us. Admittedly, some philosophers (Gert, for example) are not optimistic about such convergence. They contend that, at least in many areas, impartial, rational, well-informed assessment cannot reasonably be expected to produce it. In contrast, I hold out the hope that impartial, rational, well-informed assessment would produce convergence. Perhaps this is in part because of the central role I take moral principles to play in interpersonal justification and conflict resolution.

Let me illustrate how the requirement that rules be evaluated agent-neutrally might not lead to convergence between us. Suppose you think that the best songwriters are the most admirable people. And suppose that you evaluate rules primarily in terms of their effects on the best songwriters. Now your assessment of alternative possible moral rules is agent-neutral. It is *not* that, *because of some special connection to you*, you focus on how much the best songwriters benefit from this or that set of rules. For example, it is not that you yourself are a songwriter, or have a songwriter as a family member or friend. Nor is it the connection between songwriters and your sentiments that underwrites your focusing on the advantages and disadvantages to songwriters of this or that set of rules. Rather, the best songwriters just are the most admirable people, according to you. So that is how you evaluate rules.

Now suppose that the most admirable people, according to me, are sports stars. Again, suppose it is *not* that, *because of some special connection to me*, I focus on how much sports stars benefit from this or that set of rules. I'm not a sports star, nor is anyone with whom I have a special connection. So, in evaluating rules by their effects on sport stars, I am evaluating these rules agent-neutrally.

The group of people to whom you are giving priority in your assessment of rules overlaps very little if at all with the group of people to whom I'm giving priority in my assessment of rules. Hence, the set of rules ranked highest by you almost surely isn't the set ranked highest by me. In this example, you and I are both evaluating rules agent-neutrally, but without much serious chance of converging on the same set of rules.

Another and perhaps even more devastating objection to the thesis that rules are impartially justified as long as they are selected by agent-neutral assessment is that evaluating rules agent-neutrally is far from sufficient to obtain plausible results. Your agent-neutral assessment of rules privileges songwriters. For example, the rules you favour might place little demand on songwriters to do good for others, because songwriters need to be left as free as possible to do their songwriting. And my agent-neutral assessment of rules privileges sports stars. The rules I favour might place little demand on sports stars to do good for others, because they need to be left as free as possible to focus on their sports. But such concessions for songwriters or sports stars are intuitively wrong. So neither of us ends up with a plausible set of rules, though we both did our respective assessments agent-neutrally.

In short, evaluating *impartially in the sense of agent-neutrally* does *not* entail evaluating with *equal concern* for everyone.[10] The examples of assessment biased towards the best songwriters and assessment biased towards sports stars are merely special cases of agent-neutral perfectionism. In the spirit of offering a less idiosyncratic agent-neutral perfectionism than the one privileging songwriters and than the one privileging sports stars, someone might hold that rules are to be evaluated in terms of the effects on the most talented, whether they be in the arts, literature, science, engineering, business, sports, military activities, etc. This evaluative stance gives priority to benefits for the talented. It is a kind of elitism of the talented.

As I said a moment ago, agent-neutral assessment of rules is better than agent-relative assessment of them. The agent-neutral assessment 'Whether or not I or anyone connected with me is talented, everyone's accepting these rules would be good because this would benefit the most talented' is better than the agent-relative assessment 'Everyone's accepting these rules would be good because this would maximize benefits for me, or for my group'.

Yet elitist assessment of the basic rules of morality is unacceptable. We've seen that elitist assessment can be agent-neutral. So an evaluative stance's being agent-neutral isn't enough to make it acceptable. Thus, if 'impartial' is taken to mean 'agent-neutral', we have to reach the conclusion that an evaluative stance's being impartial isn't enough to make the evaluative stance acceptable. Far better if we can find a meaning for 'impartial' that does make an evaluative stance's being impartial enough to make it acceptable.

And, clearly, there is a perfectly obvious and straightforward sense in which the elitist evaluative stance isn't impartial. This elitist assessment gives priority to benefits to the most talented (or most accomplished). It does not count a benefit to the untalented for as much as the same-size benefit to the talented. In this obvious sense, elitism is not impartial as between the talented and the untalented.

In fact, the most obvious form of impartial concern is utilitarian concern, i.e. concern that takes a benefit to any one individual to have exactly the same importance as the same size benefit to any other individual.

One worry about this sort of impartial assessment of rules is that there will be slippage between the levels. At the deepest level, rules are to be assessed impartially. The set of rules with the highest expected net benefit will require certain kinds of partiality in everyday decision-making about how to allocate one's own time, energy, money, etc. The set of rules with the highest expected

---

[10] This point is another that Cottingham has noted; see his 'Ethical Credentials of Partiality'. pp. 4–5.

net benefit will also include a rule allowing agents to focus their lives on their own projects. But the worry is that the impartialism in the assessment of rules will seep into everyday decision-making.[11]

This worry is misplaced. How many people do you know who manifest too much impartial concern in their day-to-day decision-making? Selfishness, strictly confined generosity, concern for the neighbour that doesn't extend to the people on the far side of the neighbour, concern for members of one culture that doesn't extend to members of other cultures—all these are very common. In contrast, people who give their own welfare and the welfare of their near and dear too little consideration in comparison with the welfare of strangers can hardly be said to be teeming in the streets. That is hardly surprising. After all, natural inclination and the desire for gratitude from near and dear line up on the side of partiality. Impartial concern is the side having to fight an uphill battle.

Another objection to impartial *utilitarian* assessment of rules is that the best rules are instead the ones that maximize expected value where this is calculated by giving some degree of *priority to benefits to the worse off*. This view about what selects the best rules is called weighted prioritarianism.[12]

How much priority do benefits to the worse off get in weighted prioritarianism? Well, definitely *less* than *absolute* priority. But how much less? Different weighted prioritarians will give different answers. And maybe no weighted prioritarian will be very certain or specific about their answers. There is thus an understandable tendency for weighted prioritarianism to be somewhat vague about how much priority should be given to benefits for the worse off.

Admittedly, at least some such versions of weighted prioritarianism generate a very plausible ranking of possible sets of moral rules. But perhaps the intuitively plausible implications that these versions of weighted prioritarianism has are the flip side of their vagueness. (Or, at least, the vaguer a principle is, the harder to find cases where the principle's implications clearly are intuitively implausible.)

If weighted prioritarianism is not vague, it specifies a specific degree of priority. But any particular specific degree of priority will be difficult to defend as better than every other degree.

---

[11] For one example of this objection, see Cottingham, 'Morality, Virtues and Consequences', in D. Oderberg and L. Laing (eds), *Human Lives* (London: Macmillan, 1997) pp. 128–43, at p. 139.

[12] For influential discussions, see Joseph Raz, *The Morality of Freedom* (Oxford: Clarendon Press, 1986), p. 227; Thomas Nagel, *Equality and Partiality* (New York: Oxford University Press, 1991), ch. 7; Derek Parfit, 'Equality and Priority', *Ratio* 10 (1997), pp. 202–21; and David Miller, *Principles of Social Justice* (Cambridge, MA: Harvard University Press, 1999), pp. 223–5. For an important recent discussion, see Marc Fleurbaey, Bertil Tungodden, and Peter Vallentyne, 'On the Possibility of Nonaggregative Priority for the Worst Off', *Social Philosophy and Policy* 26 (2009), pp. 258–85.

Another argument against weighted prioritarianism is that it cannot serve as an *impartial* foundational principle for morality. Though agent-neutral, weighted prioritarianism gives priority to benefits for the worse off, and in this way is a form of partiality towards the worse off, much as forms of elitism are forms of partiality towards an elite. If elitism is not a form of impartiality, weighted prioritarianism is not either.[13]

The argument I have just rehearsed takes impartial benevolence—in which benefits or harms to any one individual have the same importance as the same size benefits or harms to any other individual—as the most natural form of impartiality in the assessment of rules. But that view can be challenged. While agreeing that rules should be assessed impartially, we might think that this requires them to be assessed in terms of justice or fairness as well as, or even instead of, in terms of net aggregate benefit. There is a variety of views about what constitutes justice or fairness. One prominent view is that justice or fairness requires that each gets what he or she deserves. Another is the view that each gets what he or she needs. Another is the view that the worst-off position should be as good as possible. Weighted prioritarianism is another rival here. And so on.

The point in mentioning this variety of views is that each of them makes a distinction that itself needs defence. What makes someone morally deserving or undeserving? What are needs and why is satisfying them, rather than (say) increasing net aggregate benefit, pivotal? Why is a benefit for someone who is worse off better than the same-size benefit for someone who is better off?

Most theorists answer this question by arguing that the distinction in question is a (or the) focus of justice or fairness. Debate then ensues about the plausibility of such claims. I now accept that no appeal to impartiality by itself can resolve the question of which agent-neutral considerations and distinctions do, and which do not, have foundational importance. I hence withdraw my previous complaint against weighted prioritarianism that it fails as a form of impartiality.

The last objection to my approach I consider here is one of John Cottingham's. He complains that consequentialists 'see the value of individual lives as essentially derivative from their contribution to impersonally defined goodness'.[14] He writes, 'Human lives are valuable not in virtue of how far they

[13] This is an argument I first presented in *Ideal Code, Real World*, pp. 60–2. I lay out the argument at greater length in 'Up and Down with Aggregation', *Social Philosophy and Policy* 26 (2009), pp. 126–47, at pp. 141–2. In the present essay, however, I shall go on to take a different line on the relationship between impartiality and prioritarianism. And I am especially grateful to Brian Feltham, Peter Vallentyne, Andrew Williams, and Michael Otsuka for pushing me to this line.

[14] 'Ethical Credentials of Partiality', p. 8.

contribute, individually or collectively, to some giant amalgam called "the good", but in so far as they are lived in ways which make the short journey each of us has to undergo meaningful and precious.'[15]

I don't understand this objection. Impartial consequentialists typically take aggregate goodness to be made up of the welfare of individuals, and the welfare of individuals is determined by how well their lives go. Since the aggregate good is a function of the good of individuals, the good of individuals is prior to (rather than derived from) the aggregate good. If anything, the aggregate good is derived from the good of individuals.

My discussion of impartiality in the assessment of moral rules has concentrated on impartial consequentialist assessment of rules. But I do not mean to suggest that consequentialist impartiality is the only kind. Contractualism and Kantianism are often offered as accounts of fundamental moral impartiality. Most famously, John Rawls offered his original position and veil of ignorance as an alternative to utilitarian impartiality.[16]

As far as I know, the most plausible development of Kantian and contractualist lines of thinking appears in Derek Parfit's recent work.[17] Parfit argues that the most plausible form of Kantian contractualism holds that an act is wrong if and only if it is forbidden by principles that everyone can rationally will that everyone accept. Parfit goes on to argue that the only principles that everyone can rationally will that everyone accept are the ones whose universal acceptance would make things go best. If Parfit's arguments are sound, Kantian contractualism leads to the same principles, or rules, that rule-consequentialism endorses. There is, of course, room for dispute, e.g. about which interpretation of the phrase 'universal acceptance' makes the theory come out most plausible. But suppose those disputes can be satisfactorily resolved without undermining Parfit's arguments. In that case, the leading forms of impartial assessment of rules, i.e. Kantian/contractualist and rule-consequentialist forms of impartial assessment, will have been shown to converge on the same set of rules. That in itself would be a discovery of immense importance.

Suppose Parfit is correct that the leading forms of impartiality converge on a certain set of rules. It might be that the rules converged upon are seriously counterintuitive. Or it might be that these rules are instead intuitively plausible.

Let us consider those two possibilities. If the rules that the leading forms of impartiality converge upon are seriously counterintuitive, those who have

---

[15] Cottingham, 'Morality, Virtues and Consequences', p. 139.
[16] John Rawls, *A Theory of Justice* (Cambridge, MA: Harvard University Press, 1971), sections 3, 4, 5, 24, 30.
[17] Derek Parfit, *On What Matters* (Oxford: Oxford University Press, forthcoming).

been rejecting impartial assessment of rules will feel vindicated. On the other hand, if the rules that the leading forms of impartiality converge upon *are* intuitively plausible, then this not only enhances the credibility of those rules but also undercuts the only credible objection to impartial assessment of rules, i.e. that such assessment leads to implausible rules.

That is, the following meta-ethical principle about evaluating moral theories seems overwhelmingly plausible:

> For any two moral theories, if they are roughly equally good at cohering with independently credible intuitions about which possible rules are good ones, and if one of these theories identifies a fundamental moral principle that provides impartial justification for these rules and the other theory doesn't, then the theory that identifies a fundamental principle that provides impartial justification for the right rules is better.[18]

[18] I am grateful to the British Academy of Humanities and Social Sciences for a Research Readership, during which I worked on a project of which this is a part. For helpful comments on this chapter, I'm grateful to John Cottingham, Jonathan Dancy, David Estlund, Brian Feltham, John Kekes, Brian McElwee, William O'Brian, Andrew Williams, Jo Wolff, and two anonymous reviewers for Oxford University Press.

2

The Demands of Impartiality and the Evolution of Morality

GERALD F. GAUS

1. Impartial Reason or/and the Evolution of Morality?

Let me begin with a stylized contrast between two ways of thinking about morality. On the one hand, morality can be understood as the dictate of, or uncovered by, impartial reason. That which is (truly) moral must be capable of being verified by everyone's reasoning from a suitably impartial perspective. If we are to respect the free and equal nature of each person, each must (in some sense) rationally validate the requirements of morality. If we take this view, the genuine requirements of morality are a matter of rational reflection and self-imposed law. For Kant it seemed to be a matter of reflection by a rational individual, testing the impartiality of his maxims. For Rawls, under the proper conditions, collective deliberation by rational and reasonable parties could yield agreement on impartial rules of justice.

From another point of view, moralities are social facts with histories. The heroes of this tradition are Hume, Ferguson, and Smith. The morality we end up with is, to some extent, a matter of chance. This is by no means to say that morality is entirely arbitrary, but it does contain a significant arbitrary element. The evolution of morality is path-dependent: only because our morality started somewhere, and has changed in response to unanticipated events, can we explain why we ended up where we have, and different societies end up in different places.

In this chapter I argue that Kantian-inspired conceptions of morality—or, as I shall call them, 'public reason' conceptions—must embrace significant parts of the evolutionary view. Morality is properly seen as consisting of self-imposed requirements verified from the impartial perspective *and* as having a history that is path-dependent. Indeed, I argue that only an evolved morality can be justified to everyone, and so only an evolved morality provides the basis for each treating all as free and equal moral persons.

I begin in Section 2 by sketching a family of moral views that are committed to what I call the Public Justification Principle. It is important to begin by reminding ourselves why respect for others requires the public justification of moral requirements from the impartial perspective, and why only moral requirements that in some sense are universally self-legislated are consistent with treating our fellows as free and equal moral persons. Once I have sketched the grounding of the Public Justification Principle, I then consider in Section 3 what seems to be an insuperable problem for public reason views of morality: reasonable persons are characterized by a deep pluralism about the basis for self-legislation. Section 4 briefly considers Rawls's early proposal for solving the problem of public justification under evaluative pluralism. Section 5 points the way to a more adequate approach to the problem, but we shall see that the solution is indeterminate; Section 6 argues that social evolutionary processes can complete the justificatory process. I reflect on some of the implications of the analysis in Section 7.

2. Respect for Persons and the Impartial Authority of Morality

2.1. Morality, Authority, and the Threat of Subjugation

Social morality provides a set of principles that provides the basis for a person to make moral demands on others. As John Stuart Mill rightly recognized, when one appeals to social morality one makes a claim to something like moral authority over another:[1] one is claiming that, on this matter, the other is not to do as she wishes, but as you require. Stephen Darwall has recently stressed the way in which interpersonal morality involves 'authority relations that an addresser takes to hold between him and his addressee'.[2] To make a moral demand on another is to assume a practical authority over her to make demands and to demand compliance.[3] To make a moral demand is not simply to call attention to your claim and its merits, but to insist that the claim be backed up

---

[1] See John Stuart Mill, *On Liberty* [1859] in *The Collected Works of John Stuart Mill*, ed. J. M. Robson (Toronto: University of Toronto Press, 1977), vol. 18, ch. 1.

[2] Stephen Darwall, *The Second-person Standpoint: Morality, Respect and Accountability* (Cambridge, MA: Harvard University Press, 2006), p. 4.

[3] *Ibid.*, pp. 10–11.

with an authoritative moral reason for the other to do as you demand.[4] Now although this form of authority is as commonplace as our moral life, it is by no means unproblematic. One person (Alf) is supposing that his view of what the other (Betty) must do (whether Betty wishes to or not) trumps her view of her reasons to act, and so what she must do. If she does not comply, he will normally deem her blameworthy, and liable to moral criticism. As Darwall points out, when Alf makes a moral claim on Betty he is not requesting or calling attention to his claim: he is demanding that Betty complies. Alf thus seems to be claiming that Betty is subject to his authoritative demands. She must obey even when she disagrees. But now we are faced with the question: by what right does Alf claim such authority over the life of Betty?

Alf's answer to the challenge, no doubt, will be that it is not his authority, but the authority of morality to which Betty is subject. But 'morality' only 'speaks' through its interpreters, and Betty dissents from Alf's interpretation. As Hobbes recognized, '[a]ll laws, written and unwritten, have need of interpretation'.[5] So the question becomes: on what grounds does Alf claim that his interpretation of the demands of morality has authority over Betty? Alf is claiming that his reason is 'right reason'—but in almost every dispute, each party claims that his or her reason is right reason. Hobbes was deeply worried about this problem:

when men that think themselves wiser than all others clamour and demand right reason for judge, yet seek no more but that things should be determined by no other men's reason but their own, it is . . . intolerable in the society of men . . . For they do nothing else, that will have every of their passions, as it comes to bear sway in them, to be taken for right reason, and that in their own controversies: bewraying [sic] their want of right reason by the claim they lay to it.[6]

As always, Hobbes's concern is social stability—a concern that should not be dismissed or trivialized. His general point, though, is profound and goes beyond stability. Because of *course* each party to a dispute claims that his reason is right reason, for Alf to demand that others conform to his reason *because* it is right reason betrays his lack of true reason by ignoring the nature of the dispute: the deep disagreement about the demands of right reason and the interpretation of social morality. For Kantians, however, not only is Alf's attitude anti-social and rationally suspect; it evinces a lack of respect for the moral freedom and equality of Betty. Alf appears to be claiming that he is a superior interpreter of morality, and so Betty is under his moral authority, though the crux of

[4] Stephen Darwall, *The Second-person Standpoint: Morality, Respect and Accountability*, p. 76.
[5] Thomas Hobbes, *Leviathan* [1651], ed. Michael Oakeshott (Oxford: Basil Blackwell, 1948), p. 180 (ch. 26).
[6] *Ibid.*, p. 26 (ch. 5).

their dispute is precisely about who is the superior interpreter. Although it is something of a rhetorical overstatement, we can appreciate the force Jeffrey Reiman's worry that Alf's assertion that he 'has a higher authority' over how Betty should act raises the spectre of 'subjugation'—that 'the very project of trying to get our fellows to act morally' may be 'just pushing people around'.[7]

This worry about using claims to superior moral insight as a way of 'pushing others around' is, I think, quintessentially liberal. Recall that Locke's canonical liberal text, *The Second Treatise*, with its adamant denial of natural authority, was written as a response to Robert Filmer's assertion that some were naturally the moral superiors of others. Filmer vigorously upheld his view against those who advocated the 'dangerous opinion' of the 'natural freedom of mankind'.[8]

Every man that is born, so far from being born free, that by his very birth he becomes a subject to him that begets him: under which subjection he is always to live, unless by immediate appointment from God, or by grant or death of his Father, he became possessed of that power to which he was subject.[9]

If there is any sense in saying that men are born free, Filmer insisted, it is that men are not born subjugated as servants, but as sons.[10] Filmer did not deny that fathers (and so monarchs) are bound by the (true) laws of nature to act justly towards their subjects and to care for their welfare, but he insisted that the authority to interpret this law resided in the father: the upshot is that the family is governed by the reason of the father.[11] Although Filmer was distinctive in deriving natural moral authority from patriarchal authority, he is by no means unique in upholding a claim that some people have intrinsic moral authority over others. Aristotle's account of the status of slaves as 'living tools' incapable of friendship,[12] Mill's own acceptance of authoritarianism for 'races' in their 'nonage',[13] and even, I think, Sidgwick's principle that 'enlightened Utilitarians' may advocate an 'esoteric morality' that is the criterion of genuine moral requirements but is not revealed to *hoi polloi*[14]—all seem to conform to

---

[7] Jeffrey Reiman, *Justice and Modern Moral Philosophy* (New Haven, CT: Yale University Press, 1990), p. 1.

[8] Robert Filmer, *Patriarcha, Patriarcha and Other Political Works*, Peter Laslett, ed. (Oxford: Blackwell, 1949), p. 53.

[9] Filmer, 'Directions for Obedience to Government in Dangerous or Doubtful Times', in *ibid.*, p. 231.

[10] Filmer, *Patriarcha*, pp. 73–4.   [11] *Ibid.*, p. 96.

[12] Aristotle, *Nicomachean Ethics*, trans. Sir David Ross (Oxford: Oxford University Press, 1954), p. 212 [1161a30–b19].

[13] Mill, *On Liberty*, ch. 1, para. 10.

[14] Henry Sidgwick, *The Methods of Ethics*, 7th edn [1907] (Chicago, IL: University of Chicago Press, 1962), pp. 489ff.

the picture of claims to superior insight into morality as being ways that some people employ to push others around.[15]

2.2. Universal Self-legislation

Social morality presupposes that we claim authority over others, yet liberals insist that we are all free and equal moral persons, and so each has an equal status as moral interpreter; each should be free to interpret her own moral obligations for herself. The authority of morality cannot be partial: it cannot privilege the perspective of some free and equal moral person over another's such that one simply occupies the role of legislator while the other is subject. How can liberalism's commitments to moral freedom and the absence of natural authority of one person over another be reconciled with the authoritative nature of moral demands? Kant's ideal of the realm of ends provides the core insight: 'A rational being belongs to the realm of ends as a member when he gives universal laws in it while also himself a subject to these laws. He belongs to it sovereign when he, as legislating, is subject to the will of no other.'[16] Kant insists that for morality to be consistent with 'the dignity of a rational being', a rational being must obey no law other than that he gives himself. The individual is both legislator and subject.

Kant's depiction of the self-legislative nature of a free and impartial morality stresses that each rational being has a will that is legislative for every other will, giving laws to all to which he is, *qua* subject, also subject. Our moral freedom consists in being a legislative member in the realm of ends,[17] but we are also subject to such legislation. Now it is important that by 'realm' Kant meant 'the systematic union of different rational beings through common laws'.[18] So Kant does not think it is fine if you legislate in one way and I in another. Implicit in Kant's analysis of morality, then, is a unanimity requirement: we legislate common laws. The same morality thus must be legislated by all rational beings.

2.3. The Generic Public Justification Principle

If we take seriously the unanimity requirement implicit in Kant's notion of universal legislation, we are led to a view of an impartial moral justification along the lines of:

[15] For a general characterization of moral authoritarianism, see my *Social Philosophy* (Armonk, NY: M.E. Sharpe, 1999), pp. 6ff.
[16] Immanuel Kant, *Foundations of the Metaphysics of Morals* [*Grundlegung zur Metaphysik der Sitten,* 1785] ed. and trans. Lewis White Beck (Indianapolis, IN: Bobbs-Merrill, 1959), p. 52. [Akademie 434].
[17] *Ibid.*, pp. 51–2 [Akademie 433–4].   [18] *Ibid.*

The (Generic) Public Justification Principle: M is a (*bona fide*) moral requirement only if each and every Member of the Public *P* has sufficient reason(s) *R* to accept *M* as a binding requirement on her.

The Public Justification Principle, as Rawls puts it, conceives of impartial moral principles as mutually acknowledged 'by free persons who have no authority over one another'.[19]

Because I am concerned with a family of 'public reason views', I focus on a generic formulation of the principle. Because this is a generic principle, I leave open the crucial problem of just how to specify *P* (whether the Members of the Public must all be reasonable, fully rational, etc.). The Public Justification Principle supposes that there is some specification (and almost certainly some idealization) of *P* such that if each member were so described, each would rationally endorse *M*.[20] One Kantian specification of Members of the Public (which I employ as a term of art) is the realm of rational beings—in so far as we act as Members of the Public, we act in accord with our status as rational moral beings; Rawls's parties are reasonable and rational.

For simplicity's sake, in this essay I suppose that Members of the Public are conceived of as deliberating about specific moral requirements. We can think of the problem posed to Members of the Public as: what should be the moral requirement, *M*, regulating matter *X*? This is closest to the Kantian-inspired view of the problem as legislating. It is more accurate, however, to suppose, as Rawls did in 'Justice as Fairness', that the object of justification is a moral practice: an interlocking set of moral requirements, permissions, and prohibitions that distinguishes certain roles and obligations. Thus the Members of the Public should probably be thought of as considering sets of moral requirements such as those that comprise the practices of ownership, personal privacy, protection of the person, and so on. Everything said here can be translated into the notion of a moral practice. What concerns Members of the Public is whether they have reason to endorse the same requirements or practices.

2.4. The Companion Deliberative Model

One of Rawls's fundamental insights was that the justificatory problem—what moral requirements do Members of the Public have reason to endorse?—can

---

[19] John Rawls, 'Justice as Fairness' [1958] in *John Rawls: Collected Papers*, ed. Sammel Freeman (Cambridge, MA: Harvard University Press, 1999), p. 55.

[20] It might be argued that an egoist has reason to accept *M* as a binding requirement, but to ignore *M*. We must recall that we are considering certain idealized persons (e.g. reasonable); in a fuller account we would also have to explicate what is involved in 'accepting' a moral requirement, and whether the egoist we are considering can be said to have accepted *M*. I am indebted to Jim Sterba for pressing me on these points and pointing out the inadequacy of an earlier formulation.

be translated into a deliberative problem.[21] Suppose we understand a member *i* of *P*, deliberating under some conditions *C*, as consulting her relevant evaluative standards—the full set of considerations that is relevant to her decision whether to accept some moral requirement (§3). After consulting her evaluative standards, *i* proposes her preferred moral requirement, M_i: the moral requirement that, on her (somewhat idealized) reasoning, best conforms to her evaluative standards. (This procedure is akin to that utilized by Rawls in 'Justice as Fairness'.)[22] Suppose also that, on the basis of her own evaluative standards, each *P* under *C* ranks everyone's proposed requirement.

This simple statement of the deliberative problem—as I said, inspired by Rawls's first formulation of his own theory—has real advantages over more familiar formulations. One of the problems with much contemporary contractualism is that it typically employs a notion of reasonable acceptability (or rejectability) without being clear about the feasible set: to ask what one can reasonably accept (or reject) without knowing the feasible alternatives is an ill-formed choice problem. 'Rationally rejectable in relation to what options?' is the crucial question. In our deliberative problem the feasible set is defined by the set of all proposals. Rawls never made this common mistake: the parties to his original position in *A Theory of Justice* choose among a small set of traditional proposals, so their choice problem is well defined. However, Rawls built into his later and more famous formulations of the deliberative problem a host of controversial conditions (as we shall see in Section 4, the aim of making the choice problem determinate must lead to demanding and controversial conditions). Instead, our deliberative problem is a straightforward articulation of the Public Justification Principle that it is meant to model: if one accepts the Public Justification Principle as posing the correct justificatory problem, there is strong—indeed, I think compelling—reason to accept this deliberative model. The only elements it adds is some specification of the conditions under which people deliberate (for example, that they are not bargaining, and the nature of the information sets) and the interpretation of what one has a reason to accept in terms of a ranking of the proposals advanced by each member of *P* under *C*, translating the idea of 'rational acceptance' into each person's ordinal rankings based on his evaluative standards. As I said, doing so is a compelling way to make the deliberative problem well formed, providing a non-arbitrary feasible set from which the members of *P* under *C* are to choose.

---

[21] John Rawls, *A Theory of Justice*, rev. edn (Cambridge, MA: Belknap Press of Harvard University Press, 1999), p. 16 (p. 17 of the original edition).

[22] 'Their procedure . . . is to let each person propose principles . . .' ('Justice as Fairness', p. 53). As will be seen, in a number of ways I am proposing going back to the project begun in that classic essay, which posed a simple and compelling Kantian deliberative problem.

But this leads directly to the really basic question: what are their evaluative standards?

3. Evaluative Pluralism and Moral Disagreement

As stated, most moral theories can endorse the Public Justification Principle and its companion deliberative model: if the parties are so specified that they all accept, say, a certain substantive moral theory, moral requirements justified by that moral theory would also be justified by the Public Justification Principle. The Public Justification Principle and its companion deliberative model would do little or no work. The Public Justification Principle becomes a substantive test of a moral requirement if we accept Rawls's claim that a wide range of rational disagreement is the 'normal result of the exercise of human reason'.[23] Suppose, then, that we accept reasonable pluralism in the sense that our characterization of the members of P deliberating under conditions C includes that members of P reason on the basis of different values, ends, goals, etc. This does not prejudge whether values are 'ultimately' plural, for perhaps fully rational, omniscient beings would agree on what is valuable: the important point for public reason views is that the characterization of Members of the Public allows for diversity in the basis of their reasoning about what moral requirements to endorse. Abstracting from the notions of goods, values, moral 'intuitions', and so on, let us say that Σ is an evaluative standard for Member of the Public Alf if holding Σ (along with various beliefs about the world) gives Alf a reason to endorse M_1 over M_2.[24] Evaluative standards, then, are to be distinguished from justified moral requirements: as I have characterized them they need not meet the test of public justification, but are the reasons Members of the Public draw on to devise proposals and rank proposed moral requirements. Evaluative standards are prior to justified moral claims only in the sense that they are the bases of public justification. This priority does not imply, though, that they are logically prior, or developmentally prior, to moral codes and convictions, as if evaluative standards are somehow formed independently of the moral environment in which one lives. To some extent, a person's evaluative standards are the result of moral convictions that she has gained

---

[23] Rawls adds: 'within the framework of free institutions of a constitutional regime'. *Political Liberalism*, paperback edn (New York: Columbia University Press, 1996), p. xviii.

[24] I leave aside here whether Σ is itself a belief about the world, or supervenes on one, as ethical naturalists would have it. Nothing in the analysis precludes moral realism as a meta-ethical or metaphysical thesis. The rationality-based constraint on justificatory reasons is the crucial principle on which the analysis rests.

through living in a community. But until these moral convictions are publicly justified they are merely her own view of morality, or her moral intuitions, which cannot form the bases of demands that treat others as free and equal.

I suppose, then, plurality of evaluative standards for P under C. How great is this pluralism? Again, each public reason view will specify a different characterization. Any plausible liberal public reason view, however, must admit (i) great diversity of evaluative standards (and so recognize the importance of reasonable pluralism) while (ii) also limiting the range of considerations that may be drawn upon in justification. Some of these limits (point ii) are implicit in the very idea of public justification. The point of public justification is for Alf to treat Betty as a free and equal moral person while also demanding that she conform to certain moral requirements. He can do this if, from her own evaluative perspective, she too has reason to accept these requirements. Suppose, then, Alf seeks to justify requirement M to Betty by appealing to her standard Σ_B, which leads her to endorse M. But suppose that Alf also holds that Σ_B is not an intelligible or reasonable basis for endorsing M; on his view, either she has no good reason to hold Σ_B, or there is no sound deliberative route from it to M. If so, then he cannot understand himself to have justified M. As a Member of the Public, he cannot think that deliberation based on that standard provides Betty (as another Member of the Public) with a reason to endorse a requirement if in his view it is an unintelligible or unreasonable basis for her deliberation. That her unreasonable standard leads her to accept M cannot lead him to think Betty has a reason to endorse M: garbage in, garbage out. A plausible conception of evaluative pluralism, then, must accept some version of what we might call 'mutually intelligible evaluative pluralism' *at the level of members of P*. Members of P will see themselves as deeply disagreeing about the basis for accepting a requirement, but will acknowledge that the bases of others' reasoning is intelligible and is relevant to the justificatory problem. As Isaiah Berlin might say, the range of plausible pluralism of members of P is limited by the 'common human horizon'.[25] Moreover, there is empirical evidence that our actual value disagreements are not so much about what is or is not valuable, but how we order shared (and so mutually intelligible) values.[26]

The problem for liberal public justification now is manifest. If the parties employ their evaluative standards to evaluate different proposed moral requirements, so long as their disagreements in evaluative standards are great, these

---

[25] See my *Contemporary Theories of Liberalism: Public Reason as a Post-Enlightenment Project* (London: Sage, 2003), ch. 2.

[26] See Milton Rokeach, *The Nature of Human Values* (New York: The Free Press, 1973), p. 110; Milton Rokeach, 'From Individual to Institutional Values', in his *Understanding Values* (London: Collier Macmillan, 1979), p. 208.

disagreements will seem inevitably to result in great disagreement in their rankings of candidates for moral requirements. If a Member of the Public Alf holds ranking $\Sigma_1 > \Sigma_2$ (read as 'Σ_1 is ranked above Σ_2') while Betty maintains that $\Sigma_2 > \Sigma_1$, then if these are the only relevant standards, and, if within a perspective the degree of justification of moral requirements varies monotonically with the ranking of evaluative standards, Alf will hold $M_1 > M_2$, while Betty will rank the requirements $M_2 > M_1$. To be sure, the Members of the Public may display consensus on some basic moral requirements (as Berlin suggests, they may all see as wrong pushing pins into babies for fun), but given the depth of evaluative pluralism, and the importance of Members of the Public's evaluative standards in their deliberations about what moral requirements they have most reason to accept, we would expect that great disagreement in evaluative rankings would result in great disagreements in the rankings of possible moral requirements. If the basis for judging moral requirements is diverse, so too will be the evaluations of moral requirements. Deep moral disagreement would seem the inevitable result of deep evaluative pluralism. The public reason liberal seems to have embraced incompatible requirements: justified morality requires rational consensus, but evaluative pluralism leads to disagreement. What's a liberal to do?[27]

4. Rawls's Great Idea

Because we have attributed significant evaluative pluralism to our Members of the Public in the deliberative model, the Kantian project of uncovering moral principles that can be legislated by all (and apply to all) is best cast in terms of a collective-choice problem. Rawls was the first to see this. As he notes in his seminal 1958 paper on 'Justice as Fairness', we could try to derive the principles of justice 'from *a priori* principles of reason, or claim that they were known by intuition'.[28] Instead, Rawls proposed to look at the choice of principles to govern social practices as a collective-choice problem in which rational individuals compromise with each other when deciding on principles of justice.[29] Rawls was clearly aware how closely this project resembled certain problems in game theory. For now, I call attention to four points:

(i) A point of some interest (that is typically overlooked, especially by philosophers) is Rawls's remark that the reasoning of a party in the deliberative

---

[27] One way out of the problem—which I think is Kant's—is to bracket pluralism and suppose that we have the same basic human aims. I criticize this Kantian 'solution' in 'Recognized Rights as Devices of Public Reason', *Philosophical Perspectives: Ethics* 23 (2009), pp. 112–36.
[28] Rawls, 'Justice as Fairness', p. 52.   [29] *Ibid.*, p. 55.

situation might be conceived of as 'if he were designing a practice in which his enemy were to assign him his place'.[30] It is seldom appreciated that if this assumption were justified, maximin reasoning by the parties would be uncontroversially correct. This would, essentially, make the parties' deliberations mimic reasoning in a zero-sum game, and, as Rawls well knew, von Neumann demonstrated that maximin is the correct solution to such games.[31] So *if* it were correct to see the choice problem in this way (which, Rawls is driven to admit, it isn't), *then* the deliberative problem would have a determinate, uniquely rational, solution.[32]

(ii) Rawls, however, did not pursue this justification of maximin. In 'Justice as Fairness' he explicitly stated that the parts of game theory that most closely related to his project were cooperative games and group decision-making, not zero-sum games.[33] It is remarkable that in 1958 Rawls already recognized that cooperative bargaining theory was relevant to his collective-choice problem. Rawls thus began to develop a bargaining solution.

(iii) Rawls, however, rejected formal bargaining theory such as that proposed by R. B. Braithwaite in 1955. Rawls's objection—and this applies to other formal accounts such as John Nash's—is that threat advantage is relevant to the final bargain, and 'To each according to his threat advantage is hardly a principle of fairness'.[34] Thus, while Rawls clearly saw the choice problem as one that involved a sort of bargaining or compromise, he insisted that formal game-theoretic approaches were inappropriate. The parties do not,

as in the theory of games . . . decide on individual strategies adjusted to their respective circumstances in the game. What the parties do is to jointly acknowledge certain *principles* of appraisal relating to their common *practices* either as already established or merely proposed. They accede to standards to judgment, not to a given practice; they do not make any specific agreements, or bargains, or adopt a specific strategy. The

---

[30] Rawls, 'Justice as Fairness', p. 54. This remark, which has puzzled many commentators, is repeated in both editions of *A Theory of Justice*, p. 133 (p. 152 of the 1971 edition).

[31] See my *On Philosophy, Politics and Economics* (Belmont, CA: Wadsworth, 2007), section 4.1.

[32] Because, in the end, the conditions that would render maximin the uncontroversially correct choice rule do not characterize the original position, Rawls advances different considerations in its favour. In particular he argues that because the parties choose under radical uncertainty, reliance on the maximin rule is plausible. This is consistent with decision theory at the time; in 1951, for example, L. T. Savage noted that the minimax principle was central to the theory of choice when the actor cannot assign probabilities. However, more recent treatments of decision-making under such conditions do not favour minimax (or maximin). See L. T. Savage, 'The Theory of Statistical Decision', *Journal of the American Statistical Association*, vol. 46 (March 1951), p. 59. See also Edward F. McLennen, *Rationality and Dynamic Choice* (Cambridge: Cambridge University Press, 1990), pp. 25–8.

[33] See 'Justice as Fairness', note 9, which points the reader to these chapters of R. Duncan Luce and Howard Raiffa, *Games and Decisions* (New York: Wiley, 1957), i.e. chs 6, 14.

[34] Rawls, 'Justice as Fairness', p. 58n.

subject of their acknowledgement is, therefore, very general indeed; it is simply the acknowledgement of certain principles of judgment, fulfilling certain general conditions to be used in criticizing the arrangement of common affairs . . . One could, if one likes, view the principles of justice as the 'solution' of this highest order 'game' of adopting, subject to the procedure described, principles of argument for all particular 'games' whose peculiarities one can in no way foresee.[35]

Formal bargaining solutions appear to give determinacy to the collective-choice problem. Their determinacy, though, is largely illusory: they yield clear determinate solutions only if we accept their controversial frameworks. The most favoured solution today is Nash's, but it can have counterintuitive implications. Even disregarding this, the determinacy is only at the level of mixes of cardinal utility satisfaction: until we specify the utility functions, the formal solution is of little help.

(iv) Having rejected formal bargaining solutions, Rawls was left with two principles of choice: equality and the Pareto Principle.[36] Equality, Rawls argued, would be accepted since 'there is no way for anyone to win special advantage for himself'.[37] (However, he also employed a version of maximin: since a practice that allows special treatment may turn against you, it is safer not to allow it.) The Pareto Principle was invoked as a defeater of the equality presumption: if some inequality-inducing improvement is preferred by everyone, then it will be agreed to. We thus get early formulations of the two principles: the first principle, which requires the greatest equal liberty, and the second, which allows inequalities that work to the advantage of all.

Because Rawls rejected formal bargaining solutions, his choice problem was indeterminate. The argument for egalitarian bargains is often a case of informal 'splitting the difference' bargains, and, while these bargains will sometimes arise, it is hard to see how, without a great many more assumptions, egalitarian bargains are the right general result.[38] The Pareto Principle, however, is much more solidly grounded as a principle of rational collective choice (if in everyone's ordering M_1 is ranked as better than M_2, then M_1 should be ranked as better than M_2 in the social ordering). But, as Rawls came to realize, the Pareto Principle is often indeterminate.[39] If we wish to generate a collective moral deliberation situation with a determinate choice, we must specify the

---

[35] *Ibid.*, p. 57.

[36] For an excellent analysis, see Robert Paul Wolff, *Understanding Rawls* (Princeton, NJ: Princeton University Press, 1977), chs 4 and 5.

[37] Rawls, 'Justice as Fairness', p. 55.

[38] This is brought out by Ken Binmore's complex argument for an egalitarian contract in *Natural Justice* (Oxford: Oxford University Press, 2005), ch. 11.

[39] See Rawls, 'Distributive Justice' [1967] in Freeman (ed.), *John Rawls: Collected Papers*, p. 136. The indeterminacy of the Pareto Principle in Rawls's first formulation of his contract is stressed by Wolff.

motivations and information sets of the parties in a detailed way so that they all reason in the same way and will choose the same point on the Pareto frontier. Hence the path that led to *A Theory of Justice*: its strengths and weakness are well known. Although Rawls began by posing a problem of collective choice, ultimately, as he tells us, the problem is reduced to the reasoning of a single person. If we exclude 'knowledge of those contingencies which set men apart . . .', then since 'everyone is equally rational and similarly situated, each is convinced by the same arguments'.[40] Instead of (to put the matter uncharitably) rigging the deliberative problem to give us a determinate result, let us explore the ignored option: learning to live with the Pareto Principle's indeterminacy. *That is, let us consider what our theory of a morality among free and equal persons will look like if we accept that the problem of collective legislation for members of P under C is inherently indeterminate.*

5. Paretian Collective Deliberation

5.1. *Unanimous Legislation I: The First Application of The Pareto Criterion*

Let us now return to the companion deliberative model. Given the plural basis of the parties' deliberation, we cannot preclude that some members of *P* under *C* will propose requirements that others might find objectionable. To be sure, given that all are employing evaluative standards that all as members of *P* under *C* see as relevant to moral deliberation, there will not be out-and-out immoral or absurd proposals, such as 'It required that all others be my slaves because that will be best for me,' but our differences in evaluative standards can still lead some to endorse moral requirements that others find highly objectionable. Suppose we are deliberating about moral norms to regulate speech. Based on a ranking of not giving offence to others over freedom and other political values, a person may propose a highly restrictive doctrine according to which in all public speech, including political debate, one is morally prohibited from speaking in ways that any other citizen considers offensive. To some free and equal moral person, such a proposed moral requirement M_x may be worse than a full Hohfeldian liberty regarding political speech. If we all have Hohfeldian moral liberties regarding speech, each would have no moral duty to refrain from any sort of speech, though no one would have a duty to refrain from

Understanding Rawls, p. 51. On the indeterminacy of the principle, see Russell Hardin, *Indeterminacy and Society* (Princeton, NJ: Princeton University Press, 2003), ch. 4.

[40] Rawls, *A Theory of Justice*, pp. 17, 120.

interfering with the speech of others. Now at the point in a person's ordering at which she would place, on the basis of her evaluative standards, a Hohfeldian moral liberty—a 'no moral requirement'—over this area of social life to all remaining proposals, she has what we might call a 'no agreement point'. She would rather not have a collective agreement than endorse, say, a palpably unfair requirement. There are, of course, generally great costs to this: a shared morality is in many ways fundamental to our social life and to treating others as fellow moral persons. But we cannot insist that a person hold that every proposal is better than failure to legislate: there may be some proposed moral requirements that she simply cannot see as in any way endorsed by her evaluative standards. We thus bifurcate each individual's ordering into an eligible set (requirements that are better than Hohfeldian moral liberties) and an ineligible set (those that are ranked worse than moral liberties by a member of P under C).

5.2. Unanimous Legislation II: The Second Application of the Pareto Criterion

According to the first application of the Pareto criterion we can eliminate as a possible moral requirement among 'citizens of the realm of ends' (members of P under C) any proposed moral requirement that is in the ineligible set of any Member of the Public. Only requirements that everyone holds are better than no requirements at all are in the eligible set. For us to appeal to a moral requirement outside the eligible set in our relations with the rejecter would, as Rawls says, be insisting on standards of judgement that, as a free moral person, she cannot accept as legitimate: she cannot will them to be universal laws regulating all Members of the Public. One thing we might mean by the inability to will a law—or its rational rejectability—is that no law at all would be better than such a law.[41]

We can invoke the Pareto criterion again: we can exclude any proposed requirement that, while in the eligible set of each individual, is Pareto-dominated by another proposed moral requirement. Requirement M_2 is Pareto-dominated by M_1 if and only if in each Member of the Public's ordering, $M_1 > M_2$. If everyone holds that M_1 is better than M_2, then the morality should be M_1 rather than M_2. Acting on M_2 would manifest a sort of collective irrationality: even though everyone sees it as inferior to M_1, we follow it anyway. What remains after our two invocations of the Pareto criterion is a set of

---

[41] If we interpret the idea of a person having reason to accept M as a member of P under C as implying that she does not think that there is *any* superior alternative requirement, then we will get a null set of 'universally willed requirements'. This interpretation of universal legislation is plausible only if we can justify a determinate deliberative solution—an idea I have argued we should abandon.

optimal eligible moral requirements: no proposed requirement in the set is ineligible in anyone's ranking, nor is it dominated by any other member of the set.

5.3. *The Deliberative Model Is Indeterminate*

It has been the traditional aim of contractualist moral theory to whittle the set of optimal eligible requirements (over any area of social life or any practice) to a singleton. If we could design a choice situation among suitably described individuals such that one proposed requirement remained in the optimal eligible set, we would have discovered the uniquely correct moral duty. In this way moral philosophy could uncover the correct morality governing the realm of ends. The move to a much thicker description of the choice situation in *A Theory of Justice* was motivated by the aim of ensuring that the same requirement be at the top of everyone's ranking.[42] I believe that, along with the more noticed move to the political in Rawls's later work, he also abandoned the idea that only one set of principles of justice remained after the contractualist argument. Justice as fairness, as Rawls interpreted it in his later work, is simply one liberal conception of justice, because each of its constituent 'elements can be seen in many different ways, so there are many liberalisms'.[43] Rawls acknowledges that there are diverse interpretations of the basic concept of a liberal political order. Indeed, he insists that 'it is inevitable and often desirable that citizens have different views as to the most appropriate political conception; for the public culture is bound to contain different fundamental ideas that can be developed in different ways'.[44] Rawls also accepted that citizens arguing in good faith and employing public reason will not accept 'the very same principles of justice'.[45] Thus, in the end, Rawls tells us that the answer provided by public reason 'must at least be reasonable, if not the most reasonable'.[46] In his last work he abandoned the aspiration that the contractual argument reduce eligible conceptions of justice to a singleton. As I think Rawls ultimately realized, the collective-choice problem we have been discussing is indeterminate. We are left with a (non-empty) set of optimal eligible proposals.

---

[42] Rawls, *A Theory of Justice*, p. 121. Emphasis added:

The restrictions on particular information in the original position are, then, of fundamental importance. Without them we would not be able to work out any definite theory of justice at all. We would have to be content with a vague formula stating that justice is what would be agreed to without being able to say much, if anything, about the substance of the agreement itself. . . . The veil of ignorance makes possible a unanimous choice of a *particular conception of justice*. Without these limitations on knowledge the bargaining problem of the original position would be hopelessly complicated.

[43] John Rawls, *Political Liberalism*, p. 223.   [44] *Ibid.*, p. 227.   [45] *Ibid.*, p. 214.
[46] *Ibid.*, p. 246.

6. Coordinating on a Morality

6.1. A 2 × 2 Toy Game Analysis

I am supposing, then, that the public justification of morality among Members of the Public leads, for every area of social life in which moral regulation is justified, to a set of optimal eligible interpretations that is not a singleton. Having taken rational collective self-legislation as far as we can go, we arrive at a number of possible requirements, all of which are evaluated as better than no moral regulation at all (i.e. pure Hohfeldian liberties), but none of which dominates any other.

At this point our Members of the Public face an impure coordination game along the lines of Figure 2.1. Suppose that M_1 and M_2 are alternative moral requirements in the optimal eligible set. The numbers in the matrix refer to ordinal utility, with high numbers indicating highly ranked options; Alf's utility is in the lower left, Betty's in the upper right, of each cell. *It is crucial to stress that by 'utility' here I mean simply a measure of the ranking of the options based on each person's evaluative standards. Utility here does not mean 'self-interest', nor is it an independent value: it is simply a summary measure of how well an option satisfies the evaluative criteria of the individual qua member of P under C.*[47] The uncoordinated outcomes indicate no shared moral requirement on this issue. Looked at *ex ante*, Betty's evaluative standards give her reason to accept practice M_1; Alf's lead him to accept M_2. *Ex ante*, Betty does not have reason to accept M_2 over M_1, nor does Alf have accept M_1 rather than M_2. They do, however, have reason to coordinate on either of the two requirements rather than none at all.

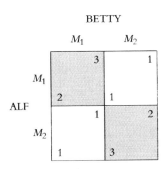

Figure 2.1. A simple impure coordination game
Note: (3= best, 1 = worst)

[47] This is fundamental point. I defend it in 'Reasonable Utility Functions and Playing the Cooperative Way', *Critical Review of International and Social Philosophy*, vol. 11 (June 2008), pp. 215–34.

Should Alf and Betty find themselves at M_1/M_1, neither would have reason to change his or her action. Given each of their evaluative standards, they have the most reason to act on practice M_1. Should they instead find themselves at M_2/M_2, each will then have most reason (given his or her evaluative standards) to act on M_2. Note that in neither case is any party induced by some external consideration to conform to a requirement that is not, from his or her perspective, optimal: *consulting simply his or her own evaluative standards, each has decisive reason to freely endorse whichever moral requirement they have coordinated on.* At M_1/M_1 Betty can demand that Alf conform and, consulting only his own evaluative standards, he will have a reason to conform; and at M_2/M_2 Alf can demand M_2, and Betty will have reason to act on it. And this even though, from the initial deliberative perspective, neither had reason to act on the other's preferred moral requirement.[48]

6.2. The Kantian Coordination Game: An N-Person Iterated Toy Game

A one-shot two-person game can give us some insight, but it is clearly an inadequate way to model the selection of a moral requirement from the optimal eligible set. The relevant coordination problem is not a single-play game, but an iterated game. We have a number of encounters with others, and each can be understood as a play in a series of impure coordination games. Now in an iterated game a person's utility (again, remember this is defined solely in terms of her evaluative criteria) is a combination of her utility in this play, plus her expectations for utility in future games. Thus a person might sacrifice utility in one play to induce play in future moves that will yield her a more favoured result. Moreover, it is certainly the case that in iterated games the play can move from one equilibrium to another. Peter Vanderschraaf and Brian Skyrms have shown how taking turns on each of the two equilibria emerges in iterated two-person impure coordination games.[49]

However, in large N-person impure coordination games with multiple equilibria, such solutions are, I think, practically impossible. In such large iterated games a bandwagon effect takes over. To intuitively see the driving force behind bandwagon effects, let us assume a cardinal utility measure (10 = best, 0 = no coordination) in a game with just two equilibria and nine players, as in Figure 2.2.

---

[48] Again, we should not be misled by the language of 'preference'. To prefer M_1 to M_2 is simply to rank M_1 over M_2 for purposes of choice; in our terms one's evaluative standards indicate reason to rank M_1 over M_2 this is all that is implied by saying one has a preference for M_1 over M_2.

[49] Peter Vanderschraaf and Brian Skyrms, 'Learning to Take Turns,' *Erkenntnis* 59 (2003), pp. 311–46.

	A	B	C	D	E	F	G	H	I
M_1	2	3	4	5	6	7	8	9	10
M_2	10	9	8	7	6	5	4	3	2

Figure 2.2. Different evaluations of two moral requirements

If player A coordinates with another player on his preferred moral requirement (M_2), he ranks that option as satisfying his evaluative standards to degree 10; if they coordinate on M_1, he ranks the outcomes as 2. If he fails to coordinate—he acts on, say, M_2 while the other acts on M_1, they each get 0.

Now what is a member of P under C to do given these differences in evaluative standards? Consider a simple-minded but illustrative policy. Each begins play by employing her favoured requirement (i.e. making demands based on it) in all her interactions (except for player E, who flips a coin and, given the flip, acts on the M_2 requirement). Again, if a player coordinates with another player on the same requirement, each gets her coordination payoff in Figure 2.2; otherwise each player receives 0 since they fail to coordinate. At the close of each round a player compares the score she received in that round with what she would have received if all others had played just as they did, but she played the opposite. If the opposite play would have resulted in a higher score, she changes her move. Assuming that each player meets every other player once in the first round, we have the payoffs shown in Figure 2.3.

Partner→	A	B	C	D	E	F	G	H	I	Total
Player A	–	10	10	10	10	0	0	0	0	40
Player B	9	–	9	9	9	0	0	0	0	36
Player C	8	8	–	8	8	0	0	0	0	32
Player D	7	7	7	–	7	0	0	0	0	28
Player E	6	6	6	6	–	0	0	0	0	24
Player F	0	0	0	0	0	–	7	7	7	21
Player G	0	0	0	0	0	8	–	8	8	24
Player H	0	0	0	0	0	9	9	–	9	27
Player I	0	0	0	0	0	10	10	10	–	30

Figure 2.3. N-person Kantian coordination game, round 1

In round 2, player F, given his own evaluative criteria, should switch his allegiance to M_2; if F had played M_2 in round 1, he would have received 25 (5×5) rather than 21. Once F switches in round 2, at the end of round 2 G will find that she would have done better (24 rather than 16) by changing to M_2, so G then will also change to M_2. Obviously, once G also has changed to M_2, H and I shall also do so. We quickly reach an all-M_2 equilibrium.

It is crucial to realize that the all-M_2 equilibrium is not reached through a collective decision procedure. Because in our example the entire process began with E's toss of a coin, it may seem as if we have simply assumed that a toss of the coin is a justified procedure for identifying a specific equilibrium. This, of course, would simply beg the question: how did we come to view this procedure as publicly justified? The Kantian coordination game is important because we can see how a *social process that is not itself justified can yield a publicly justified outcome*. As we saw in Section 2.3: 'M_2 is a (*bona fide*) moral requirement only if each and every Member of the Public P has sufficient reason(s) R to accept M_2 as a binding requirement.' Now the upshot of the first stage of the Kantian justification procedure was that M_2 is eligible as a binding, moral, requirement; and according to the second, iterated interaction, stage, each Member of the Public has sufficient reason (simply given one's own evaluative standards) to follow M_2 over every other member of the optimal eligible set as the common binding requirement. It cannot be stressed too much that the Members of the Public do not see themselves as bound by the result of the process, as if they had agreed to adopt that member of the optimal eligible set identified by a random procedure, or as if there were an independent justification for employing this procedure. Although a random element begins the process, each acts simply on her own standards, and does what she has most reason to do given the actions of others.

6.3. *The Increasing Returns of Shared Moral Requirements*

The Kantian coordination game is, of course, still terribly oversimplified, depending on a rather dumb decision rule, and an assumption that all players meet all others an equal number of times.[50] And of course we have supposed

---

[50] As Brian Skyrms shows, if players can detect other players with complementary utility functions, the analysis of the game is very different. See his *Evolution of the Social Contract* (Cambridge: Cambridge University Press, 1996), ch. 1. There has not been a great deal of work modelling what equilibrium will emerge in iterated impure coordination games; some experiments cast doubt on whether any simple mechanism, such as the most 'salient' solution, will be adopted. See Morton D. Davis, *Game*

a certain population distribution. It is by no means inevitable that the public converge on a common convention. If in Figure 2.2 the entire population were evenly divided between A-type and I-type utility functions, the population could settle into a 'polymorphic' equilibrium, with A-types always playing M_2 and I-types always playing M_1. Note that this is more likely to occur with populations split entirely into radically opposing groups and where each group ranks the other's alternative as only marginally better than no coordination at all.[51]

Despite its obvious limitations, the Kantian coordination game brings out a crucial feature of moral life among free and equal persons with a commitment to respecting each other's status: the increasing returns of coordinating on a common understanding of moral requirements. We can think of each member of P under C as having two distinct morality-related desiderata: (1) to act on the moral requirement that best satisfies her evaluative standards and (2) to act on moral requirements that are embraced by others, so that in her interactions she can make moral demands that respect their equality and moral freedom. Other things equal, a member of P under C has reason to seek a common moral life that conforms to (1), but as more and more other free and equal persons come to act on some member of the optimal eligible set, the second desideratum comes increasingly into play (even for those such as player I who place very little weight on it). Coming to accept the moral requirements that others do, so long as it is in the optimal eligible set, turns out to be the actual way in which each Member of the Public can best satisfy her entire set of evaluative standards.

Formally, converging on a common morality is an instance of increasing returns: the more others come to embrace a certain moral requirement, the more reason others have to also embrace it.[52] As we see in Figure 2.2, some people's evaluative standards may strongly favour an alternative moral requirement (consider player I), yet so long as everyone places significant importance on acting as others do (the second desideratum), our Members of the Public can still end up coordinating: as more and more adopt an alternative, even those who strongly favour another option come on board. As one option (perhaps simply because of some random event) becomes slightly more popular than the others, people will gravitate to that option (as it stands the best chance

---

Theory (Mineola, NY: Dover, 1983), pp. 133–5. On uncertainty in coordination games, see Fernando Vega-Rodondo, *Economics and the Theory of Games* (Cambridge: Cambridge University Press, 2003), pp. 188ff.

[51] This raises the interesting possibility of a Kantian account of moral multiculturalism.

[52] The path-breaking work on increasing returns was done by W. Brian Arthur. See his *Increasing Returns and Path Dependency in the Economy* (Ann Arbor, MI: University of Michigan Press, 1994).

of universal acceptance), and we witness a 'bandwagon' effect based on the increasing returns for everyone of adopting the more popular option. This dynamic is illustrated in Figure 2.4.

ALL M_1 ALL M_2

Figure 2.4. Increasing-returns dynamics
Source: Adapted from Arthur, *Increasing Returns and Path Dependency in the Economy*, p. 3

As we can see, starting out with a population evenly split between advocates of M_1 and of M_2, random events can lead the population to all M_1 or all M_2 equilibria. Which equilibrium emerges will be path-dependent: at time zero there is no reason why one or the other should emerge as the *unanimously selected choice*. Chance events, people's reactions to what they perceive as the favoured option, the publication of *A Theory of Justice* in 1971—any can lead an idealized population of Kantians to converge on one member of the eligible set. But once we have arrived at such a convergence, each Member of the Public, consulting only her own evaluative standards, will freely act on the chosen moral requirement. For our purposes, what is crucial is that the contingent and accidental way in which large groups can come to coordinate on a common practice is no bar to there being a determinate morality that all can endorse given their evaluative criteria *once it has been arrived at*.

7. The Implications of the Analysis

That our Kantians could come to share moral requirements through iterated coordination games—or more generally convergence over time because of increasing-returns dynamics—does not, of course, show us that our social morality actually evolved in this way. In so far as having a common morality is necessary to treat others as equal moral persons in one's daily interactions, the dynamics I have been considering are part of an adequate account of how we have come to share a morality, but it would be pressing credulity to think that this is the complete story. Some may go further and insist that it isn't even an important part of the story: why we have actually come to have certain moral practices and rules, they will say, depends on biological evolution, social power, and a host of other hard-headed concerns, not something so ideal as respecting others. This sort of hard-headedness seems more appealing at first sight than after reflection: that we are concerned with how our moral claims appear to others, and whether they can see a reason to abide by them, is probably a far more important factor in moral thinking than we are apt first to think. Unless the requirements of morality are affirmed by the reason of most people, it is unlikely in the extreme that a society's moral order will be stable over the long run.

The main implication of the analysis, however, does not concern the explanation of how we have arrived at our morality, but our understanding of what moral theory is, and what is demanded by the requirement that we respect others under conditions of deep evaluative plurality. Today, it seems to me, we tend to think of moral theory and rational reflection as seeking to provide determinate answers to what morality requires. We first reflect on what a rational justified morality is, and then examine our actual morality to see if it measures up. The history of thinking in this way gives us ample cause to doubt whether such rational determinacy is to be had. We have witnessed in the last thirty or so years a plethora of normative theories, each giving determinate but widely diverging pronouncements about the content of our *bona fide* moral requirements. I have suggested that there is good reason to conclude that, under conditions of evaluative pluralism, the idea of impartial rational reflection is indeterminate. Rational reflection can narrow the field, but actual interactions of good-willed people are needed to fill in the large gaps, and give us a morality that we all can will.

Once we realize that arriving at a fully justified morality could—indeed must—involve chance and path-dependency, we are apt to see moral theory in a different light. In the view of a previous generation of moral philosophers such as P. F. Strawson and Kurt Baier,[53] the starting place of moral philosophy is our actual moral practices. The question for the moral philosopher is: can these actual moral practices be justified as ones that would be acceptable from the impartial moral point of view? In our terms, the task of the moral philosopher is to determine whether our current moral practices are in the optimal eligible set: that is the best (and it is quite a bit) that impartial rational reflection can do.

---

[53] I have in mind here P. F. Strawson, 'Social Morality and Individual Ideal', *Philosophy* 36 (Jan. 1961), pp. 1–17; Kurt Baier, *The Moral Point of View: A Rational Basis for Ethics*, abridged edn (New York: Random House, 1965).

To respect others as free and equal persons does not require that we show the moral demands that we make on them are uniquely rational from the impartial perspective. Because so many moral philosophers have thought that respect requires this, they have either sought to ignore the extent of evaluative pluralism (if we all value the same thing, our rational judgements *must* converge) or invented powerful philosophical devices that (miraculously?) take our diverse evaluative judgements as inputs and yield a single, uniquely rational, determinate, answer. As philosophers we enjoy such constructions (and finding inevitable flaws), but the supposition that respecting others as free and equal requires such unequivocal answers generated by controversial devices is ultimately morally corrosive. The plausible lesson many draw from these repeated failed attempts is that respecting all as free and equal must ultimately be impossible. A moral theory that justifies our current practices if they are eligible moral requirements has a more modest ambition, but fulfilling it is all that is needed to dispel the fear that our moral demands might be just a way of pushing others around.[54]

[54] I have presented my thoughts on these matters to a number of audiences, and have greatly benefited from their questions and comments. I would like to thank the participants in the Research Triangle Ethics Circle, the Workshop on Equal Respect for Persons held at the University of Genova, the Political Theory Project at Brown University, the Philosophy Departments at the University of Reading, North Carolina State University, and the University of Georgia, and especially my colleagues and students at the University of Arizona, in particular Kevin Vallier. My special thanks go to my good friend Fred D'Agostino for encouraging this unorthodox line of inquiry.

3

Impartiality and Ethical Formation*

JOHN COTTINGHAM

1. Interpersonal versus Interior Morality

The territory of morality covers two principal domains. The first, which occupies most of the attention of present-day philosophers, covers interpersonal relations—broadly, how we should treat our fellow human beings. The second, which was the main preoccupation of many of the great moral philosophers of the ancient and early-modern periods (and which in my view is too often neglected by present-day moral philosophers), is concerned with intra-personal ethical formation—with the individual's journey towards self-knowledge, self-development, and harmonious living.[1] Of course the two domains are not unconnected: one might reasonably suppose that individuals whose inner moral life has been enriched by self-reflection, and who have made progress towards psychological maturity, will manifest this growth among other things in their attitudes and relations to others. Nonetheless, the two domains are genuinely distinct; and this is reflected in the kinds of philosophical treatment accorded to each. Investigation of our relations with our fellows rapidly involves us in a forum of public debate, covering notions such as those of mutual obligation,

* The paper was originally written for the first of the three annual conferences held by the Philosophy Department at the University of Reading as part of its three-year AHRC-funded research project on Impartiality and Partiality in Ethics (2005–8). I am grateful to participants at that first conference for helpful comments on the paper, and to all the participants in the three-year programme for the stimulus of extended discussions in this area. I am also grateful to the two anonymous readers for Oxford University Press for raising a number searching questions, some of which have prompted caveats and qualifications in this final version, although I am conscious of the shortcomings that remain.

[1] For example, self-knowledge was a primary goal of ancient Greek ethics, encapsulated in the famous motto found inscribed on the temple of Apollo at Delphi (compare Socrates' remarks in Plato, *Apology* 19Eff). For the goal of achieving a harmonious life, or in the Stoic Zeno's phrase a good 'flow of life', see A. Long and D. Sedley, *The Hellenistic Philosophers* (Cambridge: Cambridge University Press, 1987), 63A and B.

of fairness and justice, of social norms and codes. Enquiries into the nature of individual moral growth and enrichment tend instead to be concerned with the interior life, with the conditions for each person's psycho-ethical equilibrium,[2] the relationship between reason and the passions, and with the task of self-transformation—the progressive struggle to improve not just our patterns of outward conduct but our intellectual and emotional grasp of the ethical significance of our lives.

The broad contrast I am invoking here has an important bearing on the topic of impartiality and partiality in ethics. In asking about my relations with others, I am already raising a question that lays me open, at least in principle, to considerations about impartiality and fairness. For unless I try, absurdly, to deny that other people share a humanity with me, my very addressing the question of how I should behave towards them lays me open to a possible charge that in any given decision I may be giving unwarranted weight to the interests of one human being—myself—as against those of another.[3] To be sure, the potential charge may be easily rebuttable, for there may be all sorts of relevant reasons why the balance of interest tips in my favour rather than in yours, or why some network of duties or obligations singles out me and mine rather than you and yours as the recipient of my justified special concern. But the bare possibility, at least, of a charge of unjustified weighting seems at least to be in the background whenever I seriously ask the question 'How should I treat another?' In contrast, asking the more general question 'How should I live?' does not automatically seem to open me to the possibility of such interrogation. Of course part of how I should live is how I should treat others, so there is a straightforward sense in which the first question entails the second, thereby exposing me to the implications of asking the second question. But there remain many aspects of the first question that do not automatically seem to expose me to challenge in this way. Suppose I ask: 'How can I deepen my intellectual perceptions and emotional responses, so as to achieve a better insight into who I really am, and where my life should be going?'; 'How am I to ensure that my deliberations are free from the emotional distortions and projections deriving from early childhood (or from other sources) which may make some goods seem more attractive, or some ills more fearful, than they in reality are?'; 'How can I respond to the fact that the moral life is not exhausted by what I now value, given my present concerns, but embraces what I ought,

---

[2] For the term 'psycho-ethical' and its implications, see J. Cottingham, *Philosophy and the Good Life* (Cambridge: Cambridge University Press, 1998), ch. 4, §§6–8.

[3] Challenges about assigning unwarranted weight to my interests as against those of others may of course arise even when shared humanity does not apply—for example in my treatment of my pet animals; what will here be relevant is some other shared characteristic, e.g. sentience.

if I mature morally, to come to value, even though I may now resist such a change?' These are questions it seems appropriate for every morally serious human being to address, without there necessarily having to be any immediate issues hovering in the background about my status *vis-à-vis* that of others.

In religious accounts of how one should live, we often find stories of people being called to lives of contemplation, or self-purification, in seclusion from normal society, or even in complete isolation, as hermits. Religious vocations may include calls to inner transformation as well as to outward saintliness.[4] The idea that God may call an individual, sometimes to the service of others, but sometimes to a path of inner reflection, meditation, and self-examination—to the kinds of activity featured in some of the traditional programmes of 'spiritual exercises'[5]—can be interpreted in secular terms as one way of expressing an important fact about human nature. Not only, on the social level, is the record of our species marked by a long history of discord and violence, but also (and perhaps connectedly), on the individual level, each of us is born and grows up weak and vulnerable, with limited intelligence and often inadequate nurturing, beset by all manner of (often unacknowledged) inner turmoil and self-delusion, and with a tantalizingly short time at our disposal to 'sort ourselves out' and build the conditions for a mature and flourishing life. In such circumstances, quite apart from the need for the kinds of beneficial and equitable social norms variously advocated by modern moral and political theorists, there seems an equally pressing need for the kind of inner transformation sought by many of

[4] Some may object that invoking such examples moves outside the proper secular field of philosophical inquiry. But blanket exclusions of religious themes—like a recently published critique of some Pascalian arguments about the human condition, which rejected them out of hand on the grounds that they were 'based on the [false] assumption that a historical "Fall" of man actually took place'—are, it seems to me, misguided for two reasons: first because scriptural and religious ideas do not always have to be construed in a fundamentalist or crudely literalist way; but second, and more important, because such secular dismissals are curiously blind to what follows from their very assumption of the falsity of religious belief. For if (in Descartes's phrase in the First Meditation) 'we grant that everything said about God is a fiction', it must follow that such fiction has been devised by humans consciously or unconsciously for some reason or reasons—and these may well include, for example, pointing to a deep human need, or capturing a vital moral insight. The hardliner who wishes to exclude all religious reference as irrelevant to moral philosophy is thus faced with a dilemma: either religion is true, in which case such reference may be highly relevant; or else it is false, in which case it is a human invention, whose potential moral content seems *prima facie* at least as worthy of examination as that of any other human construct (for example the moral insights found in poems or novels or plays). We thus often seem to me to do our students a serious disservice by solemnly insisting, for example, that they plough through Aristotle's pompous pronouncements on 'great-souledness' while denying them the enormous moral riches of scriptural writings of a similar status and antiquity, often for no discernibly better reason than that the former are taken to be respectably secular. For the quoted critique of Pascal, see J. L. Schellenberg, *Divine Hiddenness and Human Reason* (Ithaca, NY: Cornell University Press, 1993), p. 146; cited in J. L. Kvanvig, 'Divine Hiddenness: What Is the Problem?', in D. Howard-Snyder and Paul K. Moser (eds), *Divine Hiddenness: New Essays* (Cambridge: Cambridge University Press, 2002), p. 151.

[5] See J. Cottingham, *The Spiritual Dimension* (Cambridge: Cambridge University Press, 2005), ch. 1.

the ethicists of the past. The project of morality, if one may so call it, embraces the goal of self-understanding and self-improvement, as well as—and perhaps as an inescapable condition of—the goal of better relations with our fellows.

2. The Quest for Self-improvement

Granted that the quest for self-improvement is a legitimate moral undertaking, I want to underline one aspect of it that seems to me inescapable. I have already suggested that embarking on this quest does not automatically raise impartialistic questions about the relative weightings of my interests as against those of others. But more than that, I want to argue that the quest is one that by its very nature requires me to adopt a perspective that in a sense (to be explained shortly) accords my own life a special importance, or centrality.

I have previously called this the '*autocentric*' perspective; this is not to be confused with 'egocentric' in the sense of selfish, since the *content* of the insights I achieve and the goals I make my own, as a result of interior reflection on my life and its projects, may turn out to be quite altruistic in character.[6] But even with this caveat, the label 'autocentric' now strikes me as potentially misleading, since it may have unfortunate ontological or epistemic connotations. Ontologically, it may be suggestive of the blasphemous or megalomaniac view that I am the true centre of the universe—that my life is indeed the main one that matters, or that my role in the drama of life is of prime significance.[7] According to some psychologists, this is how infants start out; and the blind fury of the two-year-old's tantrums is the first phase in the hard process of coming to learn that each ego is simply one among many. Part of our ordinary moral education is to recognize that what is central from my perspective may be peripheral from another's—a point nicely illustrated in Tom Stoppard's drama *Rosencrantz and Guildenstern are Dead*, where two of Shakespeare's faintly comic minor parts become the principals, and Hamlet a mere walk-on, with all sorts of complex resulting shifts in what occupies centre stage.[8]

Moving to the epistemic dimension, the label 'autocentric' may be misleading in another way, by suggesting that I have specially privileged access

[6] J. Cottingham, 'The Ethics of Self-Concern', *Ethics* 101 (July 1991), pp. 798–817; see esp. pp. 805, 813.

[7] Compare Stephen Darwall: 'we are prone to a kind of self-importance that involves, not just an inclination innocently to reckon values and reason from our own point of view, but to see our point of view as exclusively reason-giving, as the source of all reasons'. 'Responsibility within Relations', Chapter 7 in this volume, p. 154.

[8] Tom Stoppard, *Rosencrantz and Guildenstern are Dead* (London: Faber & Faber, 1967).

to my own thoughts and concerns, but only indirect or derivative knowledge of those of others. Whether or not this is the case—one of the well-worn stamping grounds of philosophy—I leave aside; but even if it is, it is hard to see how of itself it could carry decisive moral significance. For what is directly known, or easier to know, is by no means always what is more important from an ethical point of view.

The centrality I wish to stress, in contrast to these ontic and epistemic varieties, is an ethical centrality, a centrality of responsibility. The perspective that is mine, the place that I occupy, is such that I have a unique and special control over, and responsibility for, the activities and resources that constitute what I am. To put it very crudely, I am in charge of my life in a way no one else can be. One might suppose that an appropriate way of referring to this responsibility-based idea, given that we have discarded the label 'autocentric', would be to talk of each of us having '*autonomic*' perspective on our lives: each human being occupies a position such that they properly see their life as falling under their own autonomous control. But this alternative label also turns out to be far from ideal for my purposes, in part because the concept of autonomy is a radically ambiguous one. On one interpretation, the goal of autonomy may suggest the perfectly reasonable aim of making my life as a moral agent free from the tyranny either of irrational internal impulse or of unwarranted external control—an aim we should all share. But the goal of autonomy can also be interpreted in a much stronger way—in what may loosely be called the 'Nietzschean' or 'existentialist' way—as invoking the dangerous fantasy that I can somehow create or legislate my own values.[9] The moral quest for self-development, in my view, is most emphatically not an operation of raw will, an exercise in laying down my own self-generated goals, but rather an exercise in *discernment*, in discovering what is objectively good, and then progressively orienting myself towards it. Avoiding talk of autonomy, then, I propose, in order to convey the idea I want of a 'centrality of responsibility', to make a Greek-based coinage, and speak of the *auto-tamieutic* perspective, where the etymology connotes something like 'self-stewarding'.[10]

In being 'thrown' into the world, as Heidegger put it,[11] I find myself, whether I want to be or not, the possessor of certain gifts, or resources that

---

[9] A view sometimes (I think wrongly) seen as stemming from Kant's notion of the rational will as 'self-legislating' (*selbstgesetzgebend*). For more on the relatively benign Kantian notion of autonomy, and how it differs from the hubristic Nietzschean idea that values can be created or overturned by human fiat, see Cottingham, *The Spiritual Dimension*, ch. 3.

[10] Greek ταμιευτικος (*tamieutikos*): 'relating to a steward'.

[11] Martin Heidegger, *Being and Time* [*Sein und Zeit*, 1927], trans. J. Macquarrie and E. Robinson (New York: Harper and Row, 1962), §38.

only I am in a position to foster and utilize. Andrew, born with a gift for music, has musical opportunities which the tone-deaf Brian cannot pursue; whereas on the other hand he cannot implement Brian's gift for painting, because he lacks it, and vice versa. The various talents are capacities and faculties that characteristically require the continuing efforts of the possessor in order to bear fruit.[12] Those efforts, moreover, must, if they are to have ethical value, be responsive to objective moral facts about the kinds of good the talents are fitted to promote: the possessor of a talent does not have absolute control to use it in any way he sees fit, but is in this sense more of a 'steward', working according to predetermined conditions of appropriate use. By the same token, the possession of talents carries with it a responsibility that they should to be utilized fruitfully: this cannot be evaded by a denial of the gifts, or a wilful refusal to develop them. Talk of innate 'gifts', incidentally, need not be construed in an objectionably elitist way; for I take the parable of the talents found in the New Testament to be saying *not* that a more gifted person is more valuable than a less, but rather that much is required of those to whom much is given.[13] The man with five talents is, whether he wishes it or not, responsible for developing his resources properly—something only he can do. And the man with only one talent has no less a responsibility, one he cannot evade by complaining that he has fewer than others, or by simply letting his talent atrophy or lie dormant.

The thesis, then, is that the moral quest for self-knowledge and self-improvement requires me to adopt an 'auto-tamieutic' perspective: one from which I acknowledge the special and unique responsibility I have for understanding and properly developing my moral character, and the unique set of abilities that has been given to me. I am in an important sense steward of my own personal resources.[14] This means, in the first place, that I am responsible

[12] Of course we have innate gifts that seem to fall into our lap: some people can sing beautifully without effort; but such talents can bear fruit only if developed properly. A gifted singer who confines herself to aimlessly intoning snatches of banal popular songs, and can't be bothered to train her voice to tackle more demanding and enriching music, is wasting her talents.

[13] A man travelling into a far country called three servants, and gave to the first five talents, to the second two, and to the third one. On return he called them to account, and found the first servant had used his five to make five more, and the second had used his two to make two more; but the servant who had received but one had 'hidden his talent in the earth'. The first two are highly praised, but the third is censured and punished (see Matthew 25: 14–30).

[14] The notion may strike some readers as inappropriate because of the association with a fiduciary relationship towards another. Yet that is, of course, exactly what is conveyed by the parable of the talents, which suggests that life is a gift, the use of which I am called to account for by God. Even from a secular perspective, however, we often talk of someone's wasting their lives or failing to use their gifts properly. Whether such language is coherent if we are here, as it were by accident, and our existence with the package of abilities we happen to possess is a chance process rather than a gift, is an interesting question that cannot be dealt with here.

for developing my own moral character and talents in a way I cannot be for anyone else's. (A parent is of course responsible for developing their children's talents, but this is only, as it were, temporarily and on trust, against the day when they mature into full responsibility and self-stewardship.) In the second place, and crucially, the idea of self-stewardship means that I cannot and should not view the allocation of my time and energies in this respect as something that could be determined entirely from an impartial perspective, in accordance, say, with the demands of global welfare-maximization. For my duty of self-discovery and self-perfectioning carries with it, as it were, an *automatically implied pre-assignment of time and energies*: the goods in question are ones that are achievable only by me, and by my investments of time and energy. It is rather as if each of us is born with a key we cannot get rid of, and which can turn only a particular lock, accessible only to that one person: it makes no sense to ask if a given key could not better be used for some other purpose, since only the keyholder is in a position to use it, and the only purpose for which it is fitted is to open the particular lock to which only he or she has access.

3. Talents, Moral Character, and Resources

At this point, some critical probing is in order. First, it may be objected that I seem to be trying to mark out a certain privileged ethical zone reserved for the individual's development of her own moral character and talents; yet any privilege (runs the objection) is just that—a special entitlement or exemption accorded to one particular individual or group, and as such it surely cannot escape being required to justify itself at the bar of impartial scrutiny. In this case, however, talk of 'privilege' or a 'privileged zone' is in some respects misleading. It is not as if the 'auto-tamieutic' agent is claiming treatment or entitlements that are somehow 'special', or require particular exemptions or favoured status when viewed from an impartial standpoint. It may be helpful here to consider a parallel with the famous Cartesian 'Cogito' argument. A point frequently stressed by Descartes is that the 'validity' of the Cogito does not apply, as it were, timelessly and externally, but is something that requires to be 'activated' by each individual thinker. You cannot just read off the conclusion from the outside, as if it were on a list of 'blackboard' propositions or theses being advanced (there is, after all, nothing certain or necessary about your existence—it could cease at any moment). Rather, says Descartes, the Cogito is something each of you has to 'do', by actually thinking and meditating along with the author; only then will you see that you cannot, so long as you are engaged in this process, cease to exist.[15] In somewhat similar fashion, the good that is the development of this talent, or the deepening of this moral character, is something that cannot be realized except in the life of the individual that is me. So it is not as if I am claiming some privilege that allows me a special extra resource or consideration that is denied to others, or that might be dubious when viewed from a neutral position. I am the only vehicle for this good, its only potential implementer; if I do not realize it, it will eternally be lost.

A second possible worry about the position so far reached is that talk of each individual's responsibility for developing their own 'moral character and talents' appears to lump together two heterogeneous categories whose ethical significance is rather different. With regard to character development—the goal of interior change and self-purification, aimed at for example by the kinds of spiritual exercise mentioned earlier—one may perhaps be inclined to grant it a certain moral aura that might partly insulate it from requirements stemming from the demands of global welfare and equity: as steward of my own moral life, I cannot ethically allow it to decay in the name of some impersonal and general goal. But the development of my talents on the other hand (intellectual, artistic, athletic, and so on) seems less easy to insulate from the wider moral context. Bernard Williams, perhaps at this point over-influenced by Nietzsche, once suggested that Gauguin's decision to ditch his family might retrospectively be justified if he turned out to be a great painter; but unless we want to go all the way down the Nietzschean road, there are surely some limits to how far the potential artistic genius can be justified in putting his own self-development above the needs of others.[16]

We are here up against what might be called the problem of *resources*—a problem that in fact arises irrespective of whether we are talking about the deepening of moral character or the developing of one's own particular repertoire of skills and talents. It is an unavoidable fact that the pursuit of the relevant goods cannot be cost-free: it requires, at the very minimum, much investment of time and energy (and indeed, as a prerequisite for this, a secure infrastructure of more basic physical resources such as food and shelter and clothing). Unless we propose, like John the Baptist, to go off into the

[15] René Descartes, *Meditations* [1641], Second Meditation, AT VII 25–7: CSM II 17–18. Cf. Synopsis, AT VII 9: CSM II 8. 'AT' refers to the standard Franco-Latin edition of Descartes by C. Adam and P. Tannery, *Œuvres de Descartes* (12 vols, rev. edn, Paris: Vrin/CNRS, 1964–76), and 'CSM' to the English translation by J. Cottingham, R. Stoothoff, and D. Murdoch, *The Philosophical Writings of Descartes*, vols I and II (Cambridge: Cambridge University Press, 1985).

[16] B. Williams, *Moral Luck* (Cambridge: Cambridge University Press, 1981), ch. 2. For discussion of the moral implications of the Gauguin case, see J. Cottingham, *On the Meaning of Life* (London: Routledge, 2003), p. 30.

wilderness clothed in camel hair and living on locusts and wild honey (an option unfortunately no longer available on our now mostly wilderness-free planet),[17] we cannot, even for the most isolated auto-tamieutic projects, ultimately avoid the question of how we propose to support them. And even the Baptist must have got his camel hair from somewhere.

The question of resources is allied to the question of time, or, more generally, *extent*. I ought to reflect on my life and develop my moral character and talents—but for how much of the time, or to what extent? In his *Tugendlehre*, or 'Doctrine of Virtue' (the second part of the *Metaphysics of Morals*), Immanuel Kant's answer is, roughly, 'it's up to me' (with the proviso that I keep my nose clean in terms of the strict requirements of justice and rights: for example, I mustn't kill or steal or lie to obtain the required resources).[18] What Kant calls the strict or 'narrow' obligations of the moral law (determined by the categorical imperative) give me rigid rules for action; but the wider obligations of what Kant calls 'ethics' leave, he says, a 'latitude for free choice'.[19] Thus we do have a duty to cultivate our talents, and also a duty to 'cultivate morality in ourselves', but such duties, says Kant, are 'merely ethical, that is, duties of *wide* obligation':

No rational principle prescribes *how far* one should go in cultivating one's capacities (in enlarging or correcting one's capacity for understanding, i.e. in acquiring knowledge or skill). Then too, the different situations in which human beings may find themselves make a man's choice of the occupation for which he should cultivate his talents very much a matter for him to decide as he chooses.[20]

At first sight, this appears to sidestep some important questions. The choice of whether to develop my career in a philosophical direction, rather than, say, as a hospital orderly, may indeed be up to me; but the pursuit of philosophy entails my expending considerable energy in areas that may enrich my own life, but that make a marginal contribution to the lives of most others (many of whom are in urgent need and would benefit from just that time and attention lavished on philosophical research)—not to mention my drawing on

[17] Mark 1: 6.

[18] Bernard Gert makes the interesting and important point that these [Kantian] prohibitions are such that it is possible to follow them with complete impartiality: 'If I do not do the prohibited kind of action, I am not violating the rule with regard to any moral agent, so I am acting impartially with respect to these moral rules with respect to a group large enough to include all moral agents.' 'Impartiality and Morality', typescript.

[19] Immanuel Kant, *Metaphysics of Morals* [*Metaphysik der Sitten*, 1797], *Doctrine of Virtue* [*Tugendlehre*]. Introduction, §vii (Ak. 6: 390), trans. M. Gregor (Cambridge: Cambridge University Press, 1996), p. 153. 'Ak.' = *Kant's gesammelte Schriften*, Akademie edition, Berlin: Reimer/De Gruyter, 1900–).

[20] *Doctrine of Virtue*, Introduction, §viii (Gregor, p. 155; Ak. 6: 392).

the hardly luxurious but nonetheless comparatively comfortable infrastructure that supports a modern Western academic lifestyle. In approaching this sort of problem, Kant again seems to invoke the idea of *latitude*:

It is impossible to assign determinate limits to the extent [to which I ought to sacrifice a part of my welfare to that of others]. How far it should extend depends, in large part, on what each person's true needs are in view of his sensibilities, and it must be left to each to decide this for himself. For, a maxim of promoting others' happiness at the sacrifice of one's own happiness, one's true needs, would conflict with itself if it were made a universal law. Hence this duty is only a *wide* one: the duty has in it a latitude for doing more or less, and no specific limits can be assigned to what should be done.[21]

The phrase 'left to decide for himself' may appear to make the extent to which one should divest oneself of surplus resources within the arbitrary power of an individual to settle at whim—a procedure that might seem too capricious to carry any normative weight. Note, however, that a freedom to decide a question of extent, or degree, does not imply a completely unfettered discretion. As Kant earlier puts it, 'a wide duty is not to be taken as permission to make exceptions to the maxim of actions, but only as permission to limit one maxim of duty by another (for example, love of one's neighbour in general by love of one's parents)'.[22] The duty of beneficence remains a genuine and binding duty, which I cannot evade in my life, even if it may legitimately be subject to limits in any specific instance.[23]

In order properly to unravel the Kantian take on these matters, we have to recognize the two poles that according to Kant determine the privileged sphere of my own self-development. He insists, on the one hand, that a maxim of complete self-sacrifice could not be a rational, that is consistent, universal maxim; but on the other hand, that the duty of beneficence, though not of unrestricted scope, is a genuine, rationally binding duty. To take the second first, Kant argues that beneficence, doing good to others, must be a duty because, 'since our self-love cannot be separated from our need to be loved (helped in case of need) by others as well, we therefore make ourselves an end for others; and the only way this maxim can be binding is through . . . our will to make others our ends as well'.[24] This is a line well known from other parts of Kant's moral philosophy, and needs little comment or justification. Essentially, it is a variant of the truism that no man is an island. Human vulnerability and

---

[21] *Doctrine of Virtue*, Introduction, §viii (Gregor, p. 156: Ak. 6: 393).

[22] *Doctrine of Virtue*, Introduction, §vii (Gregor, p. 153: Ak. 6: 390).

[23] Brad Hooker, though coming from very different theoretical territory from Kant, makes a similar point about the duties of beneficence requiring to be discharged *over a lifetime* (as opposed to on any given occasion). *Ideal Code, Real World* (Oxford: Oxford University Press, 2000), ch. 8.

[24] *Doctrine of Virtue*, Introduction, §viii, 2 (Gregor, p. 156: Ak. 6: 393).

interdependence are such that I cannot honestly deny my potential need to call on the assistance of others; and in the light of that, I cannot rationally isolate myself from a potential call for me to respond to their needs. Yet to set against this, Kant also insists on the other pole of his argument, namely that a rule of total sacrifice of one's own needs would be rationally self-defeating: the maxim 'promote others' happiness at the cost of sacrificing one's own true needs' would 'conflict with itself'.

Why should this be? Mere universalizability ('Could it be willed as a universal maxim?') does not satisfactorily explain it;[25] but there is an alternative Kantian explanation available. Kant once famously said that it would be better that human beings should no longer walk the earth than that justice should be allowed to perish.[26] For very different reasons, but in somewhat analogous manner, the Kantian thought in this present case is that there would be no point left to human life if human beings did not exercise their unique capacity to set themselves goals and projects, and to pursue them without fear of their being subject to wholesale dissolution in the name of some impersonal good. It is, in Kant's words, a 'duty in itself' to cultivate those capacities by which the animal is 'first raised into the human being'. Embarking on chosen goals and projects in this way is the essence of our very humanity.[27] This, to put it in somewhat solemn language, is the source of the dignity common to all human vocations, which, from this point of view, are all equal. They differ according to individual circumstance; but none should be wasted, because all are valuable.[28]

We may thus draw from Kant's discussion a broad framework for addressing the 'problem of the extent'—the limits of an individual's legitimate use of time and resources on self-development. On the one hand the individual does not

---

[25] As has often been observed, to ask 'What if everyone did x?' cannot be a satisfactory test for the morality of an action of type x, since it would rule out, for example, shopping or going to the bank on a Tuesday (which, if everyone did it, would cause chaos). The test therefore has to be modified to be something like 'What if everyone was prepared to x under appropriate circumstances and taking into account the likely behaviour patterns of others?'; but in that case there seems nothing contradictory or absurd about adopting a maxim of sacrificing oneself when appropriate circumstances demand it.

[26] Metaphysics of Morals, Doctrine of Right [Rechtslehre], pt II, §49E.

[27] 'The capacity to set oneself an end . . . is what characterises humanity (as distinguished from animality).' Doctrine of Virtue, Introduction, §viii, 1 (Gregor, p. 154: Ak. 6: 392).

[28] Substitute 'Christian' for 'human', and the last two sentences in the above paragraph are an almost exact quotation from a discussion of the idea of vocation by Karol Wojtyla (John Paul II) in Rise, Let Us Be On our Way [Wstancie, Chodzmy!, 2004] (London: Cape, 2004), p. 37. For the requirement that 'nothing be wasted', cf. John 6: 12. Kant himself of course did not use the language of vocation, preferring to preserve a highly secular and rationalistic tone here as in so much (though not all) of his moral philosophy. Nevertheless, his conception of self-development and commitment to rationally chosen goals as part of our human birthright seems to me far from wholly discontinuous with the long tradition of religious thought that centres around the concepts of gift and vocation.

have *carte blanche*: she may not insulate herself from the duty of beneficence. But on the other hand her very humanity places her within an inalienable zone of latitude that must allow space for rational choices relating to individual character formation and self-improvement.

4. Self-development or Self-creation?

To sum up so far: I have sketched the notion of an 'auto-tamieutic perspective' from which each of us can discern a set of personal goals that are ethically immune to wholesale dissolution in the name of some externally defined goal; and I have suggested, partly following Kant, that the possibility of being able to take up such a perspective is inherent to my status as a human being. But an important caveat now needs to be entered about the interpretation of the framework so far invoked.

I have already underlined the dangers of the ideal of autonomy, if this is taken to mean that humans have the power somehow to create value in their lives, or to determine the validity of projects simply by an exercise of will. The normative status of an 'auto-tamieutic' zone ultimately makes sense only against a background of objective value, that is to say the existence of a good or goods that are logically independent of my actual preferences and choices. Thus, forms of 'preference utilitarianism' that make the good dependent on what people want, or forms of Kantianism that make the good simply a function of what can without inconsistency be chosen as a goal, are both, in my view, ethically unstable; what they lack is the anchor of a substantive theory of the good—a substantive account of the kinds of things human beings must, whether they like it or not, be directed towards if they are to achieve fulfilment.

Our unique human ability to set ourselves projects and goals is of no value in itself if those projects and goals are bad. And the development by each of us of our unique individual set of talents is of no value unless they are *bona fide* talents, that is to say, genuine gifts whose development and exercise is, independently of what we might contingently happen to want for this or that purpose, genuinely productive of human good.

At this point someone might object to the whole concept of stewardship, presupposed here and throughout this chapter, on the grounds that it tacitly presupposes or logically requires a religious worldview—involving the idea (roughly) that our 'talents' are divinely bestowed gifts that we are responsible to a higher power for developing properly. I do myself happen to hold that a theistic framework provides an appropriate, perhaps *the* appropriate, metaphysical framework for an objectivist view of moral values and a substantive theory of the good.[29] But even if one were to concede the falsity of the religious framework, thereby judging it to be merely a human fiction, this would not automatically evacuate the value and significance from the ethical concepts involved in such a framework.[30] The concept of stewardship may still carry a series of important moral insights that can readily be acknowledged even from a thoroughgoing secular perspective. To spell them out: (i) a person's talents are abilities that are naturally fitted for the production of some good (as someone with an ear for music is better able to make beautiful sounds than her tone-deaf counterpart); (ii) they are not entirely of the individual's own making (they involve a good measure of what is often called 'moral luck'); and (iii) their use is not wholly within the autonomous power of the possessor to develop or abrogate at will. The last point may perhaps seem questionable from a secular viewpoint: to call me a steward suggests that I am responsible to a higher authority; but if there is no such authority, is it not lawful for me to do what I shall with mine own? I take the parable of the talents to provide an answer to this that the secularist cannot in good faith dismiss. The servant who simply buried his one talent in the ground was indeed blameworthy—for laziness, for timidity, or simply for wasting a precious resource. Irrespective of whether one sees the gifts of nature as divinely bestowed or as the result of a genetic and environmental lottery, I see no way round these intuitions. The commonly heard phrase 'It's my life' is true and important if taken to mean that I have an inalienable responsibility for how I develop and direct it; but if said with the appropriating voice of the petulant ego 'It's mine and I can do what I want with it', it is just false.

Alexander Nehamas, in his recent book *The Art of Living*, talks about the need to 'establish a mode of life that is appropriate for [each particular individual] and not necessarily for anyone else'.[31] Invoking the ancient Socratic ideal of 'care of the self', he argues that each of us should be on a quest to find that unique mode of living that expresses who we truly are. In itself this is fine: there is a great multiplicity and diversity in the human character, and each of us has to search to realize the special pattern of self-development that arises from our distinctive blend of talents and opportunities. But as it featured in Socrates' talk of 'care of the self', this ideal had a deeply moral dimension

---

[29] At the very least one may plausibly regard a theistic metaphysics and an objectivist ethics as 'mutually supportive', to borrow the notion developed (albeit in connection with a distinctly unorthodox form of theism) by Tim Mulgan ('How should impartialists think about God?', typescript).

[30] See footnote 3, above.

[31] Alexander Nehamas, *The Art of Living: Socratic Reflections from Plato to Foucault* (Berkeley, CA: University of California Press, 1998), p. 105.

(Socrates' 'inner voice' is the voice of courage, of determination, of integrity); yet in Nehamas it becomes the far more open-ended claim that 'everyone's life [can] become a work of art'[32]—an idea that seems (like the Nietzschean model that inspired it) to risk exalting originality and autonomous will at the expense of all else.

'Care of the self' is thus a highly ambiguous notion. In one sense it invokes self-examination and self-improvement: in the tradition inherited from Augustine, this is the essentially humble or confessional project of uncovering the depths of one's true nature (a nature one did not create), so as to purge what is defective and develop a truly fulfilled and abundant human life, oriented towards the good. In quite another sense, the sense that comes to dominate Nehamas's approach, it becomes the project of 'self-creation', an ideal that starts to look increasingly arrogant and anarchic: it requires its exponent, as Nehamas puts it, to 'dislodge what was in place as the good and the true in order to find a place for himself, for his *own* truth and goodness'.[33] The idea of self-stewarding that I have been exploring in this chapter is radically at odds with this morally suspect and philosophically problematic vision.[34] What self-stewarding presupposes instead is something that is found in many traditional religiously oriented philosophers, but that is also increasingly found in recent secular work on ethics:[35] a firmly objectivist conception of the good for humankind.

5. Individual Motivation and Wider Concern

Even if self-discovery and self-formation are related to an objective structure of human goods, we are still left with the problem of striking a balance between self-concern and wider concern: how much weight should I give to those self-developmental goods that loom so large from the perspective of my own particular self-responsibility, as against the goods of others, which from a more

---

[32] Alexander Nehamas, p. 177.   [33] *Ibid.*, p. 183 (emphasis supplied).

[34] Morally suspect because it led Nietzsche to argue (terrifyingly) that the exalted superman should steel himself against the 'weak' impulses of compassion towards the vulnerable; see Friedrich Nietzsche, *Beyond Good and Evil* [*Jenseits von Gut und Böse*, 1886], §37. Philosophically problematic since I cannot make something valuable by choosing or willing it (as if I could make cardboard nutritious by deciding to eat it); indeed, this idea precisely puts the cart before the horse, since in reality my choices or acts of will can be worthwhile only in so far as their objects already have independent value. I am of course aware that these summary comments broach enormously complex issues and would require extended argumentation in order to be properly supported.

[35] See, for example, R. Shafer-Landau, *Moral Realism* (Oxford: Oxford University Press, 2003), and (from another direction) P. Bloomfield, *Moral Reality* (Oxford: Oxford University Press, 2001).

impartial perspective may seem to cry out for more urgent attention? At its crudest, how much should 'care of the self' subtract from my response to others in distress? The Kantian ideas discussed earlier give us a useful ethical framework for situating the problem, but do not in the end offer any normative procedure for tackling it.[36]

I doubt if ultimately there can be any simple philosophical template for resolving this.[37] The Western moral tradition is remarkably unhelpful in this area.[38] Aristotelian ethics, full of insights into the structure of individual virtue, simply fails to acknowledge an impartial perspective from which one might advert to the wider needs of humanity as a whole: Aristotle's good life is the good life within the closed circle of membership of the city state. The nearest he gets to glimpsing a more impartialist perspective is in his use of the striking phrase *allos autos* ('another self') when discussing the status of a friend—although of course here he is still confining himself to the strictly limited sphere of private affection.[39] In somewhat similar vein, the Hebrew Bible, in Leviticus,[40] introduces the ethically resonant requirement to love one's neighbour *as oneself*—although the term 'neighbour' still carries its literal meaning, and does not extend outside the tribal community. Later, in the Hellenistic period, Stoic ethics contains hints of a widening concern,

---

[36] Running through this whole question, moreover, there is a certain problematic slippage between what might be shown about 'us' as human beings, and what might be thought to apply to me personally. For example, it might be true that *our* lives as human beings reach their most valuable form if, on the one hand, we set ourselves personal goals and projects, and, on the other, we extend our concern to others. But how does that block either (a) the hyper-altruistic thought that I should sacrifice the value of *my* life to realize value in the lives of others, or (b) the hyper-egoistic thought that I should benefit myself most by not realizing that value? I owe these questions to an anonymous Oxford University Press reader. I explore one approach to answering (a) in 'The Ethics of Self-Concern'; an approach to tackling (b) is outlined in the remainder of the present chapter, although I would not claim that it does more than indicate a possible strategy for a response.

[37] That suggested by Liam Murphy, that the duties of benevolence are limited by the extent of non-compliance with those duties among the population at large, is aptly criticized by Michael Ridge as too lenient (since it implies, counterintuitively, that we have no duty to pick up at least some of the slack caused by others' ignoring their duties). See L. Murphy, *Moral Demands in Nonideal Theory* (Oxford: Oxford University Press, 2000), and M. Ridge, 'Fairness and Non-Compliance', Chapter 9 in the present volume.

[38] Whether the Eastern tradition is any more helpful is a moot point. The Buddha found it necessary to withdraw from human society in order to achieve personal enlightenment—although we are told that he subsequently went back into the world, out of compassion for his fellow humans still trapped in the world of illusion. However, the relevant 'illusion', on the Buddhist view, turns out to be the belief that any individual selves exist, so what is ultimately involved in the Buddhist vision is not so much a balance between individual and wider good as a denial of ultimate significance to *any* individual life. This might be thought of as impartialism, or rather impersonalism, carried to the extreme, although it seems to carry a heavy cost—that of enjoining us to let go of the very projects of commitment and rational self-development that are (as in Kant's vision) our human birthright.

[39] *Nicomachean Ethics* [c. 325 BC], bk IX, ch. 8.

[40] Leviticus 19: 18.

with the idea of moral principles as 'laws of human nature, transcending all accidents of birth and local identities'.[41] The precise import of this idea is, however, disputed among scholars of Stoicism, and it is probably only later, in early Christian thought, that we see a decisive shift to a genuinely universalist perspective. Jesus of Nazareth construes the term 'neighbour' in a very wide sense—the parable of the Good Samaritan, produced in answer to the question 'Who is my neighbour?', seems to make a neighbour anyone in need of assistance.[42] Despite this significant shift, however, the problem of balance between self-concern and wider concern is left in the end unresolved in Christianity: the actual teachings and actions of Christ continue to reflect a special concern for his own (compare the stories about his weeping for Lazarus, or the particular relationship with the 'beloved' disciple), while at the same time advocating a wider and more universal vision (as in the command to 'leave your father and mother' in order to follow the gospel).[43]

The old question of balance thus recurs, and maybe it is wrong to search for a philosophical formula or algorithm that could provide a neat solution. What can perhaps be done instead is to see how, on the level of motivation or ethical formation, the individual might be led to widen his perspective from that of self-stewarding to something broader. One way of doing this might be by arguing that, despite initial appearances, partialistic concerns and wider concerns turn out to be susceptible of *integration*—that is, that they relate to interconnected rather than to conflicting goals.[44] By way of a coda to this

<hr/>

[41] A. A. Long and D. N. Sedley, *The Hellenistic Philosophers* (Cambridge: Cambridge University Press, 1987), §67 (discussing the supposed 'internationalism' of Zeno of Citium, the founder of Stoicism, and citing sources from Plutarch and Cicero, but with reservations as to how far these ideas can be traced back to Zeno himself).

[42] Matthew 22: 37–40.

[43] For Jesus' special love for Lazarus see John 11: 35–6; for the 'beloved disciple', see, e.g., John 19: 26. For the injunction to forsake one's family for the sake of the gospel, see Matthew 19: 20; Luke 14: 26.

[44] In an earlier attempt to explore this idea I suggested that self-fulfilment and working for the fulfilment of others were contingently interlinked, by relying in Humean style on empirical facts about human character formation. Although there are no general guarantees, so ran the argument, the typical psychological profile of at least very many human beings is such that successful engagement in meaningful projects of personal involvement will progressively tend to lead them to feel the importance of making sure as many others as possible have the means to do the same. (J. Cottingham, 'The Ethical Credentials of Partiality', *Proceedings of the Aristotelian Society* 98 (1997–8), pp. 1–21.) Perhaps such a contingent claim may broadly be true; plausible variants of it are to be found in many of the psychology-oriented ethicists of the early-modern period, for example Pierre Nicole, *De la charité et de l'amour propre* [1675] (excerpted in J. B. Schneewind (ed.), *Moral Philosophy from Montaigne to Kant* (Cambridge: Cambridge University Press, 1990), vol. II, pp. 370ff.). But I now think that a proper account of the relationship between self-concern and wider concern needs to be underpinned by much heavier materials—by a teleological thesis about human nature and its goals, and a metaphysical thesis about the objectivity (and perhaps even the essential unity) of goodness.

chapter, I shall offer a very brief sketch of such an argument. Just as Aristotle observed that the good of bridle-making cannot be disentangled from the good of horsemanship,[45] so, in somewhat analogous manner, I shall suggest that the realization by each human being of his or her individual goals cannot be conceived in isolation from the realization by others of their goals.

Suppose someone asks: 'given that I am happy developing my own character and talents, and working for the good of those immediately close to me, what reason have I for adopting a more impartial perspective, and devoting more of my resources to the wider world?' To reply, 'you just ought to, because they need your help' (or, in the favoured modern jargon, 'the fact that they need your help gives you *reason* to help them') may end up seeming more like browbeating than answering the question. For the questioner still wants to know why that so-called 'external' reason gives them an incentive to offer their assistance.

I argued earlier that choices have normative status only if they are directed towards the good; and that the good cannot be a free-floating notion, but must be tied to something like the fulfilment of our nature as human beings. For the individualist, for example the (Gauguin-style) lone artist, who, when reminded of the needs of others, asks 'Why should all this concern me?', a small but significant point of leverage has now appeared. For such an individual is working to develop his talents not presumably as a random piece of compulsive behaviour, but because he seeks the fulfilment of his creative nature.[46] The 'duty of genius', the development of talents, is taken by him to be good for just this reason. But now, having gone this far along a teleological route, he cannot easily restrict his purview to that of his own individual fulfilment. For he is not some abstract Cartesian ego, but a *human being*; and human beings are not pre-social entities but are (as Aquinas insists, following Aristotle)[47] intrinsically social beings. The fostering and development of his own resources therefore has to involve him, whether he likes it or not, in close interaction with immediate others. But once that is acknowledged, it will no longer be possible to think of the good as compartmentalized into individual packages of fulfilment: the cooperation of others, and indeed their potential approbation or disapprobation, is automatically involved in any such interactions. Thus the good at which the artist aims includes the expression of insights that can be recognized and appreciated by others. There is a reciprocal network here: the

---

[45] *Nicomachean Ethics*, bk I, ch. 1.

[46] I do not of course mean that creativity is necessarily something self-absorbed or introverted; in most cases, the artist's characteristic focus and concentration in seeking the fulfilment of his creative nature is on his art rather than on himself.

[47] Aristotle, *Politics* [325 BC], bk I, ch. 2; Aquinas, *De regimine principium* [1265–7], bk I, ch. 1.

desired recognition and appreciation are integrally linked to the pursuit of the good aimed at by the artist; and the desired responses are the responses of others embarked on similar teleological paths, themselves striving to fulfil the human nature shared by all.

The argument here rests, essentially, on the nature of human goods, which, because of the kind of species we are, and because of the types of good that fulfil our nature, require not just the manipulation or use of others, nor even just their willing cooperation in providing the circumstances we need for our own pursuits, but their *involvement as responsive and developed human agents*. The musician, by the nature of her activities, requires responsive and artistically sensitive listeners—so the good she pursues cannot be isolated from their good. To summarize, then: the development of our personal resources involves us in the pursuit of the good; the good so pursued is part of the necessarily linked good of an essentially social species; hence the more zealously we pursue the good, and the better we come to understand it, the more our self-concern will necessarily be implicated in a wider concern for other humans.

But could not one draw a line, and include for consideration only those within a closed circle of like-minded *cognoscenti*, leaving the world at large to go hang?[48] Whether such partialism is psycho-ethically viable seems to me to depend partly on the stage of development which the human race has reached. If we are considering Aristotle, who knew nothing of the conditions in central Africa, and could have done virtually nothing about them even had he known, there is little sense (given that 'ought' implies 'can') of talking about either his duty or his motivation to respond to the relevant human needs. But for us today, who have both the knowledge and the means to help, it *does* make sense: the wider our power and knowledge extend, the greater the scope of our responsibility.[49] What is more, in the pursuit of our activities we are, via

[48] Did not Aristotle, for instance, fulfil his human nature, even though he failed to extend the kind of respect he accorded to his fellow citizens to, for example, his slaves? (I owe this objection to one of OUP's anonymous assessors for this volume.) This is a less extreme example of the imaginary case I have discussed elsewhere of the Nazi concentration-camp guard, who (we are invited to suppose) goes home each evening to enjoy a fulfilling life with his friends and family. My response is, in very crude summary, that the compartmentalization and blunting of sensibilities involved in such blinkered modes of living is, in the end, incompatible with the full flowering of the subject's humanity. See further J. Cottingham, *On the Meaning of Life*, ch. 1, final three sections, and (for the question of whether Don Giovanni's selfish life was fulfilling) section 3 of Cottingham, 'Demandingness, Moral Development and Moral Philosophy', in T. Chappell (ed.), *The Problem of Moral Demandingness* (Basingstoke: Palgrave Macmillan, 2009).

[49] Compare the following: 'Thus, far from thinking that works produced by man's own talent and energy are in opposition to God's power, and that the rational creature exists as a kind of rival to the Creator, Christians are convinced that the triumphs of the human race are a sign of God's grace and the flowering of His own mysterious design. For the greater man's power becomes, the farther his

the global economy, every day implicated in literally hundreds of planet-wide networks of mutual exchange and dependence. There is no going back, no removing this knowledge from our minds. To shut ourselves off from the wider good of others, of *any* others on the planet, would thus involve a wilful blunting of our sensibilities and responsiveness—the very sensibilities and responsiveness that our own personal creative projects, since we are human beings, inescapably require.

Although the schema outlined here does I think offer the beginnings of a motivational link between self-concern and wider concern, it evidently remains resistible, in the sense that there is nothing that compels any given person to internalize it. Indeed, given the extent of human selfishness and other weakness, any hope that it could be widely and deeply internalized might seem either naively optimistic, or to rest more on faith than on reason—and perhaps it does. But if so, it is a faith that has had numerous secular incarnations, in concepts such as 'the human family' or 'the brotherhood of man', which command widespread admiration irrespective of religious belief or its absence. What these notions point towards, I take it, is the fact that our very nature as human beings cannot, in the end, find proper fulfilment unless the care and respect we learn close to home is extended throughout the human community. Learning how to steward our own individual resources is one of the first and most indispensable parts of the ethical formation of a human being; truly recognizing and responding to the need for each one of our fellow humans to do likewise is its inescapable corollary.

individual and community responsibility extends. Hence it is clear that men are not deterred by the Christian message from building up the world, or impelled to neglect the welfare of their fellows, but that they are rather more stringently bound to do these very things.' *Gaudium et spes*, Second Vatican Council Document [1965], §34.

4

The Bishop, the Valet, the Wife, and the Ass: What Difference Does it Make if Something is Mine?

MAXIMILIAN DE GAYNESFORD

I

We can describe cases, real and imagined, where we have the greatest difficulty in settling the question 'what difference does it make if something is *mine?*' By this, I mean not just whether it makes a difference to what we should do, but what kind of difference. The inability to provide a satisfying answer is not due to any lack of interest in the question. The issue plays a considerable role in debates about the relative weight to be given to impartial and partial features in deciding what we should do. Nor is it because these cases fail to arouse strong beliefs. Quite the opposite. The problem is that the convictions aroused are extreme, polarized, and so completely at odds that often the preconditions of debate are not met. Either pole contrives to be blind to what is cogent or otherwise appealing about the alternative.

Consider, for example, the familiar kind of case in which a husband recognizes his wife among those in desperate need of aid. The tendency I am referring to polarizes the options, so that the fact 'she is my wife' is conceived either as making no difference at all, or as making all the difference in the world. These poles are commonly associated with, respectively, William Godwin and Bernard Williams. This may be a spurious interpretation of either or both authors. I suspect it is at least very dubious. But what matters for our purposes is the attraction that the interpretation holds. If polarization is not to be found in these texts, it is nevertheless routinely imposed on them. So we may well ask what grounds (or permits, or excuses) it. The answer provides us with clues about a variety of background preconceptions that determine the way partialist and impartialist considerations are heard in current debate.

II

William Godwin is best known, in moral and political philosophy at least, for a rhetorical question: 'What magic is there in the pronoun "my". . .?'[1] The phrase occurs at the end of a thought-experiment that Charles Lamb quickly dubbed 'the famous fire cause':[2]

The illustrious Archbishop of Cambray was of more worth than his valet, and there are few of us that would hesitate to pronounce, if his palace were in flames, and the life of only one of them could be preserved, which of the two ought to be preferred . . . Suppose I had been myself the valet; I ought to have chosen to die, rather than that Fénelon should have died . . . To have done otherwise would have been a breach of justice. Supposing the valet had been my brother, my father or my benefactor. This would not alter the truth of the proposition. The life of Fénelon would still be more valuable than that of the valet; and justice, pure, unadulterated justice, would still have preferred that which was most valuable . . . What magic is there in the pronoun 'my', that should justify us in overturning the decisions of impartial truth? My brother or my father may be a fool or a profligate, malicious, lying or dishonest. If they be, of what consequence is it that they are mine?[3]

The passage makes a number of claims, some of which Godwin clearly supposes are linked by entailment. The archbishop is of more worth than the valet. Most of us would say that the archbishop should be preserved rather than the valet. The archbishop should be preserved rather than the valet. The valet should have chosen to die to preserve the archbishop. It would have been a breach of

---

[1] Godwin's philosophical reputation rests squarely on the writings he composed in mid-career (1793–1800). In particular, the straightforwardly philosophical *Enquiry concerning political justice and its influence on modern morals and happiness* ([1793]; 2nd rev. edn [1796]; 3rd rev. edn [1798]); and the novel that most successfully re-presents his philosophical ideas of that time: *Things As They Are; or The Adventures of Caleb Williams* [1794], ed. Maurice Hindle (London: Penguin, 1988). Godwin's views changed dramatically later in his life, when he recanted his anarchism and some of the principles that had led him to endorse it. His *Thoughts occasioned by a perusal of Dr Parr's Spital sermon* of 1801 (London: G. G. and A. Robinson) belongs to the mid-career writings, although this set of responses to various critics of the *Enquiry* includes quite radical criticism not only of earlier formulations of his official position, but of that position itself.

[2] *Letters of Charles and Mary Lamb, I, 1796–1820*, ed. E. V. Lucas (London: Methuen, 1904), p. 237.

[3] William Godwin, *Enquiry concerning political justice and its influence on modern morals and happiness* [1798], 3rd edn, ed. I. Kramnick (London: Penguin, 1985) pp. 169–70.

justice if the valet had not chosen to die to preserve the archbishop. And the final claim is the one of interest here: that all these claims would still be true even if the valet were my father, brother, or benefactor.

Evidently it is the last three sentences that are meant to carry the weight. If they are meant to express an argument, the reasoning is weak and unpersuasive. It is more likely that they assert a view. And that view, as it is standardly represented, is as follows.[4] Many features are relevant in determining what one should or should not do. But the fact that some agency, or what is affected by it, is *mine* should not count. Moreover, we can and should understand what constitute the reasons for doing what we do without appealing to the fact that some of them are, or may be, expressed in a first-personal way. In short: the first person plays no part in justifying what to do. This is so whether or not some thought or judgement is actually formulated using the first person. That we tend to think and act otherwise, that we try to reason accordingly, Godwin does not attempt to deny; but the tendency is mistaken nevertheless.

To deny that the first person *counts* in practical reasoning is not (yet) to deny that it *matters* there. The distinction may seem slight. Many speak about what does and does not matter as if that were the same as what does and does not count. But there is a difference, and it may prove significant. Suppose, in trying to show that I can hit any small object, I shoot at and destroy your small porcelain bowl: you may say, 'That counts, but doesn't matter'. Now suppose, in trying to show that I can hit a small card, I hit and destroy your porcelain bowl: you may say, 'That matters, but doesn't count'.

What *does* count for Godwin is that things go as well as possible for all, impartially considered. To treat matters impartially is, in his view, to 'measure [them] solely by a consideration of the properties of the receiver, and the capacity of him that bestows. Its principle therefore is, according to a well known phrase, to be "no respecter of persons"'.[5] This requires, in his view, taking up a certain stance: 'the soundest criterion of virtue is to put ourselves in the place of an impartial spectator, of an angelic nature, suppose, beholding

---

[4] This interpretation is so deeply and widely held as to have become philosophical lore, with the effect that supporting references to specifics of the text itself are clearly regarded as optional, and difficulties in the argumentation are routinely ignored. Discussions that seem to depend on, but do more than merely mention, the common interpretation of Godwin's view about the first person (centred on 'the fire cause') include Isaac Kramnick, 'Introduction', in William Godwin, *Enquiry concerning political justice and its influence on modern morals and* happiness [1738], 3rd edn, ed. Kramnick (London: Penguin, 1985) p. 18; Don Locke, *A Fantasy of Reason: The Life and Thought of William Godwin* (London: Routledge and Kegan Paul, 1980) pp. 168–71; Peter H. Marshal, *William Godwin* (London: Yale University Press, 1984) pp. 100–2; Mark Philp, 'William Godwin', *Stanford Encyclopaedia of Philosophy*, http://plato.stanford.edu/.

[5] Godwin, *Enquiry*, p. 169.

us from an elevated station, and uninfluenced by our prejudices, conceiving what would be his estimate of the intrinsic circumstances of our neighbour, and acting accordingly'.[6]

The upshot is that considerations basic to ethics must be revised. For example, what we might call 'subject-oriented questions', like 'What should *I* do?', are to be understood as asking 'What does justice or morality require of any person so situated in order that things go as well as possible for all?' The first person is to be replaced in such cases. For the sake of perspicuity, the contribution it makes is made by another phrase. The position also affects some 'object-oriented questions', like 'What should be done for x?', or 'What should be done to x?', or 'Should this be done to x or to y?' The fact that x or y might be *me* or *related to me* in any way or to be considered *mine*—my body, my child, my spouse, my friend, my neighbour—counts for nothing in justifying what is done, and in deciding what to do. Since the first person has no contribution to make here, it cannot even be replaced. For the sake of perspicuity, it is presumably to be eliminated.

So call this 'Godwin's thesis': that the first person counts for nothing in practical reasoning; that impartiality is what matters; and that the former is true because the latter is true. On the standard interpretation, it is this thesis to which Godwin is committed.

Bernard Williams is well known for the phrase 'this construction provides the agent with a thought too many'. It occurs at the end of a passage in his 'Persons, Character, and Morality', where he is discussing a case that is in many respects similar to that described by Godwin. The case is due to Charles Fried: suppose '[a] man could, at no risk or cost to himself, save one or two persons in equal peril, and one of those in peril was, say, his wife'.[7] Williams writes:

Surely *this* is a justification on behalf of the rescuer, that the person he chose to rescue was his wife? It depends on how much weight is carried by 'justification': the consideration that it was his wife is certainly, for instance, an explanation which should silence comment. But something more ambitious than this is usually intended, essentially involving the idea that moral principle can legitimate his preference, yielding the conclusion that in situations of this kind it is at least all right (morally permissible) to save one's wife . . . But this construction provides the agent with a thought too many: it might have been hoped by some (for instance, by his wife) that his motivating thought, fully spelled out, would be the thought that it was his wife, not that it was his wife and that in situations of this kind it is permissible to save one's wife.[8]

---

[6] Godwin, *Enquiry*, pp. 173–4.

[7] *An Anatomy of Values* (London: Harvard University Press, 1970), p. 227.

[8] 'Persons, Character, and Morality' (1976), reprinted in his *Moral Luck* (Cambridge: Cambridge University Press, 1981) pp. 1–19; p. 18.

The idea seems to be that a husband's reason for saving his wife may be just this: 'that she is my wife'. It is false to suppose there is always a need for more, a stronger form of justification, such as that morality permits one in situations of this sort to save one's wife. This supposition in turn betrays wrong-headed notions of the way justification operates in ethics, and these notions in turn are deeply misleading when we are philosophically reflective about practical reasoning.

As with Godwin, there is little indication that an argument is being expressed here. The passage asserts a view about the significance of the first person in practical reasoning. And that view, at least as it is often heard, is diametrically opposed to Godwin's. Many features are relevant in determining what one should or should not do; among them is the fact that some agency, or what is affected by it, is *mine*. Sometimes the fact that something is mine is not only decisive but sufficiently significant that it removes the need to 'legitimate' action (it may 'justify' it, but only in a weak sense). Moreover, we cannot and should not understand what constitute the reasons for doing what we do without appealing to the fact that some of them are expressed in the first-personal way. That we tend to think and act in precisely this way is not something Williams seeks to excuse. To assert that the first person counts in these ways is not (yet) to deny that other features also matter (e.g. that there are several needy people in the wife-saving situation). It is just that, on occasion, the fact that something is *mine* may be the only fact that counts.[9]

The upshot is that ethics must *not* be revised in the thorough-going way Godwin promotes. Subject-oriented questions are to remain so phrased; the first person is not to be replaced. Indeed, it may be that questions phrased in precisely that way—'What should *I* do?'—are necessary if reflective practical reasoning is to be possible.[10] Then, far from being replaceable, the first person would be essential. Regarding object-oriented questions, the fact that someone might be *me* or *related to me* in any way or to be considered *mine*—my body, my child, my spouse, my friend, my neighbour—counts for much in justifying what is done, and in deciding what to do; and may indeed count for so much that no other considerations count. Again, the first person is essential.

To claim that the first person is 'essential' is ambiguous. It may mean that the first person is indispensable in the role it carries out. Or it may mean that

---

[9] It is worth noting, in passing, that this view need not be inconsistent with impartiality, at least as Godwin defines it. For the features Williams regards as significant and even decisive may be regarded quite legitimately as included *within* 'consideration of the properties of the receiver, and the capacity of him that bestows' (Godwin, *Enquiry*, p. 169) (at least so long as those properties include relational ones, which Godwin himself cannot afford to deny). If there is indeed such scope, it is presumably to be taken as a sign of weakness in Godwin's definition rather than in Williams's position.

[10] Williams's position in *Ethics and the Limits of Philosophy* (London: Fontana Press, 1985), ch. 4.

the role the first person carries out is indispensable. Either might be true while the other is false. So the first person might be indispensable in a role that is itself dispensable (just as Abelard cannot walk without legs, but he need not walk), or dispensable in a role that is itself indispensable (just as Heloise need not have been Abelard's wife, but *some* partner was needed if he was to count as married). On the standard view, Williams seems to be claiming both (what we may call 'strong' essentialism), although the weight, perhaps, is on the second claim.

So call this 'Williams's thesis': that the first person is strongly essential in practical reasoning.

The division between Godwin's and Williams's theses seems to be of such a sort that it precludes negotiation. These are not extreme positions at each end of a spectrum. That would imply that there are more moderate versions of each. The problem is that the very thought that counts for nothing with one, that some F is *mine*, is the thought that counts for everything with the other. There is no more moderate position that is a *version* of either. Thus someone who thinks the fact that 'this woman is my wife' gives the husband *any* reason to save her, no matter how small and how easily outweighed by any other consideration, is strictly no closer to one pole than to the other. For the advocate of Godwin's thesis, this fact counts not at all. And, conversely, someone who thinks that the husband's action in saving his wife needs *any* justification beyond the fact 'this is my wife' (e.g. a legitimation that morality might provide), no matter how small and negligible in comparison with any other consideration, is no closer to one pole than to the other. For the advocate of Williams's thesis, this fact counts not at all.

This is not, perhaps, accidental. For the very position from which it becomes possible to see the fact that some F's being *mine* as counting in the way one pole thinks it does blocks the possibility of seeing it in the way the other pole does—as in the duck/rabbit illustration. So the lure or appeal of one must always be hidden from or unapparent to those in the grip of the other. If this is correct, then it will always be impossible genuinely to confront one position *from* the other. So what may otherwise appear to be heated exchange is in fact just idling (wheels spin the more furiously when disengaged).

This predicament may remind us of another apparently irresolvable tension that Sidgwick described. In his view, there is no answer to the question 'what have we most reason to do?' when self-interest and morality are considered together and conflict over cases. Similarly, there is no answer to the question 'what difference does it make if something is mine?' when both poles are considered together and conflict over cases. But our situation is worse, perhaps. For Sidgwick's contenders give the agent equal reason to act. Neither outweighs the other. But at least they can be weighed against each other. This is impossible in our case. There *is* no weighing point, no common ground where *both* sets of considerations carry weight. So we appear to be in the position of Buridan's ass: the overly rational creature who was unable to act because there seemed to be equal reason to move in one direction as to move in the other.

III

The ass was mistaken. It would have been more rational to move in *any* direction than to starve. We may suspect that our problem is similarly based on confusion and misunderstanding. Each pole contrives to be ignorant of what is correct in the tendencies of its alternative—each assumes that to deny that the first person has magic is to deny that it has muscle. But this is evidently false. So perhaps we can domesticate the first person, neither exaggerating its competence nor denying its role. Then it may be possible to make headway. That, at least, is a hypothesis we might work on. More specifically, that confusion about how partiality and impartiality relate to the first person may help explain the polarization that troubles us.

Consider 'Godwin's thesis', which relates impartiality to the first person. It claims that impartiality is what matters in practical reasoning, that the first person does not count, and that the one is true because the other is. But if this were true, practical reasoning—reasoning leading to action—would be incomprehensible. The point touches on three related areas.

First, the preconditions for self-conscious agency. In order to recognize that acting is open to me in some situation, or that some action is mine, I have to recognize that it is *I* who am in that situation; that this situation is *mine*. Second, the preconditions for rational agency. In order to act for any reasons at all, I have to recognize that it is *I* who am related to certain reasons in such-and-such a situation, a relation that makes certain courses of action possible or impossible *for me*; (un)desirable; (im)permissible; (not) required; etc. Third, the preconditions for practical reasoning—reasoning leading to action. There may be any number of situations in which I might be, any number of facts about those situations that do or would give me reason to act. But unless I am related to this situation in certain ways, so that I can think of it as *mine*, and unless I am related to these reasons in certain ways, so that I can think of them as *mine*, reasons for *me* to act, those reasons will neither motivate me in that situation to act as I do, nor explain why I act as I do. Without these links between reasoning and action, what I do could not express or follow from what I think; reasoning could not 'lead to' action.

So the fact that at least *something* is *mine* is of the greatest consequence to practical reasoning. Unless some *situation* is *mine*, I am unable to recognize it as open to my agency or as relating me to various reason-giving facts. And unless some *reasons* are mine, I am unable to engage in reasoning that leads to action, or even to be considered as engaging in it. Without the link made by the first person, we would have nothing we could make recognizable to ourselves as 'practical rationality'. Action would not be rational because it would operate without rational constraint. And reasoning would not be practical because it would be disengaged from action, an idle wheel, no matter how furiously it might spin.

Godwin's thesis, then, is contradictory as it stands. If impartiality is what counts in practical reasoning, then it must leave that reasoning intelligible as such. But if the first person does not count, that reasoning is not intelligible as such. By admitting this, impartialists need lose nothing they value. Practical principles can still be formulated in the most rigidly impersonal terms—'Justice or morality requires action A of any person P in situated S'. If we add that each of us must recognize '*I* am the person P situated at S' and thus 'Action A is required of *me*', no compromise is required. Suppose, for example, that the impartialist advocates a scheme in which my agency is reduced to the most meagre level—e.g. the level that Williams claims utilitarian impartialism must reduce it to: I am 'just the representative of the satisfaction system who happens to be near to certain causal levers at a certain time'.[11] Still, I have to recognize that the person in this situation is *me*; that it is *I* who am called on to pull the lever; that the responsibility of doing so is *mine*; and so on. The first person secures the link between reasoning and action, which in turn ensures that the principles do not idle.

If (even) the impartialist can and should recognize these features, why might Godwin's thesis have seemed remotely plausible? We may suspect this of being a forced error, driven by a mistaken view of the position that impartialism opposes. It is often supposed that partialism is simply extended egoism—spreading one's preference for oneself to a limited set of others with whom one is in some deep or otherwise relevant sense related. What explains this is the background thought that, if it is allowed that partial considerations matter, then the first person must have a dominating significance in practical reasoning. Of course, if this *were* what partialism was committed to, then the justification for it would heavily depend on the claim that the first person has

---

[11] 'Persons, Character, and Morality', p. 4.

dominating significance in practical reasoning. So this understanding of their opponents offers impartialists a peculiarly decisive strategy. Simply deny that the first person has any such significance at all. If we support this view with claims about what impartial justice requires, we arrive at 'Godwin's thesis'.

But 'Godwin's thesis' is mistaken as it stands. And what makes it a forced error is a mistake about partialism. Treating partialism as extended egoism is akin to treating the first-person plural as the plural form of *I*. There is no such form; otherwise *we* would mean '*I* and *I* and *I*' instead of '*I* and at least one other (*you; he /she*)'. Similarly, 'extending egoism' could only mean more preference for oneself. The point of introducing a separate term, 'partialism', is to label a preference or particular concern for *certain* others. So it might justly be regarded as a form of altruism—an altruism with limited range.[12] As such, it places no special weight on the significance of the first person.

Parties to the debate mean at least two things by partiality. Some mean bias or prejudice, something that is always bad and generally wrong.[13] Others mean a preference for something, a favourable disposition towards it. It might be assumed that, once the first option were agreed on, debate would be foreclosed. For if partiality means bias or prejudice, it must be undue or unfair, unreasoned and perhaps unreasonable. What shocks partialists in the second sense is that their opponents are sometimes prepared to accept that it is permissible to be partial in the first sense. And what shocks their opponents is that anyone should be prepared to treat partiality with anything more than reluctance, as a necessary evil.

To avoid foreclosing debate, consider 'partiality' in the second sense: as the exercise of a preferential option (thus leaving it open whether doing so is fair or unfair, reasoned or unreasoned, reasonable or unreasonable). The major effect of supposing that partiality must ascribe a dominating significance to the first person is that an unbridgeable gulf opens up between partialism and the impartial distribution of goods. This must be a mistake. For it is consistent with partialism, and may in certain circumstances be required for it, that one exercise impartiality.

Consider one's treatment towards those to whom one is partial—parents, say, towards their children; teachers towards their own students. Being partial

---

[12] Partialism need not be limited in depth, perhaps—there might be 'nothing one would not do for' one's wife. To think of partialism as limited altruism is to be free of the solecism involved in thinking of it as egoism. But thinking of partialism in this way is not wholly innocent; it may reflect a certain poverty of the imagination infecting philosophizing at this point. Why must we think of this form of attitude or behaviour as a qualified version of other forms, rather than as a form proper to itself?

[13] Bishop Hooker gave purpose to this usage early on (1593): he wrote 'Let not the faith which ye have in our Lord Jesus Christ, be blemished with partialities'. *The Lawes of Ecclesiastical Politie* (Preface, p. 4).

towards them does not imply that one is or should be partial *between* them. If parents show equal love, affection, care, and concern for their children, they may be heroic, but not inconsistent. Indeed, as in this case, it might seem that the very reasons that make partiality towards a particular group acceptable or permissible or justified call for impartiality between its members. One's impartiality can proceed from one's partiality.

Not always, of course. In certain circumstances, one's reasons for being partial *towards* a particular group might provide one's reasons for being partial *between* them also. This may even be true of parent–child relationships. Consider primogeniture. If I believe it is better for the good of my family members that my holdings remain as a coherent whole, then leaving all to my eldest alone may simply be what my preferential option for them requires when I make my will. But this is arguable, and the case itself is special—it stands out by contrast with a general rule: that in the central cases at least, one's reasons for being partial towards a group may provide one's reasons for being impartial between its members.

The notion that there *is* so complete a gulf between partialism and impartiality plays deeply in the debate. It supports the assumption that, when we know it would be right to act impartially, that cannot be due to partialist considerations. This assumption turns up in discussion of cases like the following. Suppose my friend and a complete stranger are dying of the same rare disease; I have a pill that would enable my friend to live one second longer, or give the stranger an extra decade of happy life.[14] In the absence of any other relevant facts, it would be right to give the pill to the stranger, wrong to give it to my friend. We appeal to considerations of impartiality to explain this. So, given the rift, it is assumed that we have appealed to non-partialist considerations—partialism may be unable to endorse them; it may even have to reject them; it certainly cannot generate them.

This is a mistake. As in the parent–child case, partialism can explain why one should be impartial. For these are the things one can say. I give preferential treatment to my children because I am their parent, and again, *because I am their parent*, I try to be impartial between them. I give preferential treatment to my friend because I am his friend, and again, *because I am his friend*, I give the pill to the stranger. I might try to explain myself thus. Friendship is not possible in a cocoon; it is interdependent with the way one treats oneself and anyone else. Doing special things for my friend *because he is my friend* is interdependent with doing ordinary things for others because they have a call on me—because

---

[14] Brad Hooker describes a similar case and discusses it in ways to which I am objecting (Chapter 1, this volume, pp. 26–41).

they are in pain, for example, or in need. So giving the pill to my friend in this case would make me incapable of being a friend; it would be to deafen myself so completely to the call of others on me as to reject the possibility of the interdependence that makes friendship possible. Hence precisely *because* I am his friend, I do not give him the pill. (This is how I might explain myself to myself—e.g. in my journal—or to another close acquaintance. It is exactly to the point that, so long as my friend were *compos mentis*, I would not need to explain myself, in this or any other way, to *him*. This is a specific case of a rich ethical issue: which of one's reasons for action one gives in which circumstances, to whom, and for what purposes.)

To think this reply unavailable to a partialist is, I suspect, to assume one of two things: either that having a preference for someone is to exercise it, or that exercising a preference for someone is to distribute goods to them. Neither assumption is correct. I have a preference for my friend in this case, and that leaves me with various choices. One is that I do not exercise it. Another is that I do exercise it, but in such a way as to distribute goods so that they go to others.

To be clear: I am not here defending the partialist's decision or his reasoning, but trying to show that—and how—it is available. One can act as the impartialist supposes one should act in cases of this sort, but nevertheless do so for partialist reasons, and justify oneself in partialist terms. We can no doubt manufacture ever-weightier cases that resist resolution ever more impressively. My friend becomes my closest relative, the stranger becomes an entire species, and I am called on to decide who should survive. But this is all strictly beside the point. I am not arguing about what one should do; not even about what the partialist should do. I am simply trying to show that the options available to the partialist are broader than is sometimes thought; that he has greater scope in what he is free to do, and what he can say in defence or justification of what he does. One consequence is that it is less easy for the impartialist to find cases with which to convict the partialist, cases in which the former and the latter disagree about which actions to permit, require, or forbid. Or to put this in more eirenic terms, there is greater scope for agreement between the two about what should be done, notwithstanding continuing disagreement about why.

Such attempts to establish and extend common ground can proceed in a number of directions. Impartialists, for example, are proud to proclaim the universal aspect of their view. As Godwin writes, 'the same justice that binds me to any individual of my fellow men binds me to the whole'.[15] So it is

---

[15] Godwin, *Enquiry*, p. 174.

important to recognize that the partialist can endorse this same move, replacing 'justice' with the mode of partiality in question—friendship, say, or paternal love.[16]

Assumptions about the relation between partiality and the first person take other forms. Some assume that, to be partial to Fs, I must be an F myself, or at least personally related to Fs. It would follow that, if I am not an F or not related to anyone who is, no action of mine towards Fs can be described as partial. But suppose I decide, on a complete whim, to leave everything I have to any aliens who arrive on earth. This would be to be partial towards—to exercise a preferential option towards—aliens.

This misconception—that partiality places special weight on the significance of the first person—can take a subtler form. It is assumed that partiality is always agent-relative—i.e. that reference to the agent forms an ineliminable and non-trivial part of the principle reflecting partialist reasons. To see what is wrong with this, we need to be more precise about what it is to practise a preferential option. One way of doing so is to distinguish such behaviour into categories by reference to object-giving answers to the question 'why [what reason do you have to] practise a preferential option for x?', e.g.

1. Other-object; e.g. because x is *poor*; or x is *English*; or x is *female* (i.e. a preferential option for the poor, the English, women)
2. Self-object; i.e. because x is *one's own* (in some way)—i.e. first-personal partiality (each agent will translate the principle for themselves as 'because x is *mine* [or ours]'

We can also distinguish into categories by reference to subject-giving answers to the question 'who practises a preferential option for x?', e.g.

3. Other-including-subject: one does/one should (depending on the normative status of the reason)
4. Other-excluding-subject: I do/I should (depending on the normative status of the reason)

By cross-categorizing, we then obtain (for the case of 'should' rather than 'do'):

(a) One should because x is poor
(b) I should because x is poor

---

[16] This is too brief on a controversial point; but it is enough here to sketch the possibility of such a reply. Scanlon draws a similar conclusion, though from different considerations, in his discussion of friendship (*What We Owe to Each Other* (London/Cambridge, MA: Harvard University Press, 1998), pp. 88–90; 123–4; 160–2; 164–6; particularly pp. 164–5).

    (c) One should because x is one's own
    (d) I should because x is mine

This helps in various ways. For example, it immediately reveals what is wrong with claiming partiality is always agent-relative. This approach is wrong-headed, and for three main reasons.

First, because it treats some principles as impartial when they are clearly partial, i.e. one can exercise partiality towards a group for reasons independent of oneself. For example, one might exercise a preferential option for the poor in circumstances where that is so. The principle would be 'One should practise a preferential option for x because x is poor'.[17] Second, because it treats some principles as partial when they are not; they may even be impartial. Consider, for example, Captain Vere in the much-discussed Melville story *Billy Budd*. His actions as judge at the trial are interpretable as reflecting adherence to the idea that 'It would be wrong *for me* to exercise any preferential option', where the 'for me' is irreducible and ineliminable; it is crucial to Vere that it might be permissible for another captain to exercise a preferential option in this case. So the principle on which he acts could not be 'Captains should never exercise a preferential option'. Third, because it is not fine-grained enough, i.e. reference to the agent can form an ineliminable and non-trivial part of the principle reflecting the reason in at least two ways: because that is essential to the object-giving answer (because x is *mine*); or because that is essential to the subject-giving answer (*I should*).

It is important to distinguish the two because (as we know from discussion of 'Godwin's thesis') the second is essential to practical reasoning while the first is not. Moreover, the first is often objectionable. So of course misconceptions occur if the presence of either is sufficient to make a principle partial.

This chapter began by describing cases where we have no idea how to settle the question 'what difference does it make if something is *mine*?' This is characteristic of polarized views about the first person and of its role in practical reasoning. A working hypothesis was then offered: that each pole contrives to be ignorant of what is correct in the tendencies of its alternative; that each extreme assumes that the first person either has quasi-magical powers of conferring significance, or that its powers are mythical, conferring no significance at all; that polarization would collapse if the first person were regarded as neither mythic nor magical but simply allowed its muscle.

Finally, the chapter surveyed the evidence relevant to this hypothesis. It found that, indeed, debates about partialism and impartialism thrive on tacit

---

[17] Those who suppose that the only reasons that count as partial are agent-relative reasons face an additional problem here: this principle is evidently not agent-relative.

assumptions about the way each relates to the first person. These assumptions rest on mistakes and confusions that make incomprehensible the role of the first person in practical reason. This makes practical reasoning itself incomprehensible and gives false impressions of what partialists and impartialists must be committed to. To suppose that the first person has no significance in practical reasoning is false. 'Godwin's thesis' should be rejected. But this does not imply partialism. For impartialists need not and should not hold that thesis. To suppose that the first person has a dominating significance in practical reasoning is also false. But partialists need not and should not hold that it has. So this does not imply impartialism.

Having a clear view of practical reasoning requires that we give some significance to the first person, but not a dominating one. If we hold to this, it may be possible to resist those entrenched false assumptions that induce polarization. Dismounting from this particular seesaw does not render debate between impartialists and partialists unnecessary. On the contrary, it makes such debate possible.[18]

[18] For comments and advice, I am most particularly grateful to Brian Feltham, and also to John Cottingham, Roger Crisp, Jonathan Dancy, Brad Hooker, Elinor Mason, Michael Ridge, Galen Strawson, and Bart Streumer.

5

Morality and Reasonable Partiality*

SAMUEL SCHEFFLER

1. Introduction

What is the relation between morality and partiality? Can the kind of partiality that matters to us be accommodated within moral thought, or are morality and partiality rival sources of normative considerations? These are questions that moral philosophy has struggled with in recent decades.[1] They may not have much intuitive resonance, because the term 'partiality' is not used much in everyday discourse. The June 2005 draft revision of the online *OED* offers two primary definitions of the word. The first definition is '[u]nfair or undue favouring of one party or side in a debate, dispute, etc.; bias, prejudice; an instance of this.' The second definition is '[p]reference for or favourable disposition towards a particular person or thing; fondness; predilection; particular affection; an instance of this.'[2] To someone unfamiliar

* This essay is also published in Samuel Scheffler, *Equality and Tradition* (New York: Oxford University Press, 2010). Printed here by agreement with the publisher.

[1] See, for example, David Archard, 'Moral Partiality', *Midwest Studies in Philosophy* 20 (1995). pp. 129–41; Marcia Baron, 'Impartiality and Friendship', *Ethics* 101 (1991), pp. 836–57; Lawrence Blum, *Friendship, Altruism, and Morality* (London: Routledge and Kegan Paul, 1980); John Cottingham, 'Ethics and Impartiality', *Philosophical Studies* 43 (1983), pp. 83–99, and 'Partiality, Favouritism, and Morality', *The Philosophical Quarterly* 36 (1986), pp. 357–73; Owen Flanagan and Jonathan Adler, 'Impartiality and Particularity', *Social Research* 50 (1983), pp. 576–96; Marilyn Friedman, 'The Impracticality of Impartiality', *Journal of Philosophy* 86 (1989), pp. 645–56, and 'The Practice of Partiality', *Ethics* 101 (1991), pp. 818–35; Barbara Herman, 'Integrity and Impartiality', *The Monist* 66 (1983), pp. 233–50; Diane Jeske, 'Friendship, Virtue, and Impartiality', *Philosophy and Phenomenological Research* LVII (1997), pp. 51–72; Troy Jollimore, 'Friendship Without Partiality?' *Ratio* 13 (2000), pp. 69–82; John Kekes, 'Morality and Impartiality', *American Philosophical Quarterly* 18 (1981), pp. 295–303; Thomas Nagel, *Equality and Partiality* (New York: Oxford University Press, 1991); David Velleman, 'Love as a Moral Emotion', *Ethics* 109 (1999), pp. 338–74; Bernard Williams, 'Persons, Character, and Morality', in his *Moral Luck* (Cambridge: Cambridge University Press, 1981), pp. 1–19; and Susan Wolf, 'Morality and Partiality', *Philosophical Perspectives* 6 (1992), pp. 243–59.

[2] http://dictionary.oed.com/cgi/entry/50172138 (last accessed 15 June 2006).

with debates in moral philosophy over the last quarter century, these definitions might seem to give us all the tools we need to answer the question of whether morality and partiality are compatible with one another. If, by 'partiality', we mean bias or prejudice, then surely morality and partiality are not compatible, for bias and prejudice are antithetical to the kind of *im*partiality that is a fundamental feature of moral thought. But if, on the other hand, what we mean by 'partiality' is a preference or fondness or affection for a particular person, then surely morality and partiality are compatible. Notwithstanding the importance that it assigns to impartiality in certain contexts, morality cannot possibly condemn our particular preferences and affections for one another.

Like many others who have written on these topics, I believe that this simple, commonsensical answer is basically correct. Yet the second half of the answer has been the subject of a surprising degree of controversy in recent moral philosophy. It has been challenged, from the one side, by defenders of morality—and especially by defenders of certain moral theories—who see our particular affections and preferences for one another as being in serious tension with the forms of impartiality and universality that are essential to morality. The most extreme versions of this challenge construe our particular affections and preferences as tantamount to forms of bias or prejudice; in effect, they see partiality in the second of the *OED*'s senses as tantamount to partiality in the first sense. At the same time, the second half of the commonsensical answer has also been challenged by critics of morality, who believe that, in consequence of its commitments to impartiality and universality, morality cannot do justice to the role in our lives of particular attachments and affections.

The fact that the relation between morality and partiality is seen as problematic testifies in part to the influence within modern moral philosophy of highly universalistic moral theories, especially consequentialist and Kantian theories, which have seemed to many of their supporters, and to at least as many of their critics, to make the relation between moral norms and particularistic loyalties and attachments appear problematic to one degree or another. More generally, and more speculatively, it is perhaps not surprising that, in a world where rapidly intensifying processes of global integration coexist uneasily and at times explosively with a range of identity-based social and political movements, there should be a perceived need, both within philosophy and outside of it, to revisit the ancient issue of universalism and particularism in ethics.

As I said, the commonsense view of the relation between morality and partiality seems to me largely correct, but of course I have given only a crude statement of that view. And then there is the question of how to argue for it, since there are some who are not impressed by the authority of common sense, and still others who do not find the view commonsensical at all. In this essay, I cannot hope to discuss all of the relevant issues. What I shall try to do is to extend a line of argument I have developed elsewhere that bears on some of those issues. The general aim of this line of thought is to establish that what I shall call 'reasons of partiality' are inevitable concomitants of certain of the most basic forms of human valuing. This means that, for human beings as creatures with values, the normative force of certain forms of partiality is nearly unavoidable. If that is right, then for morality to reject partiality in a general or systematic way would be for it to set itself against our nature as valuing creatures. And that, I believe, would make morality an incoherent enterprise. My ultimate conclusion is that any coherent morality will make room for partiality, not merely in the sense that it will permit or require partial behaviour in some circumstances, but also in the sense that it will treat reasons of partiality as having direct moral significance.

These are ambitious claims. I shall not be able to give anything approaching a complete defence of them here. But I hope to take some steps toward such a defence. The structure of this chapter will be as follows. In the next section, I shall make some brief preliminary points about the nature and significance of the notion of valuing. In Section 3, I shall summarize arguments I have given elsewhere about the reason-giving status of personal projects and interpersonal relationships. Projects and relationships are among the most fundamental categories of human value, and to value a project or relationship is to see oneself as having reasons for action of a distinctive kind: 'project-dependent reasons' in the one case, and 'relationship-dependent reasons' in the other. In a sense to be specified, these reasons amount to 'reasons of partiality'. In Section 4, I shall extend this line of thought by introducing another category of reasons of partiality, which I shall call 'membership-dependent reasons.' In Section 5, I shall attempt to account for an asymmetry between the normative force of project-dependent reasons, on the one hand, and relationship-dependent and membership-dependent reasons, on the other. In the sixth and longest section, I shall consider the proposal, which is implicit in the work of a number of philosophers, that morality itself may be interpreted on the model of relationship-dependent reasons and membership-dependent reasons. This proposal suggests a radical extension of the line of argument developed in earlier sections of the chapter, and has the potential to cast debates about morality and partiality in a new light. It implies that the very impartiality that we rightly see as a defining feature of morality has its roots in the same structures of normativity that give rise to legitimate reasons of partiality. More generally, it supports a 'relational' conception of morality—a conception that stands in contrast to the kind of impersonality associated with consequentialist conceptions. I shall discuss several different versions of the proposal that moral reasons can be interpreted on the model of relationship-dependent reasons. I shall articulate a number of questions and reservations about each of these versions, in the hope of identifying some of the issues that need to be addressed if some version of the proposal is ultimately to be vindicated. In Section 7, I shall consider some general issues bearing on the prospects for a compelling relational view of morality. Finally, in Section 8, I shall explain how, in the absence of a fully satisfactory relational account, I see my discussion of project-dependent, relationship-dependent, and membership-dependent reasons as bearing on the issue of morality and partiality. As I have indicated, my claim will be, not merely that morality permits or requires partial behaviour in some circumstances, but, in addition, that morality itself actually incorporates reasons of partiality. By this I mean that such reasons bear directly on the rightness or wrongness of actions.

2. Valuing

Much of the distinctiveness and appeal of utilitarianism derives from the fact that it gives priority to the good over the right, or to the evaluative over the normative. In the utilitarian view, moral norms that do not serve to advance the human good are to that extent pointless or arbitrary or worse: this is the meaning of the famous charge of 'rule-worship'.[3] To insist on obedience to a set of rules, however securely entrenched in custom and tradition they may be, is irrational and inhumane if it does not serve to secure for people the kinds of lives that they aspire to lead. Rules lack any legitimate purpose or normative significance, the utilitarian claims, if they do not serve to promote human well-being: if they fail to maximize value.

One response to utilitarianism is to point out that 'value' is a verb as well as a noun. We can talk about value or values, but we can also talk about what *we value*. In asserting that right acts are those that maximize aggregate value, utilitarianism in effect privileges the noun over the verb. But the general idea that the evaluative has priority over the normative does not by itself dictate this choice. Since it is not obvious that the maximization of aggregate value coincides with what we do in fact value, it is reasonable to ask about the relation between these two notions. Is the maximization of aggregate value

---

[3] See J. J. C. Smart, 'An Outline of a System of Utilitarian Ethics', in *Utilitarianism: For and Against*, ed. J. J. C. Smart and B. Williams (Cambridge: Cambridge University Press, 1973), pp. 3–74, at p. 10.

itself something that we do or should value? Is it at least compatible with what we value? Positive answers cannot be ruled out *a priori*, but to make such answers compelling would require sustained attention to questions about the nature of valuing, and these are questions that utilitarianism, with its emphasis on maximizing 'the good', has tended to neglect. If utilitarianism says that the right thing to do is at all times to maximize aggregate value, and if doing this is incompatible with what people actually—and not unreasonably—value, then utilitarianism may itself be vulnerable to a version of the charge of 'rule-worship'. For, on these assumptions, the norm of rightness on which utilitarianism insists is disconnected from basic human concerns, from what people themselves prize or cherish. And if that is so, then the utilitarian's allegiance to the norm may begin to look like a case of venerating the rule for its own sake, in isolation from any contribution it may make to the fulfilment of basic human purposes. It may begin to look, in other words, like an instance of the dreaded rule-worship.

Of course, one need not be a utilitarian for questions about the nature of valuing to be significant. Indeed, my position will be that questions about the nature of valuing lead us away from utilitarianism and other forms of consequentialism. To that extent, I am in agreement with the position defended by Thomas Scanlon in chapter 2 of *What We Owe to Each Other*.[4] But Scanlon is also interested in the nature of valuing because he regards it as a 'helpful stepping-stone'[5] in the development of his 'buck-passing account' of goodness and value. By contrast, I shall not be presenting any account of goodness—or of 'value as a noun'—and, as far as I can see, my arguments are neutral with respect to the truth or falsity of the buck-passing account.

I take valuing in general to comprise a complex syndrome of dispositions and attitudes. These include dispositions to treat certain characteristic types of consideration as reasons for action. They also include certain characteristic types of belief and susceptibility to a wide range of emotions. For the purposes of the arguments I shall be developing in this chapter, the connection between valuing and the perception of reasons for action is particularly important. However, the role of the emotions is also important and must not be overlooked. To value something is in part to be susceptible to a wide range of emotions, depending on the circumstances and on the nature of the thing that is valued. We learn what people value by attending not merely to what they *say* they value but also to the emotions they say they experience in different circumstances. Someone

---

[4] Cambridge, MA: Harvard University Press, 1998.
[5] *What We Owe to Each Other*, p. 95.

who values a personal project, for example, may feel anxious about whether the project will be successful, frustrated if it encounters obstacles, depressed at not having enough time to devote to it, ambivalent if forced to choose between it and other valued pursuits, defensive if other people criticize it or regard it as unworthy, exhilarated if the project goes better than expected, and crushed or empty if it fails.[6] We expect someone who values a project to be vulnerable to emotions of these types. A person may sincerely profess to value something, but if he does not, in the relevant contexts, experience any of the emotions characteristically associated with valuing something of that kind, then we may come to doubt that he really does value it, and upon reflection he may himself come to doubt it as well.

What is involved in valuing a particular thing will depend to some extent on the type of thing that it is. For example, certain emotions presuppose that the object of the emotion has the capacity to recognize and to respond to reasons. Valuing one's relationship with another person involves a susceptibility to experiencing towards that person emotions that carry this presupposition. By contrast, valuing an inanimate object—a work of art, say, or a beautiful rock formation—does not. This illustrates the point that what it is to value something is conditioned by the nature of the object that is valued. It follows that any account of valuing *in general* must remain highly abstract and limited. To make further progress in understanding what is involved in valuing, we need to proceed in a more piecemeal way by reflecting on the specific kinds of things that people value. That will be how I proceed in this chapter. I shall ask: what is involved in valuing a personal project? What is involved in valuing a personal relationship? What is involved in valuing one's membership in a group, community, or association?

3. Relationships and Projects

In a series of earlier essays, I have argued that to value one's relationship with another person non-instrumentally is, in part, to see that person's needs, interests, and desires as providing one, in contexts that may vary depending on the nature of the relationship, with reasons for action, reasons that one

---

[6] This sentence is taken, with slight alterations, from my essay 'Projects, Relationships, and Reasons', in *Reason and Value: Themes from the Moral Philosophy of Joseph Raz*, ed. R. Jay Wallace, Philip Pettit, Samuel Scheffler, and Michael Smith (Oxford: Clarendon Press, 2004), pp. 247–69, at pp. 253–4. Elizabeth Anderson makes a very similar point in her *Value in Ethics and Economics* (Cambridge, MA: Harvard University Press, 1993), p. 11.

would not have had in the absence of the relationship.[7] Of course, the needs and interests of strangers also give one reasons for action. The fact that I lack a relationship with you does not mean that I never have reason to take your interests into account or to act on your behalf. But if I do have a relationship with you, and if I attach non-instrumental value to that relationship, then I shall be disposed to see your needs, interests, and desires as providing me, in contexts of various kinds, with reasons that I would not otherwise have had, and with which the needs, interests, and desires of other people do not provide me. This means that I shall see myself both as having reasons to do things on your behalf that I have no comparable reason to do for others, and as having reason to give your interests priority over theirs in at least some cases of conflict. This is part of what valuing one's relationships involves. If there are no contexts whatsoever in which I would see your needs and interests as giving me reasons of this kind, then it makes no sense to say that I value my relationship with you, even if I profess to do so. Of course, not all of your needs, interests, and desires give me these *relationship-dependent reasons*, and even those that do may at times be silenced or outweighed or overridden by other considerations. Still, if I value my relationship with you non-instrumentally, then I shall treat that relationship as a source of reasons that I would not otherwise have. To value one's relationships is to treat them as reason-giving.

This does not mean that to value a personal relationship is to regard the person with whom one has the relationship as more valuable than other people, or to regard the relationship itself as more valuable than other people's relationships. On the contrary, valuing one's relationships is fully compatible with a recognition of the equal worth of persons and with a recognition that other people have relationships that are just as valuable as one's own. Yet, at the same time, there is more to valuing one's relationships than simply believing that they are instances of valuable types of relationship. To value one's relationships is not to regard them as more valuable than other people's relationships, but neither is it merely to believe that they are valuable relationships that happen to be one's own. To value one's relationships is also to see them as a distinctive source of reasons. It is, in other words, for the needs, desires, and interests of the people with whom one has valued relationships to present themselves as having deliberative significance, in ways that the needs and interests of other people do not.

---

[7] The relevant essays are: 'Relationships and Responsibilities', *Philosophy & Public Affairs* 26 (1997), pp. 189–209, reprinted in *Boundaries and Allegiances* (Oxford: Oxford University Press, 2001), pp. 97–110; 'Conceptions of Cosmopolitanism', *Utilitas* 11(1999), pp. 255–76, reprinted in *Boundaries and Allegiances*, pp. 111–30; and 'Projects, Relationships, and Reasons'. My discussion in this section draws on these earlier essays.

There are clear parallels between what is involved in valuing a personal relationship and what is involved in valuing a personal project. Valuing a personal project, like valuing a personal relationship, involves seeing it as reason-giving. In other words, to value a project of one's own is, among other things, to see it as giving one reasons for action in a way that other people's projects do not, and in a way that other comparably valuable activities in which one might engage do not. Again, this does not mean that one sees one's projects as being more valuable than anybody else's projects or than any other activity in which one might engage. Nor does it mean that one's *project-dependent* reasons always take priority over other reasons. Still, if I value my projects non-instrumentally, then I shall see them as a distinctive source of reasons for action, and there will be contexts in which I see myself as having reasons to pursue those projects even though doing so means passing up opportunities to engage in other equally valuable activities or to assist other people with their equally valuable projects. This is simply what valuing one's personal projects non-instrumentally involves. If I do not see myself as having any more reason to attend to my own projects and goals than I do to engage in other activities or to attend to the projects and goals of other people, then it no longer makes sense to think of them as my projects and goals at all, still less to think that I value them non-instrumentally.

There are few things to which people attach greater value than their personal projects and interpersonal relationships. I take this claim to be uncontroversial. Our projects and relationships are among the primary things that we value. They give purpose and shape to our lives. Of course, particular projects and relationships are open to criticism of various kinds. A project may be pointless, misguided, shallow, corrupt, or evil. A relationship may be unhealthy or exploitative or oppressive. The fact that someone values a particular project or relationship does not mean that it is worth valuing. Yet any suggestion that people should in general cease to value their personal projects and relationships would be difficult to take seriously. From what vantage point might such a claim be put forward? And on what authority might one presume to tell people that they should abandon these basic categories of human value? There are religious ideals that hold that one should strive to detach oneself from worldly concerns and to transcend the self altogether. Whatever the attractions of these ideals, they do not provide grounds for criticizing the particular categories of value we are discussing. They aspire to something more radical: a rejection of all valuing, indeed a rejection of the self as normally understood. I won't engage with these ideals here, since debates about morality and partiality normally take it for granted that we are dealing with human beings as creatures with values who have distinct identities as persons. So long as we proceed on that assumption, I see little basis for any credible argument to the effect that people should cease to value their projects and relationships.

If the arguments I have been sketching are correct, this means that partiality is a deeply entrenched feature of human valuing. To value one's projects and relationships is to see them as sources of reasons for action in a way that other people's projects and relationships are not. Personal projects and relationships by their nature define forms of reasonable partiality, partiality not merely in our preferences or affections but in the reasons that flow from some of our most basic values. To be sure, I have so far argued only that valuing one's projects and relationships involves *seeing them as* sources of reasons. I have not argued that these 'reasons of partiality' really exist. Yet if there is no general ground for insisting that we are mistaken in valuing our projects and relationships, then neither is there any ground for denying the validity of project-dependent and relationship-dependent reasons as a class. By virtue of what we value, we see ourselves as having reasons of these types. We may on occasion value things that shouldn't be valued, and so we may on occasion see ourselves as having reasons that we do not have. But to say that we are fallible is not to say that we are systematically misguided. Absent any reason for repudiating our valuation of projects and relationships as a class, there is no basis for denying that we have project-dependent and relationship-dependent reasons at all. Contrapositively, scepticism about such reasons is tantamount to the rejection of fundamental categories of human valuation.

4. Membership-dependent Reasons

In addition to valuing their personal projects and interpersonal relationships, people value their membership in groups and associations of various kinds. They value group membership even when the groups in question are large enough that there is no prospect of knowing individually, let alone having a personal relationship with, each of the other members. It is possible, of course, to value one's membership in a group in a purely instrumental way, as a means of achieving one's long-term goals or obtaining the discrete benefits that group membership makes available. For example, an ambitious white-collar worker may apply for membership in an exclusive club in the hope that it will enhance his career. Or, again, one may value one's membership in the American Association of Retired People solely because AARP members receive a discount on the purchase of prescription drugs. Here it is perfectly imaginable that one might receive such a discount without belonging to the

AARP, and if one could, then, by hypothesis, one would see no loss in surrendering one's membership and obtaining the discount in other ways.

Often, however, people value their membership in groups non-instrumentally. They find membership rewarding in its own right. Even in such cases, there may seem to be a sense in which they can be said to value membership for the sake of the benefits it provides. Perhaps, for example, one values one's membership in a particular community because of the bonds of trust and solidarity that members share. However, this is merely a way of characterizing the respects in which membership in the group is a good. It is not a specification of a good that is independent of membership and to which membership is a means. In other words, the 'benefits' mentioned are not separable even in principle from one's membership; one could not, even in principle, receive them without belonging to this community. One might, of course, come to develop bonds of trust in some other community, but the bonds that unite members of *this* community have a distinctive character and are not fungible. If one ceased to be a member of the community, one would experience a sense of loss even if one were assured that one would be welcomed into some other community. Since one cannot make sense of the idea that one might obtain the 'benefits' of belonging to this particular community without actually belonging to this particular community, it would be wrong to say that one values one's membership only as a means of obtaining those benefits. In valuing the benefits one is valuing one's membership.

It is not surprising that people should value group membership. Human beings are social creatures, and we express our social natures through participation in a rich variety of formal and informal groups, associations, and organizations. This is one of the basic ways in which we find fulfilment. So it is not at all surprising that we should value our membership in groups. This form of valuation is firmly rooted in our nature as social creatures. What is involved in valuing non-instrumentally one's membership in a group or association? As with projects and relationships, valuing one's membership in a group or association is in part a matter of seeing it as reason-giving, as a source of what I shall call *membership-dependent reasons*. In general, membership-dependent reasons are reasons to do one's share, as defined by the norms and ideals of the group itself, to help sustain it and contribute to its purposes. Most groups and associations have formal or informal ways of communicating what is expected of individual members. To value one's membership in a group or association is, in part, to see these expectations as presenting one with reasons for action in a way that the expectations of other worthy groups do not. One need not believe that the group to which one belongs is the most valuable group of its kind, still less that it is the most valuable group of any kind, in order for its expectations to be perceived as presenting one with reasons for action in a way that other groups' expectations do not. Nor need one believe that fulfilling the group's expectations will have better overall results, in the consequentialist sense, than engaging in other valuable activities would. The capacity of my membership in a group to provide me with reasons for action is not dependent on a conviction that the group is worthier than other groups or that fulfilling its expectations is the most valuable thing I could do. Of course, my membership-dependent reasons may in various contexts be overridden or outweighed or silenced by reasons of other kinds. And if an otherwise worthy group articulates expectations in a given case that strike me as foolhardy or unjust, then I may not see myself as having any reason to fulfil those expectations. But if I never see myself as having any more reason to respond to the group's expectations than I do to engage in other valuable activities, then it no longer makes sense to suppose that I value my membership in the group non-instrumentally.

If these arguments are correct, then, like personal projects and relationships, group membership defines a form of reasonable partiality, partiality in the reasons that flow from deeply entrenched categories of human valuation. If there is no ground for insisting that we are mistaken in valuing group membership in general, then neither is there any ground for denying the validity of membership-dependent reasons as a class. By virtue of what we value, we see ourselves as having reasons of these types. To be sure, some groups are evil or corrupt, and if we value our membership in such a group we may see ourselves as having reasons that we do not really have. As with projects and relationships, however, to say that we are fallible is not to say that we are systematically misguided. Absent any reason for repudiating our valuation of group membership in general, there is no basis for denying that we have membership-dependent reasons at all. Contrapositively, scepticism about such reasons is tantamount to rejecting a fundamental category of human valuation.

5. The Asymmetry between Projects and Relationships

Despite the strong parallels between project-dependent reasons and relationship dependent reasons, there is, as I've noted elsewhere,[8] an important asymmetry between them. Oversimplifying slightly, we may characterize the asymmetry

---

[8] In 'Projects, Relationships, and Reasons'.

as follows. We normally suppose that many of our relationship-dependent reasons are reasons on which we are required or obligated to act. It is not merely that we have reasons to attend to the needs of, say, our children or elderly parents, but that we have obligations to do so. By contrast, even when we have strong project-dependent reasons, we do not normally suppose that we are obligated or required to act on them. I may have strong reasons to complete my novel, but if I fail to do so I shall not have violated any obligation or deontic requirement. And this remains the case even though these reasons may strike me with the force of practical necessity; prospectively I may say that I 'have to' finish my novel or that I simply 'must' do so. This means that there are really two puzzles to be addressed. One puzzle is how to account for the asymmetry between project-dependent and relationship-dependent reasons. But in order to address that puzzle, we need to characterize more clearly the content of the asymmetry. If reasons of both kinds may strike us with the force of practical necessity—as reasons on which we 'must' act—then how can it also be true that we are 'required' or 'obligated' to act on reasons of one kind but not the other?

The key to solving both puzzles lies in the observation that many relationship-dependent reasons are reasons that one lacks the authority to disregard, not merely in the sense that the reasons may be compelling or rationally decisive, but in the sense that there are specific people who are entitled to complain if one neglects those reasons. If I fail to act on compelling relationship-dependent reasons to attend to my son's needs, then, other things equal, I have wronged him and he has a legitimate complaint against me. But if I fail to act on compelling project-dependent reasons to finish my novel, I have wronged no one and no one is in a privileged position to complain.[9] This gives content to the claim that, despite the fact that both relationship-dependent reasons and project-dependent reasons may strike us with the force of practical necessity, we are 'required' or 'obligated' to act on the former but not on the latter.

But why is someone entitled to complain in the one case but not in the other? Why is it the case that, if I neglect compelling relationship-dependent reasons to attend to my son's needs, then I shall have wronged him, whereas, if I neglect compelling project-dependent reasons to finish my novel, then I shall not have wronged anyone? It would, of course, be circular to reply

[9] Compare the view that Milan Kundera attributes to Stravinsky: '[W]hat an author creates doesn't belong to his papa, his mama, his nation, or to mankind; it belongs to no one but himself; he can publish it when he wants and if he wants; he can change it, revise it, lengthen it, shorten it, throw it in the toilet and flush it down without the slightest obligation to explain himself to anybody at all' (M. Kundera, 'What is a Novelist?' *The New Yorker* (9 October 2006), pp. 40–5, at p. 44).

that, in the first case, I lack the authority to disregard the reasons in question, whereas in the second case I retain that authority. Nor will it do to say that, in the first case, my failure will affect my son adversely, while in the second case my failure will have adverse effects on nobody but myself. One's failure to act on one's project-dependent reasons may well have adverse effects on other people. My failure to complete my novel may disappoint admirers of my fiction. My failure to complete the design for a new product may deprive others of its benefits. My failure to open the small business I had dreamed about may deprive the local economy of a badly needed boost. My failure to complete my medical studies may mean that someone does not receive medical care that is as good as the care I would have provided.

A more promising answer would proceed along the following lines.[10] To value our relationships is to see them as sources of reasons. In so far as we are correct to value our relationships—insofar as our relationships are valuable—they are indeed sources of reasons. So if we ask why the needs, interests, and desires of people with whom we have valuable relationships give us reasons for action, the answer lies in the fact that we have those relationships with them. A valuable relationship transforms the needs and desires of the participants into reasons for each to act on behalf of the other in suitable contexts. At the same time, it gives each of them reasons to form certain normative expectations of the other, and to complain if these expectations are not met.[11] In particular, it gives each of them reason to expect that the other will act on his or her behalf in suitable contexts. These two sets of reasons—reasons for action on the one hand and reasons to form normative expectations on the other—are two sides of the same coin. They are constitutively linked and jointly generated by the relationship between the participants. In so far as we have a valuable relationship, I have reasons to respond to your needs, desires, and interests, and in so far as those reasons are compelling or decisive, you have complementary reasons to expect that I shall do so. And vice versa. This is neither a coincidence nor a mystery. It is simply the normative upshot of valuable human relationships. The fact that two human beings have a valuable bond or tie is a source of interlocking reasons and expectations for each of them. That is the kind of normative significance that valuable relationships

---

[10] The discussion in this paragraph derives from but also revises and supersedes my earlier discussion of this issue in 'Projects, Relationships, and Reasons', pp. 266–8. In making these revisions, I largely follow the account given by R. Jay Wallace in 'The Deontic Structure of Morality', unpublished draft, 3 December 2005.

[11] The idea of holding agents to a set of normative expectations is central to the account of responsibility developed by R. Jay Wallace in *Responsibility and the Moral Sentiments* (Cambridge, MA: Harvard University Press, 1994). Here I focus on the distinctive expectations of the participants in interpersonal relationships.

have for their participants. I might have compelling pragmatic or prudential reasons to respond to your needs or desires without your being entitled to form an expectation that I shall do so or to hold me to account if I do not. But if the source of my reason to respond to your needs and desires lies in the value of our relationship, and if that reason is compelling, then my reason for action is complemented by your entitlement to expect that I shall respond. The very same consideration that gives me reason to act on your behalf gives you reason to complain if I do not. In this sense, I lack the authority unilaterally to disregard my reason to act on your behalf; I cannot waive your entitlement to complain.

This argument needs refinement and qualification, but something along these lines seems to me basically correct. And even without having the refinements and qualifications in hand, it is clear that no comparable argument applies to the case of project-dependent reasons. In so far as they arise outside the context of interpersonal relations, my project-dependent reasons are not accompanied by complementary entitlements on the part of other people to form expectations of me. Interpersonal relationships are collaborative enterprises by definition, and the normative considerations they generate for each party are constitutively linked to the normative considerations they generate for the other. In giving me a decisive reason to act on your behalf, they give you a claim that I should do so. By contrast, nobody but I need be a party to my project. And so my project can give me reasons to act without giving anyone the normative standing to complain if I fail to do so. In this sense, my purely project-dependent reasons might be described as 'normatively individualistic'. I have unilateral authority to disregard such reasons, however strong they may be, and this gives content to the idea that, even though I may be foolish or unreasonable not to act on them, nevertheless I am not 'required' or 'obligated' to do so. In practice, of course, project-dependent reasons often overlap with relationship-dependent reasons, both because the participants in personal relationships sometimes develop joint projects and because personal projects sometimes involve relationships with other people. In cases of either of these types, it may be impossible to distinguish one's project-dependent reasons from one's relationship-dependent reasons, and when this happens it is the normative character of the relationship-dependent reasons that is dominant. That is, one's reasons lose the normative characteristics of purely project-dependent reasons, and one may be required or obligated to act on them. Still, purely project-dependent reasons do exist, and they differ in their deontic character from relationship-dependent reasons.

The normative characteristics of membership-dependent reasons do not correspond precisely to those of either relationship-dependent or project-dependent reasons. On the one hand, membership in a group implicates one directly in relations of co-membership with others, and membership-dependent reasons lack the normatively individualistic character of purely project-dependent reasons. One may be required or obligated to act on them. On the other hand, the relations that are constitutive of group membership may be highly attenuated. One need not have a face-to-face relationship or even a personal acquaintance with each of the other members of a group to which one belongs, and in larger groups one may know personally only a very small proportion of them. This means that the normative significance of membership-dependent reasons has a more diffuse character than is typical of relationship-dependent reasons. Although one's failure to act on one's membership-dependent reasons does give others grounds for complaint, it may not always be clear who exactly has the standing to complain. Perhaps all the members of the group do, or perhaps only those group members who are most affected by one's failure to act, if they can be identified, or perhaps only the officials or designated representatives of the group, if it has any. It may be even less clear who can reasonably be said to have been wronged by one's failure to act: is it the entire membership of the group, or the group itself, considered as something over and above its membership, or some subset of group members? Or does it not make sense to speak of wronging in such cases? One reason for doubt is that, in large groups at least, the failure of any one individual to satisfy the group's expectations may have no perceptible effect on the other members, who may not even be aware of it. So it may seem overblown to use the language of wronging.

In any event, the answers to questions about who is wronged and who has standing to complain when an individual fails to act on his membership-dependent reasons may vary depending on the nature, size, and organizational structure of the group of which he is a member. What does seem clear is that the relatively simple pattern of reciprocal normativity that characterizes two-person relationships may not apply straightforwardly in these cases.

6. A Relational View of Morality?

I have argued that our project-dependent, relationship-dependent, and membership-dependent reasons all define important forms of reasonable partiality. This list may not be exhaustive. At the very least, though, the three types of reason I have identified cover much of the territory of reasonable partiality. So it is noteworthy that various philosophers have seen personal relationships as crucial to understanding the normative force of morality itself. On the face of it, many moral reasons are 'relationship-independent'. That is, they are reasons to treat other people in certain ways whether or not we have any personal relationship with them. Yet a number of philosophers have suggested, in effect, that these reasons are best understood as constituting a species of relationship-dependent or membership-dependent reason, and the idea that morality has an essentially relational structure has been presented as an alternative to the consequentialist emphasis on the impersonal aggregation of value. In an early essay,[12] for example, Thomas Nagel characterized the difference between utilitarianism and absolutist deontology in the following terms:

> Absolutism is associated with a view of oneself as a small being interacting with others in a large world. The justifications it requires are primarily interpersonal. Utilitarianism is associated with a view of oneself as a benevolent bureaucrat distributing such benefits as one can control to countless other beings, with whom one may have various relations or none. The justifications it requires are primarily administrative.[13]

Nagel suggests in the same essay that the key to understanding the basis of deontological restrictions may lie in 'the possibility that to treat someone else horribly puts you in a special relation to him which may have to be defended in terms of other features of your relation to him'.[14]

More recently, Jay Wallace has argued that the 'deontic structure' of morality—the fact that moral reasons present themselves to us in deliberation as requirements or obligations—can be understood by reference to the same kind of reciprocal normativity that characterizes personal relationships, such as friendship, and the reasons arising from them.[15] Just as we lack the authority unilaterally to disregard our relationship-dependent reasons because they arise from valuable relationships that also ground corresponding expectations and

---

[12] 'War and Massacre', *Philosophy & Public Affairs* 1 (2) (Winter 1972), pp. 123–44; reprinted in *Consequentialism and Its Critics*, ed. Samuel Scheffler (Oxford: Oxford University Press, 1988), pp. 51–73.

[13] *Ibid.*, p. 67.   [14] *Ibid.*, p. 66.

[15] Wallace, 'The Deontic Structure of Morality.' I am here oversimplifying Wallace's position. He also cites two other factors that may contribute to our understanding of moral reasons as having the status of requirements. These factors are the inescapability of such reasons—the fact that they apply to all people—and their weightiness or importance. However, the central argument of his paper is that the deontic structure of morality cannot be fully explained by these other factors alone. There is, he says, a 'distinct source of deontic structure' (p. 2), and he appeals to the notion of reciprocal or relational normativity to account for this additional dimension of the normativity of morality. I shall ignore this complication in the remainder of my discussion, since I don't believe that it affects the points I want to make.

complaints on the part of the people with whom we have those relationships, so too there are 'valuable relationships [that lie] at the heart of morality', and these relationships, in providing us with reasons for action, also generate legitimate expectations and grounds for privileged complaint on the part of other people. Like relationship-dependent reasons, Wallace argues, moral reasons have the character of requirements because they arise within structures of relational or reciprocal or 'bipolar' normativity.[16]

These ideas suggest a radical extension of the line of argument that I have been developing. My aim has been to argue that project-dependent, relationship-dependent, and membership-dependent reasons all represent forms of reasonable partiality, which morality should be thought of as incorporating. But the remarks of Nagel and Wallace may be taken to suggest, more radically, that moral reasons are always relationship-dependent. This suggestion has the potential to transform debates about morality and partiality. Whereas the presupposition of those debates is that there is at least a *prima facie* tension between morality and partiality, the suggestion here is that even those moral reasons that appear superficially to be relationship-independent nevertheless have their source in relations among people, so that moral reasons and reasons of partiality arise ultimately in just the same way.

I find the idea of interpreting morality in fundamentally relational terms attractive, yet I believe that a satisfactory relational interpretation continues to elude us. Several versions of a relational interpretation have been suggested in recent philosophical work. These versions differ from one another in significant ways, but in each case there are puzzles or obscurities that bar the way to unqualified acceptance. In the remainder of this section, I shall discuss three of these versions, and in each case I shall try to identify some of the issues that need to be addressed if a compelling position is to emerge.

One way of modelling moral reasons on relationship-dependent reasons is suggested by Nagel's frankly speculative proposal that 'to treat someone else horribly puts you in a special relation to him which may have to be defended in terms of other features of your relation to him'.[17] However, Nagel offers this as a suggestion about how deontological restrictions in particular might be justified or explained. He does not purport to be offering a relational account of morality as a whole. And since the 'special relation' he invokes is supposed to be called into being by mistreatment—by the violation of a deontological

---

[16] The notion of bipolar normativity derives from Michael Thompson, 'What is it to Wrong Somebody? A Puzzle about Justice', in *Reason and Value: Themes from the Moral Philosophy of Joseph Raz*, pp. 333–84.

[17] Nagel, 'War and Massacre', p. 66. The next several paragraphs expand on points I made in footnote 25 of 'Projects, Relationships, and Reasons', pp. 267–8.

restriction—it is not clear how readily this proposal could be generalized to explain moral reasons as a class. The suggestion that 'to treat someone horribly puts you in a special relation to him' implies that the relation arises from the fact of mistreatment. It is the mistreatment that 'establishes'[18] the relation. But this means that, if a person respects deontological restrictions, then there is no relation of the relevant kind between him and those who would otherwise have been his victims. Since it is unclear how the deontological reason the agent respects could have its source in a relation that doesn't exist, this raises a question about whether Nagel's appeal to the relation between agent and victim can fully explain how such reasons arise. It is even less clear how that appeal might be extended to provide a relational account of moral reasons in general.

There is a deeper point here. I have argued that personal relationships can be sources of reasons for action because they are among the most basic objects of human valuation, and because valuing is always connected to the perception of reasons. But the relevant notion of a 'relationship' requires clarification. As Niko Kolodny has observed, there is a thin, logical sense in which, whenever two people satisfy some two-place predicate, they can be said to stand in an interpersonal relation.[19] But the valuable reason-giving relationships that I have been discussing are relationships in a more robust sense. They are ongoing bonds between individuals who have a shared history that usually includes patterns of engagement and forms of mutual familiarity, attachment, and regard developed over time.[20] In such cases, we can usually say not merely that the participants *stand in some relation to* one another, but that they *have a relationship with* one another. My argument has been that relationships of this kind are among the most basic and deeply entrenched categories of human valuation and the most important sources of human fulfilment and that, as such, they have the capacity to give us reasons for action if anything does. In this sense, I have attempted to explain the source of relationship-dependent reasons.

The pertinent question to ask about relational views of morality is whether they can provide a comparable explanation of the source of moral reasons, by showing how those reasons arise from valuable human relationships of some kind. The 'special relation' between agent and victim that Nagel speaks of is not, however, a valuable relationship. Indeed, it is not a human relationship in

<hr/>

[18] Nagel, 'War and Massacre', p. 67n.
[19] Niko Kolodny, 'Love as Valuing a Relationship', *Philosophical Review* 112 (2003), pp. 135–89, at p. 147.
[20] See Kolodny, 'Love as Valuing a Relationship', p. 148. Kolodny particularly emphasizes the importance of a shared history.

the sense just described at all. Rather than being a temporally extended pattern of mutual engagement, the relation between agent and victim supervenes on a discrete interaction between two individuals who may have no independent relationship of any kind.[21] In speaking of a special relation between those two individuals, Nagel means to emphasize that what is wrong about the violation of a deontological restriction has to do with features of the interaction *between them*. It does not have to do with the wider effects or overall consequences of such a violation. In *The View from Nowhere*, he suggests that the wrongmaking feature is the fact that the agent's actions are guided by or aim at the victim's harm or injury or evil.[22] But to say this is clearly not to ground moral reasons in an ongoing human relationship, let alone in a valuable one. So it does not by itself take us very far down the road towards a satisfactory relational view of morality.

Perhaps the most straightforward way of trying to develop such a view is to argue that, in addition to their other personal relationships and social affiliations, all people share the bond of their common humanity. In Locke's words, all of '*mankind are one community*, make up one society, distinct from all other creatures'.[23] Or, in Christine Korsgaard's more Kantian formulation, each person is not only 'a member of many smaller and more local communities', but also 'a member of the party of humanity, a Citizen of the Kingdom of Ends'.[24] This argument proposes that, just as it is possible to value non-instrumentally one's relationships with particular individuals and one's membership in various social groups and associations, so too it is possible to value one's membership in the wider human community. And just as valuing one's relationships or one's membership in groups and associations involves seeing those bonds as reason-giving, so too valuing one's membership in the wider human community involves seeing it as reason-giving. Moral reasons, this proposal concludes, are simply membership-dependent reasons that arise from the value of belonging to the human community.

---

[21] Thus I find misleading Christine Korsgaard's comment that 'the relationship of agents and victims, like that of love or friendship, is a *personal* relationship' ('The Reasons We Can Share', *Social Philosophy and Policy* 10 (1993), pp. 24–51, at p. 48). Niko Kolodny makes similar points in his 'Partiality and the Contours of the Moral' (unpublished).

[22] Nagel writes that a deontological restriction 'expresses the direct appeal to the point of view of the agent from the point of view of the person on whom he is acting. It operates through that relation. The victim feels outrage when he is deliberately harmed even for the greater good of others, not simply because of the quantity of the harm but because of the assault on his value of having my actions guided by his evil. What I do is immediately directed against his good: it doesn't just in fact harm him' (*The View from Nowhere* (New York: Oxford University Press, 1986), at p. 184).

[23] John Locke, *Second Treatise of Government* (1690), Section 128 (emphasis in the original).

[24] Christine Korsgaard, *The Sources of Normativity* (Cambridge: Cambridge University Press, 1996), p. 127.

One initial worry about this proposal, which I shall mention only to set aside, is that it may provide a relatively weak motivational foundation for morality. Most people do have projects and relationships that they value, and few of them doubt that those projects and relationships give them reasons for action. But scepticism about morality is more widespread, and moral sceptics may be happy to deny that they value something called 'membership in the human community'. So if moral reasons do arise from the value of this kind of membership, this may do little to persuade the sceptic. Of course, a central aspiration of Kantian moral philosophy is to establish that one must value one's own humanity as a condition of valuing one's other relationships and affiliations, or indeed of valuing anything at all. I shall not engage with this dimension of the Kantian project here, since I want to concentrate on the prior question of whether a viable relational interpretation of morality is available in the first place.

More immediately pressing puzzles emerge if we ask the following question. If valuing one's membership in the human community involves seeing it as reason-giving, what is the content of those reasons? If they are construed on the model of relationship-dependent reasons, then perhaps they are reasons to respond to the needs and interests of human beings, reasons that one does not have to respond to the needs and interests of non-humans. I have two reservations about this proposal. First, as Locke's emphasis on our being 'distinct from all other creatures' suggests, it treats the distinction between human and non-human creatures as the linchpin of morality, as if the primary moral imperative were to give the interests of human beings priority over those of the beasts or of aliens from outer space. Second, it says nothing about the kind of response to the needs and interests of human beings that is called for, and in particular it says nothing to rule out the utilitarian idea that one should respond to those needs and interests by maximizing their aggregate satisfaction. To that extent, it does nothing by itself to flesh out the idea of a relational conception of morality as an alternative to impersonal, aggregative forms of consequentialism.

If the reasons involved in valuing one's membership in the human community are instead construed on the model of other membership-dependent reasons, then perhaps they are reasons to do one's fair share, as defined by the norms and ideals of the human community itself, to help sustain the community and contribute to its purposes. The problem, of course, is that in asking about the content of our moral reasons, the norms of the human community are precisely what we are trying to characterize. There is, by hypothesis, no independent characterization of those norms to which non-circular appeal can be made. So, on this interpretation, the proposal is vacuous.

Underlying many of these worries is a more basic doubt about the plausibility of grounding moral reasons in the value of membership in the human community. One way of articulating this doubt is to suggest that this proposal takes too literally what is in fact a metaphorical way of formulating a very different view. The alternative view is that moral reasons are grounded in the value of humanity, or of persons. This view can be expressed metaphorically by speaking of the value of membership in the human community, but the metaphor should not be taken literally. A literal reading makes morality seem too much like a matter of group loyalty—of loyalty to one's fellow humans—and in so doing it puts the accent in the wrong place.[25] It is not really the value of *membership* that gives rise to moral reasons, according to the alternative view, but rather the value of humanity—of persons—and talk of membership in the human community is simply a picturesque way of reminding us that all persons have moral standing. This contrasts with cases of genuinely relationship-dependent and membership-dependent reasons.[26] In such cases, one's reasons do not arise simply from the value of the person with whom one has the relationship or shares the group affiliation. Instead, it is one's participation in the valuable group or relationship that is the source of one's reasons, and non-participants do not have the same reasons, even though they may recognize the value of the persons involved. If this is correct, and if the doubts articulated here are well founded, then what looks like a relational conception of morality may turn out in the end not to be one after all.

A third way of grounding moral reasons in valuable human relationships is suggested by Thomas Scanlon in *What We Owe to Each Other*. Scanlon's contractualism 'holds that an act is wrong if its performance under the circumstances would be disallowed by any set of principles for the general regulation of behaviour that no one could reasonably reject as a basis for informed, unforced general agreement'.[27] Scanlon takes it to be an advantage of this view that it provides a compelling explanation of the reason-giving force of moral judgements. The core idea is that the distinctive reason that we have to avoid doing what is wrong is a reason to want our behaviour to be justifiable to others on grounds they could not reasonably reject. Scanlon

[25] I take this to be an objection to the view of morality defended by Andrew Oldenquist in 'Loyalties', *Journal of Philosophy* 79 (1982), pp. 173–93. But see Bernard Williams, 'The Human Prejudice', in his (ed. A. W. Moore) *Philosophy as a Humanistic Discipline* (Princeton, NJ: Princeton University Press, 2006), ch. 16.

[26] This is related to the contrast drawn by Niko Kolodny, in 'Partiality and the Contours of the Moral', between the 'person-based' conception of morality and the 'owed-to' conception. Significantly, Kolodny argues that a commitment to the person-based conception is what motivates the view that morality excludes partiality.

[27] Scanlon, *What We Owe to Each Other*, p. 153.

writes: 'When I reflect on the reason that the wrongness of an action seems to
supply not to do it, the best description of this reason I can come up with has
to do with the relation to others that such acts would put me in: the sense that
others could reasonably object to what I do.'[28] This suggests that moral reasons
are rooted in considerations about our relations to other people.

Scanlon elaborates on this suggestion in the course of explaining how the
contractualist account of moral motivation makes available a convincing reply
to 'Pritchard's dilemma'. This dilemma asserts that any account of moral
motivation will be either trivial (if it says that we have reason to avoid
doing what's wrong just because it's wrong) or unacceptably 'external' (if, for
example, it says that avoiding wrongdoing will conduce to our own interests).
Scanlon develops his reply by first considering the case of friendship. In this
case, a similar 'dilemma' might seem to arise, for we can ask why we should
be loyal to our friends, and any answer we give may appear either trivial (if
it says that loyalty is what friendship requires) or unacceptably external (if
it appeals to the benefits of having friends). The solution to the friendship
dilemma, Scanlon believes, is to characterize friendship in such a way as
to make clear why it is a relationship that is 'desirable and admirable in
itself'.[29] If we do this, we shall see that there is really no dilemma. Rather
than being competing answers to a single question, the two horns of the
supposed dilemma capture 'two essential aspects of friendship'.[30] On the
one hand, part of what friendship involves is seeing loyalty to one's friends
as a sufficient reason for performing what may sometimes be burdensome
actions. On the other hand, being a friend also involves an appreciation
of the way in which the friendship enriches one's life and contributes to
one's good.

Analogous points hold, Scanlon maintains, in the case of morality. Here
his solution to Pritchard's dilemma is to represent our reasons to avoid
wrongdoing as rooted in a certain ideal of interpersonal relations that is
intimately connected with morality, but that has enough independence from
it to provide a non-trivial account of those reasons. He writes:

There are obvious similarities between the case of friendship as I have described it and
that of the morality of right and wrong, and my strategy in responding to the problem
of moral motivation is analogous to the response I have just sketched to Pritchard's
dilemma in the case of friendship. The contractualist ideal of acting in accord with
principles that others (similarly motivated) could not reasonably reject is meant to
characterize the relation with others the value and appeal of which underlies our
reasons to do what morality requires. This relation, much less personal than friendship,

[28] *Ibid.*, p. 155.   [29] *Ibid.*, p. 161.   [30] *Ibid.*, p. 162.

might be called a relation of mutual recognition. Standing in this relation to others is appealing in itself—worth seeking for its own sake. A moral person will refrain from lying to others, cheating, harming, or exploiting them, 'because these things are wrong.' But for such a person these requirements are not just formal imperatives; they are aspects of the positive value of a way of living with others.[31]

Scanlon's position, then, is that a relation of mutual recognition, which is in some ways analogous to friendship but is less personal, 'underlies' our reasons to conform with moral requirements. If this is correct, then it seems that moral reasons may be thought of as relationship-dependent reasons arising from the valuable relation of mutual recognition. Furthermore, as Wallace suggests, the 'deontic character' of moral reasons may then be understood on the model of other relationship-dependent reasons, such as those arising from friendship. The suggestion, in other words, is that, in the moral case as in the case of friendship, our relationship-dependent reasons belong to structures of reciprocal normativity, which means the same considerations that generate reasons for an agent to conform to moral requirements also generate reasons for others to complain if he does not. In the moral case, the people who may complain are those to whom the action could not have been justified on grounds they would have been unreasonable to reject. As Wallace puts the point:

What makes an action of mine morally wrong is the fact that it cannot be justified to someone affected by it on terms that person would be unreasonable to reject. In a situation in which I do something morally wrong, the person adversely affected will have been wronged by me, and have privileged basis for moral complaint, resentment, and so on, precisely insofar as I have acted with indifference to the value of relating to them on a basis of mutual recognition and regard. The very principles that specify what I have moral reason to do, on this relational conception, equally serve to specify normative expectations and entitlements on the part of others. Those principles are thus implicated in a bipolar normative nexus very like the one that defines the reciprocal reasons and expectations constitutive of a relationship of friendship.[32]

This explains why, in the moral case as in the case of friendship, one's relationship-dependent reasons have the character of requirements; as elements

[31] Scanlon, *What We Owe to Each Other*, p. 153.

[32] Wallace, 'The Deontic Structure of Morality', p. 35. As Frances Kamm has emphasized in discussion, one obvious question is whether a view of this kind can account for imperfect duties, which are not owed to any particular individual. Another obvious question is whether it can account for the norms governing our treatment of non-human animals. However, Scanlon says clearly that his view is meant only to account for the portion of morality that concerns 'what we owe to each other', and that questions about the treatment of non-human animals may fall outside the scope of that part of morality. See Scanlon, *What We Owe to Each Other*, pp. 177–88.

belonging to a 'bipolar normative nexus', they are reasons that one lacks the authority unilaterally to disregard.

Attractive as this picture is, the force of the analogy between friendship and the relation of mutual recognition seems to me uncertain. Scanlon identifies one source of doubt when he says that the relation of mutual recognition may seem 'implausibly ideal'. He adds:

> The motivational basis of friendship makes sense because friends play a real and important role in one's life. But morality, as I am describing it, requires us to be moved by (indeed to give priority to) the thought of our relation to a large number of people, most of whom we will never have any contact with at all. This may seem bizarre.

Scanlon's reply to this objection is that 'if the alternative is to say that people count for nothing if I will never come in contact with them, then surely this is bizarre as well'.[33] This reply seems curiously unresponsive to the objection as stated, since the relevant alternative to Scanlon's position is not that people count for nothing if one will never come into contact with them, but rather that the reason why they count for something does not derive from the value of the relation of mutual recognition.[34] More significantly, Scanlon's characterization of the objection to his view seems to run together two different worries. The first worry is that, whereas one's friendships play a 'real' role in one's life, the relation of mutual recognition is 'ideal'. The second worry is that, whereas friends are people one actually knows, the relation of mutual recognition is supposed to be capable of holding among people who do not know and will never meet one another. Scanlon's response focuses on the second of these worries, but if we are attempting to evaluate the analogy between friendship and mutual recognition, both worries need to be addressed.

The way I would formulate the second concern is as follows. In what sense may two people be said to stand in a 'relation' of mutual recognition if they have never met or interacted, will never meet or interact, and do not even know of each other's existence? Clearly, Scanlon does not mean to be using the term 'relation' merely in the thin, logical sense identified earlier. But in what more substantive sense do people in the circumstances described stand in a relation of mutual recognition? Perhaps the idea is that, even though they do not know of each other's existence, each wants his behaviour to be justifiable to everyone, and so, by implication, each wants his behaviour to

---

[33] Scanlon, *What We Owe to Each Other*, p. 168.

[34] Scanlon goes on to consider a version of this objection, but the version he considers denies the relevance, not of the relation of mutual recognition *per se*, but rather of the idea of justifiability to others. This deflects attention away from the questions about the relation of recognition that I pursue above.

be justifiable to the other. Now if this is what is meant by saying that the two people stand in a relation of mutual recognition, the pertinent notion of 'relation' would seem to be very different from the one that is operative in the case of valuable personal relationships like friendship. As we have seen, the latter consist in ongoing relationships between individuals who have a shared history that usually includes patterns of engagement and forms of mutual familiarity, attachment, and regard developed over time. Even if we can find a use of the term 'relation' or 'relationship' that goes beyond the thin, logical sense and applies in the case of mutual recognition, it is not clear that there is enough substantively in common between that case and the case of friendship to support an analogy between the reason–giving characteristics of each.

The other worry is this. In the case of friendship, what gives rise to reasons is an actual relationship. In general, relationship-dependent reasons, as I have characterized them, are simply reasons that one has by virtue of participation in a valuable relationship, and this model applies straightforwardly to the case of friendship as Scanlon discusses it. In the moral case, however, Scanlon does not say that we do in fact stand in relations of mutual recognition with others. Nor, *a fortiori*, does he say that we have moral reasons in virtue of our participation in actual relations of mutual recognition with others (a claim that might have the awkward implication that moral norms do not apply to our treatment of those with whom we lack such relations). What he tends to say instead is that what underlies moral reasons is the 'appeal' or 'ideal' of standing in relations of mutual recognition. If I understand him correctly, the idea is that we value a certain way of living with others, which we may or may not have achieved in practice, and in so far as we respond to moral reasons, we seek to realize that way of living together. Now this may be a plausible account of how moral reasons arise. However, the role it assigns to the relation of mutual recognition in generating such reasons is not analogous to the role that a person's friendships play in generating relationship-dependent reasons. In the friendship case, it is the value of an actual relationship in which one is a participant that generates the reasons. In the moral case, as here understood, what seems to generate the reasons is not any actual relationship at all, but rather a certain ideal of how human beings should relate to one another. If this is correct, then moral reasons are not relationship-dependent reasons in the sense that I have specified. And despite what Scanlon suggests, morality does not give one reasons in the same way that one's friendships do.

This is not an objection to Scanlon's contractualism or even to the account he gives of moral motivation, except in so far as that account relies on an analogy between the way friendships generate reasons and the way relations of mutual recognition generate reasons. But it does mean that, as it stands at least,

Scanlon's contractualism does not provide us with a way of construing moral reasons as a species of relationship-dependent reason. Nor, contrary to what Wallace suggests, does it yet enable us to see how a relational conception of morality might be grounded. To be sure, contractualism as Scanlon presents it, with its emphasis on the justifiability of one's actions to others who are affected by them, coheres smoothly with an interpretation of the deontic character of morality that links it to structures of reciprocal or bipolar normativity, in which reasons for action are constitutively connected to grounds for privileged complaint. But in the case of valued personal relationships like friendship, the value of the relationships provides an explanation of how these structures of reciprocal normativity arise. The appeal to relations of mutual recognition does not play a comparably explanatory role, for the relations in question are not actual, ongoing human relationships at all. One thing that may serve to obscure this disanalogy is the fact that a structure of reciprocal normativity can itself be taken to define or constitute a 'relationship' of a certain kind between two people. If I have reason to act on your behalf and you have reason to complain if I do not, then those facts themselves might be said to define a 'normative relationship' between us. Clearly, however, structures of reciprocal normativity cannot be grounded in the very normative relationships that they are said to define, for there is no content to these relationships other than the facts of reciprocal normativity themselves.[35] In the case of friendship, the normative relationship supervenes on an ongoing historical relationship between the participants, and it is the value of that ongoing relationship that is explanatory. But nothing comparable is true in the case of the relation of mutual recognition. So, as it stands at least, the appeal to that relation does not explain how structures of reciprocal normativity arise.

To sum up: the function of the relation of mutual recognition in the contractualist arguments I have been discussing is ideal and prospective; rather than being an ongoing relationship that gives rise to moral reasons, it is a relation that is supposed to be realized or made possible by acting on such reasons. If the appeal to this relation is to explain how reciprocal moral reasons arise, we need a clearer understanding of how ideal, prospective relations can generate reasons. The character of the relation of mutual recognition also requires further elucidation. It must be a relation that can plausibly be said to obtain between people whether or not they ever meet or know of each other's existence, and whether or not the actions of either ever affect the other. And

---

[35] This is a point that has been emphasized by Kerstin Haase in her unpublished writing on this topic.

it must be sufficiently independent of the structures of reciprocal normativity themselves that it is capable of providing a non-circular grounding for them.

7. Relational Views, Deontic Character, and the Consequentialist Challenge

It is beyond the scope of this chapter to consider whether a successful account of moral reasons along these lines can be provided. Perhaps there is a way of interpreting the appeal to relations of mutual recognition that would make clear its capacity to generate structures of reciprocal normativity. Still, I take the lesson of the discussion in the previous section to be that, even if such an interpretation is forthcoming, it is unlikely to represent moral reasons in general as relationship-dependent reasons in my sense. And this, after all, is not surprising. Relationship-dependent reasons are reasons of partiality arising from the value of particular, historical relationships between specific individuals. Even if moral norms can be represented as relational in important respects, morality aspires to the regulation of behaviour among strangers as well as among intimates, and it seems implausible that moral reasons of all kinds should have their source in particular, historical relationships.[36]

However, the idea that morality is relational in the sense that its deontic character is to be understood with reference to structures of reciprocal normativity has much to recommend it. In other words, we can distinguish between a *relational view* of morality—the view that the deontic structure of morality is best understood with reference to notions of reciprocal normativity—and the thesis that moral reasons are in general *relationship-dependent*. Even if we do not accept the relationship-dependency thesis, a relational view of morality remains attractive. For one thing, the fact that the deontic character of relationship-dependent reasons is best understood in terms of reciprocal normativity speaks in favour of a relational view of morality, even if morality itself is not in general relationship-dependent. Of course, my own view is that, despite not being generally relationship-dependent, morality does incorporate many relationship-dependent reasons, and this already implies that

---

[36] In *Moral Dimensions: Permissibility, Meaning, Blame* (Cambridge, MA: Harvard University Press, 2008), Scanlon develops an analogy between friendship and what he calls 'the moral relationship'. What he says about this analogy differs in some significant respects from his discussion of the analogy between friendship and 'the relation of mutual recognition' in *What We Owe to Each Other*. I do not have space here to give Scanlon's new discussion the careful consideration it deserves. Suffice it to say that it does not allay my doubts about the plausibility of construing moral reasons as relationship-dependent (or membership-dependent) reasons in my sense.

the deontic character of at least some moral reasons must be understood in terms of reciprocal normativity. But even if one rejects this view, the fact remains that relationship-dependent reasons frequently present themselves to us in deliberation and reflection as requirements or obligations, and that their deontic character is best understood in terms of reciprocal structures of reasons and complaints. If that is right, then there is at least *prima facie* reason to think that the deontic character of other reasons that present themselves as requirements or obligations should be understood in the same way.

This consideration is reinforced by the fact that consequentialism, the most influential and best-developed alternative to a relational view, has a hard time accounting for the deontic character of morality at all. Although many consequentialists argue that promoting optimal outcomes is what we have *most reason* to do, this is not yet to explain the peculiar deontic character of morality—the fact that we see moral norms as defining a set of *requirements* or *obligations*. This is a point that Jay Wallace has made very effectively.[37] To my knowledge, consequentialists have done little to explain how morality could have this kind of deontic character, although some of them have, in effect, tried to explain the phenomenon away by construing questions about what it is to have an obligation as questions about the utility of blaming the agent. But this is a significantly revisionist move. It amounts to denying that morality has a distinctively deontic character at all, and substituting a set of very different considerations about the utility of blame. If we are resistant to this kind of revisionism, and believe that the deontic character of morality is something to be explained rather than explained away, then a relational conception of morality will seem much more promising than a consequentialist conception.

On the other hand, even if one has doubts about consequentialist revisionism in general, there is something to be said on behalf of revisionism about the deontic character of morality in particular, especially if deontic character is understood in terms of structures of reciprocal normativity. Beginning with the great utilitarian writers of the eighteenth and nineteenth centuries, one of the strengths of the consequentialist tradition—and one of its most striking features—has been its insistence on the need to think about moral questions in a systematic and holistic way, focusing not merely on individual actions in isolation but also on the way in which our actions are structured by social institutions and are related to wider patterns of human conduct. In the utilitarian view, the traditional moral norms that serve to regulate the conduct of individual agents in their dealings with one another may not, despite their commonsense credentials, be adequate to the circumstances of the modern

---

[37] In 'The Deontic Structure of Morality'.

world. Although it is understandable that people should once have thought about questions of right and wrong primarily in the context of the relationships among single individuals or the members of relatively small groups, the fates of people in the modern world are tied together in complex ways through their shared participation in vast social, political, and economic structures. Individual actions must therefore be assessed, and the norms governing them must be rationalized, from a broader perspective, which takes into account the entire web of causal connections in which both the actions and the norms are embedded.

Among philosophers, utilitarianism has been severely criticized for its many counterintuitive implications and for its insensitivity to the complex structures of value that inform our practical deliberations and interpersonal relations. But economists and social policy makers have continued to find utilitarianism's broad institutional perspective congenial, and among them its influence has never waned. In *A Theory of Justice*, John Rawls wrote:

> We sometimes forget that the great utilitarians, Hume and Adam Smith, Bentham and Mill, were social theorists and economists of the first rank; and the moral doctrine they worked out was framed to meet the needs of their wider interests and to fit into a comprehensive scheme. Those who criticized them often did so on a much narrower front. They pointed out the obscurities of the principle of utility and noted the apparent inconsistencies between many of its implications and our moral sentiments. But they failed, I believe, to construct a workable and systematic moral conception to oppose it. The outcome is that we often seem forced to choose between utilitarianism and intuitionism.[38]

Much has changed since Rawls wrote these words, not least because of the great impact of his own work. But the influence of utilitarianism endures among social and economic policy makers and theorists, and for many of the same reasons. Viewed in this light, the failure of consequentialism to explain the deontic character of morality may be cast by its defenders, not as an embarrassing omission, but rather as a deliberate challenge to more conventional forms of moral thought, a challenge that might be spelled out as follows.

The idea of 'deontic character', understood with reference to structures of reciprocal normativity, is indeed at home in a morality of interpersonal relations. But a morality of interpersonal relations is no longer an adequate morality for our world. In trying to decide how people should act, we cannot think about their actions and the implications of those actions solely or primarily in the

---

[38] John Rawls, *A Theory of Justice* (Cambridge, MA: Harvard University Press, 1971), pp. vii–viii.

context of their personal relationships with their friends, family, and associates. The most important moral questions to ask about individual actions often pertain instead to the social and institutional forms that structure the options available to individuals, and the wider social and global impact of patterns of activity to which each of a very large number of individuals makes only a tiny contribution. This is evident, for example, if we think about global warming and other environmental problems, or if we think about the relation between consumer behaviour in affluent countries and labour practices in developing countries. In this context, it is a mistake to think that what is crucial for moral thought is to preserve the 'deontic character' of morality—where this means identifying, for each act of wrongdoing, particular people who have been wronged and have privileged ground for complaint. To do this is to mistake the phenomenology of traditional morality for a fundamental feature of moral thought, and to deprive ourselves of the tools we need to address the moral problems we actually face. Some of those problems are difficult precisely because, although they have clearly been caused by the actions of human beings, no specific individuals have privileged grounds for complaint about the behaviour of any other specific individuals. So as long as we insist that structures of reciprocal normativity are essential to morality, our moral thought will lack the concepts it needs to address these problems. The task we face is not to preserve the notions of obligatoriness and privileged complaint, but rather to persuade people that they have reason to avoid certain kinds of actions even when no particular individuals have special grounds for complaint about those actions.

To describe this consequentialist challenge is not, of course, to endorse it, still less to concede that consequentialism itself represents an adequate moral outlook—in contemporary conditions or any others. I have argued in various places that, for a number of different reasons, among which its failure adequately to accommodate reasonable partiality is one of the most important, consequentialism does not provide a viable alternative to the traditional morality it criticizes. Still, the consequentialist challenge reinforces the importance of addressing the lacuna we have identified in the relational view of morality. The question is how, on the relational view, to explain the source of moral reasons in a way that preserves the view's emphasis on reciprocal normativity, while at the same time demonstrating its applicability outside the context of relatively small-scale interpersonal relationships. This means providing a sensible treatment of the structural, institutional, and aggregative phenomena that the consequentialist challenge highlights, and accounting in a plausible way for the norms that govern our treatment of distant strangers. Whatever the failings of the consequentialist position, the structural and institutional phenomena to which it calls attention are of undeniable importance, and their perceived salience is likely to grow in coming years. These phenomena are not themselves artefacts of consequentialism, and no moral outlook can ultimately be acceptable unless it addresses them in a satisfactory way. Nor can a moral outlook be acceptable if it fails to account for the norms governing our treatment of distant strangers. So it is essential to establish that a relational view of morality can be convincingly applied outside the context of actual interpersonal relationships. As I have argued, although appeals to the relation between agent and victim, to membership in the human community, and to relations of mutual recognition are all suggestive, none establishes a convincing parallel with personal relationships like friendship, and none, without further development, provides a clear explanation of the source of moral reasons in general. I continue to believe that the capacity of a relational view to provide a non-sceptical interpretation of the deontic character of morality is a great advantage. But the worry persists that this may be an illusion, deriving from an understandable but mistaken tendency to apply essentially interpersonal concepts outside the domain in which they have a genuine application.

8. Morality and Partiality

Setting relational views to one side, the question of morality and partiality remains. Even if morality is not generally relational, I believe that it incorporates project-dependent, relationship-dependent, and membership-dependent reasons, and in so doing accommodates reasonable partiality. When I say that it incorporates these reasons, what I mean is that reasons of these types bear directly on the rightness or wrongness of actions, in much the same way that the fact that one has promised to act in a certain way bears directly on the rightness or wrongness of acting in that way. In my view, moral norms aim to regulate the conduct of people who are understood from the outset as valuing creatures, creatures with projects, relationships, and group affiliations. Like other forms of regulation, morality simultaneously constrains and legitimates. On the one hand, not only does it limit what may be done in the service of our projects, relationships, and group affiliations; it shapes our understanding of what counts as a worthy project or relationship or association in the first place. It tells us not merely that there are limits to what may be done in the name of a personal project or relationship, but also that a project that is evil or corrupt, or a relationship that is destructive or abusive, lacks the value that makes it a source of reasons to begin with. Yet morality also assumes that, within these limits and constraints, it is appropriate and often obligatory that people should act on the reasons that arise from their projects, relationships, and group affiliations. It tells us that we may legitimately pursue our projects, that we are obligated to address the needs and interests of our intimates, and that we should do our fair share in the joint enterprises in which we participate.

None of this is argument, of course, and it is in fact quite difficult to argue in a non-question-begging way for this or any other view of the relation between morality and partiality. That is because the issue turns ultimately on some of the most basic and abstract questions about the nature and function of morality, and it is difficult to produce arguments about morality and partiality that do not already presuppose some answers to those questions. My strategy in this chapter has been indirect. By examining project-dependent, relationship-dependent, and membership-dependent reasons, I have sought to emphasize that partiality is a dimension of practical rationality, and so to undercut the tendency to associate morality with detached reason and partiality with non-rational feeling or affection. I have also tried to highlight two features of these reasons that, to my mind, make it implausible to situate them outside the ambit of morality. The first is the fact that they are concomitants of basic categories of human valuation; in other words, the recognition of such reasons is part of what is involved in valuing some our deepest commitments. The second is that reasons of partiality exhibit precisely the deontic characteristics that we associate with moral norms; we see ourselves, for example, as having obligations to our families, friends, and associates, as being entitled or permitted to develop and pursue personal projects, and so on. Indeed, obligations to family, friends, and associates are often viewed as paradigmatic moral requirements. Taken together, these considerations seem to me to make a strong, albeit indirect, case for incorporating reasons of partiality within morality. At the very least, they shift the burden of proof to those who would exclude such reasons from morality's ambit. Those who wish to do this cannot deny that we are valuing creatures at all. Nor can they deny that morality appeals to our nature as valuing creatures, since morality is itself a realm of value, and the capacity of moral norms and ideals to motivate and engage us depends on the fact that we are valuers. So the position must be that although humans are valuing creatures, and although morality appeals to our nature as valuing creatures, morality nevertheless gives no direct weight to some of the most basic reasons we have in virtue of what we value; instead, whatever morality asks of us, it asks of us on the basis of reasons that have some other source, and whose roots in what we actually value remain to be explained. And this despite the fact that the excluded reasons are often taken as paradigmatic moral considerations and exhibit precisely the deontic characteristics associated with moral norms. What exactly might the motivation for this 'exclusivist' position be?

The point can be sharpened. Morality aspires to regulate our conduct towards all people, strangers and intimates alike. The exclusivist position is that, at the most fundamental level, the moral reasons that apply to intimates are no different from those that apply to strangers. But once we accept that reasons of partiality are genuine reasons that flow from some of our most basic values and do in fact apply to our treatment of our intimates, the insistence that these reasons have no direct moral relevance risks making morality itself seem irrelevant. If morality were to give no weight to these reasons, then instead of looking authoritative, moral judgements might appear simply to be based on an incomplete accounting of the pertinent considerations. And if that were so, then it would be unclear why people should acknowledge the authority of those judgements or even take them into account. Ultimately, then, the basic reason for thinking that morality incorporates reasons of partiality is that no credible system for the regulation of human behaviour can possibly exclude them.[39]

[39] An earlier version of this chapter was presented as the Mala Kamm Memorial Lecture at NYU. Versions were also presented to audiences at Reading, MIT, Cornell, Oslo, Iowa, and the Ethics Centre at the University of Zurich. I am grateful to all of these audiences for helpful discussion. Special thanks to Nick Sturgeon, who served as commentator on the paper at Cornell, and to Niko Kolodny and Jay Wallace, who provided helpful comments on the earliest draft.

6

Permissible Partiality, Projects, and Plural Agency*

SARAH STROUD

We are far from impartial in the conduct of our daily lives. We devote significant care and attention to certain favoured others, while doing next to nothing to meet the possibly far more urgent needs of others not so favoured. I spend a considerable amount of time, for instance, working with my students: going over their papers, helping them to polish their writing, urging them to make their formulations more definite and more precise, suggesting counter-arguments they should consider, and so on. It is my impression that these students benefit considerably from this kind of detailed attention. But I'm sure there are many other students out there who need and would benefit from this kind of professorial attention even more; and I'm not helping them. In similar vein, consider the time and energy each of us has spent helping friends get over romantic disappointments. Given that the broken-hearted are often fairly long-winded in airing their grievances and emotions, each of us has probably spent quite a bit of time consoling friends under such circumstances. And we do so unquestioningly, without taking much note of all the other people we know less well who would also benefit from being able to talk through their hurt feelings but who may lack a readily available sounding board. (Not to mention all the people suffering from woes much worse than romantic rejection whose fates we similarly ignore while we help our friend

* The first version of this chapter was presented in the Philosophy Department of the University of Reading at the invitation of the AHRC research team on Impartiality and Partiality in Ethics. I benefited greatly from the ensuing stimulating discussion with team members and from written comments which Brad Hooker generously gave me on that occasion. I subsequently presented some of this material at a workshop on Friendships and Partiality in Ethics at the Université de Montréal: I thank Christine Tappolet for organizing the workshop, and all workshop participants for profitable discussion. That version appeared in French as 'La partialité par les projets', *Les ateliers de l'éthique* 3 (2008), pp.41–51.

through this crisis.) These are only a couple of specific examples, but these forms of devoted, asymmetric attention to our students and our friends are characteristic, it seems to me, of our deeply partial lives.

But is it morally permissible for us to favour certain others in this way? And, if so, when and why? These are the large questions on which I want to begin to make some headway in this chapter, if only in programmatic fashion. I want to focus especially on the issue of the *source* of any moral permission we enjoy to be partial to certain others. That is, if we are indeed permitted to be partial, why or in virtue of what are we so permitted? Moral philosophers who insist that an acceptable morality must leave us free to exercise partiality are pretty numerous; but even the most ardent defenders of the moral permissibility of partiality have not, I think, given this latter question the explicit attention it deserves.

In this chapter, therefore, I shall examine and assess several different possible strategies for securing the moral permissibility of partial behaviour. How, I shall ask, can partiality best be shown to be morally permissible? Along what lines can it most convincingly be argued that we are morally permitted to be partial to certain others? The suggestion I shall make is that we may best be able to secure a space for permissible partiality by deploying the notion of a person's *projects*, rather than by claiming a brute or primitive permission to be partial as an allegedly basic element of morality. One could thus say with some justice that on the view I wish to put on the table, we do not actually find within morality a permission for partiality as such. Rather, we find a permission for something else, which may correspond more or less closely to what we have in mind when we say that morality must leave room for partiality.

1. Permissible Partiality

It is worth underlining that my concern here will be *permissible* partiality, because to contemplate whether and why partiality is morally permissible is to consider only one role that partiality might play within morality. It could be very plausibly claimed, for instance, that morality actually contains *obligations* to be partial to certain people. We might, that is, be downright morally *required* to show greater consideration for the interests of certain people than we do for 'just anyone'. For example, it seems very plausible that those of us who are parents are morally required, and not just permitted, to be partial in various ways toward our children. But whether and why this is so—that is, the question of the source of *special obligations*, as they are called—is not my concern in the present chapter. To the extent that these issues can be treated separately, I want to focus here on strategies for grounding a *permission* to be partial, rather than on putative partial *obligations*.

It may seem, for two reasons, that it is not easy to keep these two issues separate. First, the specific kinds of partiality whose moral permissibility we would be most keen to establish are probably those connected to close attachments, such as to our friends, spouses, and children. But those are also the very relationships that most plausibly give rise to special obligations. So it may seem that wherever the issue of permissibility is important to us, we find associated requirements in its wake. Second, it is of course true as a general matter that one way to show that something is morally permitted is to show that it is morally required. 'Required' *entails* 'permitted', so if we are asking what is the best strategy for establishing that partiality is permissible, it may seem that the obvious answer is that we need only show that, or when, such partiality is actually required.

Despite these two considerations, I think the two questions of requirement and permission can fruitfully be considered separately. In principle, partiality could figure in morality in both, in just the latter, or in neither of these ways; and—importantly for my inquiry here—the arguments in support of its appearing in the former role would presumably be rather different from those that would substantiate the latter status. For, in general, there must be arguments for something's being morally permissible that do not pass through its being morally required. This must be so for the simple reason that the range of what is morally permissible is wider than the scope of what is morally required. Even if everything morally required is morally permitted, the converse is not true; and this shows that there must be independent ways of establishing something to be morally permitted even when we cannot claim that it is downright obligatory. There can be good reasons for holding certain conduct to be morally protected—protected, that is, by a moral permission—that are independent of whatever reasons there may be to *demand* such conduct of moral agents.

So my focus here will be the search for *independent* arguments—which in principle ought to exist—for partiality's being morally permitted (as opposed to morally required). Is partiality the content of—or protected by, as we might say—a moral permission?[1] If so, why is this: what arguments ground such a

---

[1] The issue, more precisely, is whether it is protected by a 'pure' moral permission. I say 'pure' because (as just discussed) the permission in question is supposed to be independent of, and not simply derivative from, our moral *obligations*; we are looking for a permission to do *x* that does not stand or fall on whether we are morally *required* to do *x*. When speaking of permissions and of what is permissible in this chapter, I shall generally always have in mind 'pure' permissions or 'pure' permissibility in this sense.

permission? As I mentioned earlier, I shall suggest that the most convincing such arguments draw on the significance of an agent's *projects*. Before we get to that point, however, we should clarify some aspects of the present inquiry. First: *what is partiality?* If we are going to be trying to determine why and whether partiality is morally permissible, it will be useful to be clear on what partiality is. What is the thing into whose moral status we are inquiring? This is actually less obvious than it seems. Let us say rather vaguely—but, I hope, uncontroversially—that according to common philosophical parlance, partiality is *special concern for the interests of certain people*. By 'special' I mean specifically 'greater': the idea is that S shows greater deference to the interests of those to whom she is partial than to the interests of those to whom she is not partial.[2] We can imagine, for example, that S would confer benefits on those to whom she is partial that she would not confer on others, or that she would choose to direct benefits to them in preference to others. (While this is vague, our subsequent discussion will not, I think, turn on any of the ways in which it could be refined.)

Second: *protection* from *what?* If we're going to be speaking of a permission for partiality, or partiality's being morally protected, what 'threat' to partial practices do we have in mind? What I am interested in is whether and why partiality gets protection from *what would otherwise be moral demands*. That is, I want to look closely at the basis for insisting that the moral requirements to which we are subject must 'leave room' for partial attachments. Why would such insistence even be needed? Why would there even be a worry about moral demands leaving no room for partial practices? The easiest 'threat' to envisage here is a thoroughgoing act-consequentialist morality that demands that each of us maximize agent-neutral value in all our actions. Such a view clearly threatens partial practices: not by forbidding them *de jure*, as it were, but by presenting us with untempered demands to improve the universe, which will probably occupy all our time *de facto*.

Indeed, one might feel a need to protect partial attachments in the face of *any* highly demanding set of alleged moral requirements, whether or not they were based on a global requirement to maximize agent-neutral value or a substantive general principle of impartiality. For example, Garrett Cullity argues that even the seemingly modest demands of beneficence to which we in the affluent

---

[2] Christine Tappolet has pointed out to me that strictly speaking partiality ought to include giving *less* consideration to certain people's interests (say, because one dislikes them). Certainly it is true that someone who behaves in this way is not being fully impartial. But because most philosophers who have argued that morality must leave room for partiality did not have this kind of case in mind, I limit myself to examining how one might justify especially *favourable* treatment of certain others.

world are plausibly subject will have the effect, if iterated, of driving out partial attachments and connections.[3] So whether or not they take a distinctively consequentialist form, moral claims stemming from considerations of impartial beneficence seem to have the potential—if unfettered—to swallow up the rest of our lives; and this is sufficient to make us feel a need to ensure that our partial practices receive protection from those moral claims, in the form of appropriate moral permissions.

That, then, brings us to the third question to clarify: *protection* by *what?* In response to the threat of partial practices being effectively driven out of our lives by other moral requirements, we would like to be able to substantiate the objection that certain moralities are too demanding. To do this we need to find—and deploy—some arguments or concepts or phenomena that can ground moral permissions. We want factors that we can legitimately cite to block what would otherwise be moral requirements, but that do not themselves necessarily stem from or constitute further moral requirements. (Otherwise we would justify partiality only by showing it to be obligatory—not what we had in mind.) Luckily, there is already out there an argument of just this character: a general argumentative strategy that has already been taken (by some, at least) to constitute a compelling or at least a legitimate rationale for tempering the demands of morality and motivating moral permissions. I'm referring to the appeal to *the personal point of view* that was made influential—in that formulation—by Samuel Scheffler in his *Rejection of Consequentialism*, but that is also strongly present (even if not expressed in those words) in the works of other important critics of purely impartial morality such as Bernard Williams and Thomas Nagel.[4] What happens if we hitch the present inquiry to that star? Given the power of that appeal, it seems to me that it will only strengthen the moral case for permissible partiality if we can find a place for it under the umbrella of 'the personal point of view' and the 'agent-centred prerogative' that Scheffler proposed to protect it. So I propose to piggy-back on something like these concepts in an effort to ground the permissibility of partiality.

As I shall try to show, this strategy leaves plenty of interesting work to do, even once we make the significant—although vague—assumption that 'the personal point of view' is indeed a powerful or at least a legitimate weapon to

---

[3] Garrett Cullity, *The Moral Demands of Affluence* (Oxford: Clarendon Press, 2004).

[4] Samuel Scheffler, *The Rejection of Consequentialism* (Oxford: Clarendon Press, 1982). See also Bernard Williams, 'A Critique of Utilitarianism', in J. J. C. Smart and Bernard Williams, *Utilitarianism: For and Against* (Cambridge: Cambridge University Press, 1973); Thomas Nagel's discussion of 'reasons of autonomy' in his *The View from Nowhere* (New York: Oxford University Press, 1986), ch. IX (see also ch. X); and his *Equality and Partiality* (New York: Oxford University Press, 1991).

use against the demands of impartial beneficence. The appeal to 'the personal point of view' suggests that there must be something *agent-relative* that can be set against and limit the potentially voracious demands of impartial beneficence that act-utilitarianism and act-consequentialism embrace as the fundamental moral requirements. But what, exactly, is that something? What, exactly, is 'the personal point of view'? What, exactly—*which* agent-relative elements—do 'agent-centred prerogatives' protect?

On closer examination it turns out not to be obvious what the answers to these questions are, and I don't think philosophers have been as clear on these points as we should have been. For in fact there are several *different* things one might mean by saying that morality must leave room for 'the personal point of view': the content of the rather protean concept of 'the personal point of view' is not immediately clear or obvious. So in what follows we shall look carefully at a few different ways of spelling out what it is that ought to be protected from impartial demands: *what* it is whose special significance to the agent ought to find expression in an agent-centred prerogative that puts a brake on those demands. I shall operate primarily at the conceptual level: what *concept* serves us best in this connection? That is, what concept makes this appeal most compelling as a basis for insisting on moral permissions? But I shall also be concerned with the implications for partiality in particular of these various possible disambiguations of the appeal to 'the personal point of view'. Which of these various construals, if any, is apt to ground a permission for partiality?

To recapitulate, then: we are looking for a compelling way of grounding moral permissions to engage in partial behaviour. To that end, we shall consider several distinct ways of disambiguating the appeal to 'the personal point of view', because that general strategy is already accepted—by some, at least—as a plausible basis for insisting that moral theory show special deference to certain agent-relative elements. With regard to each candidate disambiguation, our twin questions will be how compelling a case it yields for tempering the demands of morality, and to what degree the 'protection' that it affords would extend to partiality. Does partiality as such—or, more modestly, some particular form of partiality—fall within the 'protected area' that blocks the rapacious reach of would-be demands of impartial beneficence, on one or more of the following ways of delineating that area?

In short, according to the present strategy there is indeed magic in the adjective 'my';[5] the question before us now is 'my *what*?' *For what X* do

---

[5] The reference is to William Godwin, *Enquiry concerning political justice*, 3rd edn (1798), vol. 1, p. 127.

we feel that the moral demands on me must be deferential to *my* X? What concept do we want to use to cash out the relevant X? Let us consider some candidates.

Option 1: My Interests

Perhaps the most straightforward way of spelling out what allegedly requires special deference is *the interests* (or well-being) *of the agent to whom moral demands are addressed*. And the obvious way of accomplishing this is for my interests to receive extra weight when we are considering what I morally ought to do. The appropriate form for an 'agent-centred prerogative' to take would therefore be the introduction of something like a 'multiplier' that operates on *my* interests in comparison with the interests of others when we are trying to determine what I am morally required to do. In fact Scheffler's original formulation of the 'agent-centred prerogative' took precisely this form: 'a plausible agent-centred prerogative', Scheffler wrote, 'would allow each agent to assign a certain proportionately greater weight to his own interests than to the interests of other people'.[6] Associated with this appeal to *my* interests as requiring moral protection is a particular way of making out the objection that certain moralities are too demanding. On the present construal, what is, at bottom, wrong with a morality that is too demanding is that it comes at too high a cost to my well-being, or leaves me not well enough off.[7] It is not clear why this should be thought to be a fatal objection to a morality, however. It might constitute a fatal objection *if* we assumed morality were a contract for mutual advantage. In that case, if I am left worse off due to the adoption of a particular morality, that would indeed mean that morality was failing in its purpose. But that seems a very contentious assumption to make about what morality is.

We should also note, in any case, that this approach does not seem to generate *any* permission for partiality as such. On this approach, the only consideration that acts as a brake on possibly encroaching moral demands is *my* self-interest; only *my* interests get special regard. We could therefore speak of 'partiality to oneself', but surely this does not exhaust the kinds of partial attachments and practices that we were hoping to protect from competing moral claims. So whether or not this is a compelling way to

---

[6] Scheffler, *The Rejection of Consequentialism*, p. 20.

[7] Simplifying greatly, this is the tenor of Liam Murphy's rather sceptical analysis of 'the problem of over-demandingness' in his *Moral Demands in Nonideal Theory* (New York: Oxford University Press, 2000), chs 1–3, esp. pp. 16–21. Murphy distinguishes 'losses' and 'absolute-level' versions of the objection.

temper the demands of morality, it is not one especially favourable to partiality as such.

Option 2: My Interests and the Interests of those Who Stand in Certain Designated Relations to Me

In light of the observation we have just made, the present suggestion is a very natural broadening of the previous option. On this proposal, the moral requirements that apply to you must be tempered by or show deference to not just *your* interests, but the interests of other people who are related to you in certain designated ways. An 'agent-centred prerogative' that had the same structure as in Option 1 but spread the extra weight around more broadly might be structurally analogous to the concentric circles of Broad's 'self-referential altruism', although in the present case these concentric circles would be better described as 'self-referential permissions'.[8] Such a system would, I think, constitute a granting of moral protection to partiality as such—or at least to partiality toward those related to us in the designated ways.

This raises the question, however, of what these 'designated ways' might be, and how we would determine what they should be. Recall that these relations pick out, for present purposes, people whose interests we are *permitted*—not obliged—to favour, even at the expense of other morally worthy aims. How are we to characterize which relations these are? To take just one example, how are we to determine whether fellow citizenship is such a relation? One might say it is simply a brute fact that certain relations generate these permissions. It seems odd, however, to posit that what one might term 'eternal moral verities'[9] govern whose interests *may*—not *must*—be accorded special weight in your moral decisions.[10] It would be odd, for instance, for you automatically to have a permission to favour (say) your sister over others objectively more needy, even if you don't care about her at all. Under the circumstances it seems pointless—as well as detrimental to the needy—to grant you such a prerogative. A further issue: a scheme like this will probably want to assign decreasing *degrees* of extra weight to others' interests depending on the precise

---

[8] C. D. Broad, 'Self and Others', in David Cheney (ed.), *Broad's Critical Essays in Moral Philosophy* (London: George Allen & Unwin, 1971).

[9] Cf. Christine Korsgaard's use of the phrase 'eternal normative verity' at p. 315 of 'Realism and Constructivism in Twentieth-Century Moral Philosophy', in her *The Constitution of Agency: Essays on Practical Reason and Moral Psychology* (Oxford: Oxford University Press, 2008).

[10] I don't think the parallel point about obligations sounds as odd as the present claim about permissions, which is why I emphasize the difference between them.

relation in which those others stand to you (so that the interests of your fellow citizens get less of a top-up than those of your spouse, for instance). But what exactly is the metric of 'distance' that would be required to map this discounting? This is far from obvious.

These worries about the present proposal might push us out to a still more broadly based permission, extending to the next option.

Option 3: My Entire Evaluative, Desiderative, and Motivational Outlook

On this proposal, anything that is part of what Bernard Williams called your 'S'—anything you care about, prefer, or value—would receive moral deference, and would thus be capable of blocking or putting the brakes on would-be impartial moral demands.[11] In determining what you are morally required to do, morality would have to recognize the special significance to you of all these elements of your S.

This proposal has some important virtues, both in terms of its substantive implications and in terms of its possible theoretical grounding.[12] This proposal nicely responds to some of the worries we had about Options 1 and 2. Unlike Option 2, this proposal has a built-in way of demarcating the *scope* of the partiality that is covered by the permission. On this approach, the scope of the permission for partiality would be determined by the scope of what—or whom—you care about. So this proposal would not be subject to the worry we raised above about 'eternal moral verities'. On this view, there wouldn't be any such 'eternal moral verities', as the 'preferred others' for a given person would be picked out by what she cares about—not by some *a priori* demarcation of relations into those that do and those that do not confer extra weight on the relatee's interests. The present proposal could also plausibly propose a metric for *degrees* of permissible partiality: the degree to which someone cares about something (the intensity of her caring, preferring, or valuing) could serve as a metric for fixing the degree of extra weight those factors get in determining what she may do.

Note also that the elements singled out for moral protection by Options 1 and 2 will very probably also receive special deference on this proposal; whereas certain limitations built into Options 1 and 2 will be jettisoned. Option 3 will very probably extend moral protection to your interests and to those of others who are related to you in certain ways, simply because

---

[11] Bernard Williams, 'Internal and External Reasons', in his *Moral Luck* (Cambridge: Cambridge University Press, 1981).

[12] I discuss only the former here in the main text; see n. 19 for the latter.

you probably *care* distinctively about the advancement of interests falling into these two classes. But the present proposal does not insist that *only* those two categories of interests can receive special moral deference. One of the virtues of the present approach, compared for example with Option 1, is its moving away from a concern for *myself*. Preferences and desires—which of course count as part of my evaluative/desiderative/motivational profile—can be *for* anything: any state of affairs, whether it involves me or not, can be the proper object of a preference or desire on my part, and thereby something whose importance to me morality ought to respect.

This last feature of the present proposal—its flexibility—is attractive, yet also dangerous. Precisely because it is so potentially capacious, the present proposal risks extending moral protection to things that are not clearly proper subjects of such protection. We can see this by deploying a kind of 'remoteness' objection that has been effectively used in other contexts: in political philosophy, for instance, and in debates over theories of well-being.[13] Suppose, for instance, that Jerry's strongest preference is that the Red Sox win the pennant. I don't have in mind a case in which Jerry *is* a Red Sock, or a family member of a Red Sock. Rather, Jerry is just a rabid Red Sox fan, of which there are many in New England. Now Jerry doesn't take himself to be in a position to *do* anything to help them win the pennant—he's a fan, not a collaborator. But as a wish, hope, or preference, this one—that the Red Sox win the pennant—scores very high for intensity. According to the present proposal, then, Jerry ought to be morally permitted to give the interests of the Red Sox *a lot* of weight, as compared for instance to the interests of people with far more urgent needs than the Red Sox whom he could help instead. Does this seem correct? Ought Jerry to have an *agent-centred prerogative* to ignore those people and confer a benefit on the Red Sox, if he's doling out benefits?

We need not definitively settle whether we are comfortable granting the protection of an 'agent-centred prerogative' to 'remote' preferences like these in order to agree that they make a fairly dubious or problematic case for such a prerogative. In other words, if the argument for the necessity of an 'agent-centred prerogative', or for special moral permissions for elements of the 'personal point of view', must extend to cases like these—because these cases present all the features which that argument describes as relevant to grounding the prerogative—then we have not made the job of defending the necessity

---

[13] For an influential deployment of such considerations in political philosophy, see R. M. Dworkin's discussion of 'external preferences' in his *Taking Rights Seriously* (Cambridge, MA: Harvard University Press, 1977), ch. 9. For an example in the context of debates over the nature of well-being, see for instance Derek Parfit, *Reasons and Persons* (Oxford: Clarendon Press, 1984), p. 494.

of such a prerogative easy for ourselves. We would be better served, it seems, by coming up with a rationale that does not apply to just any element of an agent's S, and, in particular, that avoids committing itself to an alleged right to benefit 'remote' others.

That brings us to Option 4.

Option 4: My Projects

This proposal as to what needs or deserves protection from impartial moral demands claims that status only for a particular subset of the items mentioned in Option 3. For goals, aims, and projects are different from mere preferences. That something is one of your preferences, or something you care about, or that you have a 'pro attitude' towards the obtaining of a certain state of affairs, does not entail that it is one of your aims, goals, or projects.[14] Let's pause for a moment to bring out the *distinctive* type of pro attitude towards p that is having p as a goal or aim, in contrast to other pro attitudes towards p such as wishing, hoping, wanting, or preferring.

You and I may both very much prefer that the Democrats win the election and unseat the Republicans. But our relation to that state of affairs that we both desire is different if I volunteer with my local Democratic Party organization and spend time mobilizing voters and working with others to make decisions about campaign strategy, while you do nothing. That, roughly speaking, is the difference between a mere preference or desire and an aim, goal, or project: something's being one of your aims, goals, or projects means not just that you want it to come to pass, but that you intend to bring it about through your own efforts.[15] Your aims, goals, and projects are indeed things you care about, but they are not only things you care about: they are things towards which you are directing your *agency*.[16] Now no doubt one could make subtle distinctions among goals, aims, and projects. In particular, one's projects are not limited to things one is trying to achieve: things for which there is some state of affairs that is the object of one's pursuit. We would want to include in one's projects the *activities* one engages in, even if they are not goal-directed in the narrow sense. For present purposes, however, the important point is the way in which

---

[14] From among the authors cited in n. 4, Bernard Williams has especially emphasized the significance of an agent's *projects*. See, e.g., his 'A Critique of Utilitarianism' and 'Persons, Character, Morality' (the latter in his *Moral Luck*).

[15] Simon Keller has stressed the difference between desires and goals. See his 'Welfare and the Achievement of Goals', *Philosophical Studies* 121 (2004), pp. 27–41.

[16] What is the currency of this possibly mysterious notion of 'agency'? Roughly, time and energy, rather than mere intensity or strength of preference.

all of these concepts go beyond mere desires and preferences and involve the direction of your agency towards something.

An appeal to *projects* as the target of an 'agent-centred prerogative' has, I think, several notable virtues. First, its substantive content seems more plausible than that of the other options we have considered. An appeal to projects shares the advantages we noted earlier in connection with Option 3. Like Option 3, the present approach avoids the excessive narrowness of Option 1, because the content of your projects extends beyond your own well-being. It also avoids the 'eternal moral verities' difficulty we raised for Option 2. But an appeal to projects seems in the end more plausible than Option 3, because it avoids the latter's problematic breadth. Because the present approach distinguishes projects from mere preferences or wishes, it would not follow from this approach that the Jerry/Red Sox case presents all the features relevant to grounding a special moral permission. An appeal that is limited in this way to projects will in general be less susceptible to such 'remoteness' objections, as anything to which you are devoting your agency is not 'remote' to you in the way an object of mere preference or wish can be.

A second important virtue of this approach is more theoretical in nature. I think it counts strongly in favour of this approach that a plausible theoretical grounding for an agent-centred prerogative focused on projects can be supplied, or at least sketched. I have in mind what Garrett Cullity calls a 'broadly Kantian' argument: his useful label for arguments that seek to bring to light certain presuppositions of the moral demands to which agents are subject, but that themselves support a tempering of those demands.[17] Here is a quick argument of this kind in favour of morality's showing some kind of special deference towards an agent's projects. Moral demands are, by definition, addressed to *agents*: anything that is subject to a moral demand is, necessarily, an agent. Since morality is necessarily addressed to agents, it seems plausible that it must reflect the *nature* of agents. Here is one pertinent fact about agents: they have projects. (This seems a conceptual, or anyway a necessary, truth about agents.) Furthermore, an agent's projects are necessarily of special significance to him: for me to have something as a project *is* for me to be focusing my energies on it in a way I am not doing for other perhaps equally meritorious pursuits.[18] To ask agents not to do this would be to ask them not to be agents. Morality,

[17] Cullity, *The Moral Demands of Affluence*, ch. 6.
[18] Cf. Ibid., pp. 130–31. We could think also, in this connection, of the special structuring role in practical reasoning of plans and intentions, which Michael Bratman has stressed. To intend to do something is for that course of action to have a special role in your practical reasoning compared with equally meritorious options that you did not select. See Michael Bratman, *Intention, Plans, and Practical Reason* (Cambridge, MA: Harvard University Press, 1987).

then, must not make such a demand; it must, rather, recognize the special significance to agents of their own projects, and permit them to accord those projects special weight. Otherwise it implicitly denies their status as agents.[19]

Because of the substantive and theoretical virtues we've noted, I'm inclined to think that an appeal couched in terms of *projects* makes the best case for moral deference to (certain elements of) 'the personal point of view'. So *if* we could fit partiality under this rubric, it seems that this could only help in making the case for a moral permission to be partial to certain others. I want now to turn to that question, and explore to what extent we could get the partial permissions we are looking for from this approach to tempering morality's demands.

2. Projects and Partiality

At first glance a prerogative focusing on the agent's *projects* and *agency* might seem conceptually rather distant from partiality as such. Our initial working gloss on partiality defined it as special concern for the interests of certain others; and by 'special concern for their interests' we meant attaching more weight to their interests than to other people's, for example by directing benefits to them in preference to others. This seems to correspond poorly with any 'protected zone' we could hope to establish on the basis of an appeal to the special significance to an agent of his projects. There won't be any *direct* right to favour the interests of certain people within this picture; we shall have such a right only to the extent that, and for the reason that, such conduct counts as pursuing our projects. So if it were one of my *projects* to advance your welfare, *then* my doing so would receive some degree of deference from morality; otherwise not.[20] This kind of approach, then, does not seem liable to generate a permission for partiality as such.

---

[19] Samuel Scheffler, in his contribution to this volume (Chapter 5), appears to suggest a similar 'broadly Kantian' style of argument, but one that takes off from 'our nature as valuing creatures' rather than, as here, from our nature as *agents* ('for morality to reject partiality in a general or systematic way would be for it to set itself against our nature as valuing creatures', p. 100). Note that one could also offer an argument with this same 'broadly Kantian' structure on behalf of Option 3, asserting at the pertinent stage of the argument that agents necessarily have their own evaluative/desiderative/motivational profiles and that these necessarily involve their giving special weight to the things they care about. I cannot enter here into a full discussion of the comparative merits of these different versions of the 'broadly Kantian' argument. But because the basis of the argument I proffer in the text seems to me slimmer and narrower than the one that an argument for Option 3 would require, I would think the former argument more secure.

[20] I ignore for simplicity the possibility that my advancing your welfare might be (instrumentally) necessary for the success of some *other* project I am pursuing.

However, I think there is more to be said about the connection between the present approach and the possibility of justifying partial conduct. In this section of the chapter I want to underline some aspects of the project-based approach that seem to bring it conceptually closer to what is on our mind when we stress the need for morality to leave space for partiality. When we do this, I think, we are not so much insisting on a right to preferential treatment in the abstract, but, rather, we are thinking especially of the special concern characteristic of certain *relationships*. We want to be sure, that is, that we are morally free to manifest the special concern we have for our friends, our children, our loved ones, our students. (Let's call these, generically, our 'Rs', for 'relatees'.) But what does that 'special concern' for our Rs actually amount to? I think it is time to look more deeply into that notion: this will bring out a heretofore unnoticed connection to the strategy that highlights projects and agency.

In general—and here we begin to depart from our original working gloss on partiality —I think that 'special concern' is very inadequately characterized as simply favouring your Rs' interests, conferring benefits on them in preference to other people. To return to the case of friendship with which we opened the chapter, the 'special concern' we have for our friends certainly does not primarily take the form of a differential tendency to confer benefits on them. Indeed, that would be a caricature of the 'special concern' that friendship involves.[21] If we looked more deeply into the moral psychology of friendship (as some philosophers have done, including myself on other occasions[22]), we would find as far more salient phenomena such things as emotional openness and responsiveness to our friend, 'being there for' our friend, esteem for our friend's particular qualities, loyalty to our friend, shared activity, and simply enjoying spending time with our friend. None of these is easily reduced to a preference for our friend's interests. This is not to deny that 'we would do things for a friend that we wouldn't do for just anyone'. Admittedly, I am more likely to help a friend move house than I would be to help just anyone move house. But it would be misguided to put forward cases like these as expressing the heart of the 'special concern' that friends have for each other.

To take another example introduced earlier, I think it would be correct to say that I have a 'special concern' for my students and supervisees. As mentioned earlier, I work with them to develop the clarity and vigour of their writing,

---

[21] Cullity argues at pp. 130–3 of *The Moral Demands of Affluence* that friendship is clearly not 'about' conferring cash gifts on our friends, or, more generally, differentially advancing our friends' interests.

[22] For works on the moral psychology of friendship, see, e.g., Sarah Stroud, 'Epistemic Partiality in Friendship', *Ethics* 116 (2006), pp. 498–524, and Dean Cocking and Jeanette Kennett, 'Friendship and the Self', *Ethics* 108 (1998), pp. 502–27.

their analytic acuity, their trust in their own philosophical judgement, their standards of meticulousness, and their own distinctive philosophical interests, in a way that I don't work with other equally meritorious people at their stage who do not happen to be studying with me. So it would not be false to say that I am advancing their interests in a way that I am not advancing others' interests. But again it would seem wrong-headed to encapsulate my 'special concern' for these students as a 'special concern' to advance their interests, in the sense of attaching more weight—in some generic way—to their interests than to other people's when making decisions. For example, if I had some money that for some reason I was going to give away, I wouldn't be any more likely to bestow it on my students: I don't think it would even occur to me to make them the special beneficiaries of my *financial* largesse. My 'special concern' for them takes other forms; a generic extra weighting of their interests is too blunt an instrument to capture the sense in which I am 'partial' to *my* students over other people's students.

The partiality that is manifested in certain paradigmatic personal relationships is, then, very imperfectly conceptualized as a matter of attaching extra weight to or favouring certain people's interests in one's decisions. What seems most distinctive about the personal relationships we have discussed, I submit, is not that we have a differential concern for these people's *interests*, but rather that we devote our *agency* (our time, our energy) to these relationships and to the specific activities they consist in. This much better picks out the sense in which I devote special care and attention to my students and friends. But now a tie emerges to the conceptual framework we used in the context of the appeal to the 'personal point of view' when we settled on an interpretation of the latter in terms of *projects* and *agency*. There is after all a conceptual link, then, between the notions that we deployed to ground an agent-centred prerogative, and the type of partiality that is constitutive of close personal relationships. This suggests that the project-based approach we are presently exploring *does* have the potential to generate a permission for me to manifest these forms of special concern, in so far as I have a permission to direct my agency towards my projects and aims.

We can bring out a further relevant dimension of the project-based or agency-based approach by highlighting another inadequacy of thinking of partiality simply in terms of a preference for conferring benefits on certain people over others. Our Rs figure in that approach only as (passive) recipients of our beneficence. But that seems especially inapposite for personal relationships, because one very salient element of those relationships is joint participation, *as agents*, in some shared activity or pursuit. Here we take up the Aristotelian idea that *shared activity* is a constitutive element and characteristic expression of *philia*,[23] interpreting that claim broadly to include the joint pursuit of shared goals and aims. Indeed, when you and I are in a personal relationship, I want to suggest that we very often form a 'we' in a sufficiently robust sense that we can speak of *plural* or *collective* or *shared agency*.[24] One can clearly see this in the case of spouses, where many 'we'-statements such as 'we are having people over' or 'we decided to move house' will unquestionably be true and seem genuinely to refer to the actions of a plural agent. But the point also holds of other relationships. My students and I are jointly pursuing their intellectual and philosophical development. My colleagues and I work together to offer a well-balanced array of courses to undergraduates. My daughter and I practise piano together each evening. My fellow campaign workers and I are trying to get the vote out next Tuesday. It seems the partners in a variety of relationships often constitute a 'we'-agent.

I would suggest that these instances of co-agency are typical or even characteristic of personal relationships, and that they are much more salient in the moral psychology of such relationships than a simple favouring of your Rs' interests. As we might put it, rather picturesquely, 'with' is the preposition of choice between 'I' and 'you': it's what I do *with* you, not what I do *to* or *for* you, that we should be focusing on.[25] Let's make the bold conjecture that such co-agency is ethically significant: that my entering into plural agency with you affects the ethical landscape facing me. This might well be germane to the issue of permissible partiality. For if we are granting moral significance to the fact that I invest my agency in collective pursuits with you, this already marks you off as occupying a special moral place in relation to S.S.; this already distinguishes you from the other individuals with whom I do not form plural agents. After all, I've chosen to form a plural agent with you, which plural agent has projects of its own; and I haven't done that with others. Indeed, if we were prepared to identify my participation in joint projects together with you as the heart of the sense in which I am 'partial' to you, the fact of such co-agency could be the main source of permissible partiality.

[23] See Aristotle, *Nicomachean Ethics*, bks VIII, IX.

[24] Such 'plural agency' has been extensively explored by Margaret Gilbert and Michael Bratman, among others. See Margaret Gilbert, *On Social Facts* (London; New York: Routledge, 1989), *Living Together: Rationality, Sociality, and Obligation* (Lanham, MD: Rowman and Littlefield, 1996), and *Sociality and Responsibility: New Essays in Plural Subject Theory* (Lanham, MD: Rowman and Littlefield, 2000), and Michael Bratman, *Faces of Intention* (Cambridge: Cambridge University Press, 1999), chs 5–8, and *Structures of Agency* (New York: Oxford University Press, 2007), ch. 13. The scope and precise analysis of shared or plural agency are controversial, but we need not resolve all the metaphysical issues surrounding collective agents in order to suggest, as I do here, that plural agency is an important dimension to consider in analysing the moral standing and import of personal relationships.

[25] On this picture, for instance, we should focus more on the fact that I practise piano with my daughter every day than on the fact that I pay for her piano lessons.

But are we prepared to do this? Here are some considerations, on both the 'pro' and the 'con' sides, to think about further. On this approach, what we find by way of 'a permission for partiality' within morality is actually a permission to pursue and engage in projects, notably of the plural kind. From a theoretical point of view, then, this model is pleasingly economical, because it folds *relationships* as grounds for moral permissions under something that was playing that role anyway, namely *projects*.[26] In terms of its substantive content, this model would confer special moral consideration on those with whom we form plural agents. Indeed, this model would yield something like the concentric circles of 'self-referential permissions' that we discussed earlier under Option 2. But this time that structure would come with some added benefits that were absent the first time around. Those include a clear demarcation of who gets a 'circle': our co-agents. Furthermore, by adding a dollop of voluntarism to the picture, we would avoid the 'eternal moral verities' problem. On this view, the selection of people I am permitted to favour is sensitive to my choices, rather than being determined by some 'eternal moral verity'.[27] Finally, this line would appear to give thumbs down to moral permissions in 'remoteness' cases like that of Jerry and the Red Sox, or in cases in which someone habitually wishes to give preference to, say, his own ethnic group. The present approach would refuse to grant any special moral dispensation to those preferences and desires, because there's no plural agency present in these cases. This may in fact be a welcome result.

However, despite these important theoretical and substantive virtues, the proposal is still at least somewhat revisionist: its fit with the partiality we would like to be allowed to exhibit may seem notably imperfect. It seems to me that there are two general types of case where the present approach would have trouble justifying partiality that we might well want to see protected. (I simply

[26] Although the broad strategy of argument of this chapter obviously owes much to the work of Samuel Scheffler, the present approach diverges in this important respect from the direction Scheffler has taken in his recent work. An important theme of his recent work is that there are at least two *distinct* categories of agent-relative reasons that morality must take account of: 'project-dependent reasons' and 'relationship-dependent reasons'. See his 'Projects, Relationships, and Reasons', in R. Jay Wallace *et al.* (eds), *Reason and Value: Themes from the Philosophy of Joseph Raz* (Oxford: Clarendon Press, 2004), pp. 247–69, and his chapter in the present volume (Chapter 5), in which he proposes a further distinct category of such reasons, 'membership-dependent reasons'. While this is not the place to engage more fully with the rich picture Scheffler has developed, were one to wish to consider further the potential merits and demerits of the present approach it would certainly be important to compare it carefully with Scheffler's more nuanced but theoretically less parsimonious model.

[27] I should underline again that the present inquiry concerns only the grounding of (pure) moral *permissions*. It would not, in my view, be equally plausible to hold that there must be a voluntaristic underpinning to all special *obligations*. (On this latter issue see Scheffler, *Boundaries and Allegiances* (Oxford: Oxford University Press, 2001), chs 3, 4, 6.)

present these for your consideration here, without trying to determine what might be the most effective line of response, or indeed whether there is one.) First, because the partial permissions this approach can secure are triggered by joint agency, those permissions would apply only within the context of that joint agency. Your special moral permissions, in other words, would not extend to your Rs' interests in general: this model does not grant you a permission to favour your co-agents' interests outside the context of your respective joint projects with them. This line of argument, then, allows you to favour the *project*, but not the other person's interests *per se*. (One might even say: the project but not the person.) So if the cellist in my quintet needs a new bow and is too poor to buy one, I might be permitted to direct money that could otherwise go to famine relief to the cause of getting her one, in so far as that makes possible the continuation of a collective project in which I am engaged: playing the Schumann Quintet. But if she needs money for reasons unrelated to the quintet project, then it seems I can send my money to famine relief without any cost to *my* (or *our*) *projects*; so on the present approach I would not have the same moral case for directing it to her instead.

A second potential problem is that some cases of partial attachment that we would have thought it important to protect against voracious moral demands will not easily qualify as cases of plural agency or joint projects at all, and thus will not fall within the scope of the moral protections this approach can secure. This will be the case, notably, for all close attachments to someone who is not an agent, and thus *a fortiori* not part of a plural agent with you.[28] A leading example here might be a new parent's devotion to and love for his newborn, and the fierce concern for her interests that he will feel. This is a prime example of the kind of personal attachment to which we want to be free to devote ourselves, and yet because a newborn is arguably not an agent at all this case does not fit easily under the present rubric. It may sound forced and over-intellectualized to say that the parent and his baby are jointly pursuing some project; but if we don't say that, then it seems the notion of plural agency can offer us no assistance.[29]

---

[28] A different type of case involves an attachment between two people who *are* both agents, but whose relationship no longer involves much shared agency. Think of an old friend who has for years lived thousands of miles from you, or the relationship between grown children and parents who live in different cities.

[29] Of course, we could fall back here on an *individual* project as grounds for the relevant moral permission. For even if there is no collective project here to protect, there is at least an individual project on the part of the parent, who presumably devotes considerable time and energy (the basic currencies, if you recall, of agency) to the advancement of his child's development and welfare. It is not clear that this gives an intuitively satisfying description of the morally relevant aspects of the case, however.

In considering further a project-based approach to the question of permissible partiality we shall clearly have to think about how much revisionism we are prepared to tolerate for the sake of the theoretical and substantive virtues I have highlighted. I do hope these are sufficient to place such an approach on the menu of options that should be considered as we seek to understand and, if possible, to validate permissible partiality.

7

Responsibility within Relations

STEPHEN DARWALL

There was, beginning in the middle to late 1970s, a kind of ethical particularism that was associated less with the position that Jonathan Dancy has recently defended than with Bernard Williams's 'one thought too many', Lawrence Blum on altruism, and feminist philosophical writing on the ethics of care and love that grew out of work by Iris Murdoch and Carol Gilligan's *In a Different Voice*.[1] Partly what was at issue was how to weigh partial and impartial demands and considerations—whether friends, family members, neighbours, fellow citizens, and so on can or should weigh the interests and concerns of those to whom they stand in these special relations differently from those of others.[2] Much of this writing sounded some of the same themes as more recent particularist critiques of general or universal principles. But the strain I am most interested in stressed the idea that ethical concern is properly particularistic in the sense that its proper objects are particular individuals.

Consider Williams's famous example. We are to imagine someone who is in a position to save either a stranger or his wife, pauses to consider whether he may give preference to his wife over the stranger, concludes that he may, and proceeds to save her on this basis. Williams famously remarks:

This construction provides the agent with one thought too many: it might have been hoped by some (for instance, his wife) that his motivating thought, fully spelled out,

---

[1] Jonathan Dancy, *Ethics Without Principles* (Oxford: Oxford University Press, 2006); Bernard Williams, 'Persons, Character, and Morality', published first in Amelie O. Rorty (ed.), *The Identities of Persons* (Berkeley, CA: University of California Press, 1976); Lawrence Blum, *Friendship, Altruism, and Morality* (Boston, MA/London: Routledge & Kegan Paul, 1980); Iris Murdoch, *The Sovereignty of Good* (London: Routledge & Kegan Paul, 1970); Carol Gilligan, *In a Different Voice* (Cambridge, MA: Harvard University Press, 1982).

[2] In this vein, see, e.g., John Cottingham, 'Ethics and Impartiality', *Philosophical Studies* 43 (1983), pp. 83–99, but also Andrew Oldenquist, 'Loyalties', *Journal of Philosophy* 79 (1982), pp. 173–93.

would be the thought that it was his wife, not that it was his wife and that in situations of this kind it is permissible to save one's wife.[3]

Williams imagines the agent thinking that he may save his wife because the stranger has no greater moral claim on him—as it happens, in consequentialist terms, but this doesn't matter. It wouldn't help to deflect Williams's complaint either, however, if the agent were to have thought that his wife had a greater claim on him because of the duties that spouses have to each other. It seems clear that, as Williams and many following him saw things, either the thought that in situations of this kind it is permissible to save one's wife or the thought that in situations of this kind there is a duty to save one's wife would have been one thought too many. The point was that the husband should have been moved directly by a concern for the particular individual who was his wife. When Williams says that the agent's wife might have hoped that the agent's motivating reason would have been 'that it was his wife', he wants us to understand 'his wife' as rigidly designating a particular individual.

This idea has also been a staple of philosophical writing about care. A good example would be Nel Noddings, who understands care as a relation between particular individuals, the 'one caring' and the 'cared-for'.[4] Similarly, Carol Gilligan stresses that the 'ethics of care' is concerned with how individuals relate to one another within their specific relations, which she contrasts with a more orthodox view that conceives of others in 'general' or 'universal' terms.[5] Genuine care for others is an attitude towards them as particular individuals and not just as 'generalized others'.[6]

We can find a similar critique of Kantian ethics in Iris Murdoch's objection that Kantian respect for the dignity of persons is not really for individual persons but rather for 'universal reason in their breasts'.[7] According to this line of criticism, Kantianism and utilitarianism can be seen as partners in the crime of regarding individuals as mere 'containers' or placeholders, for pleasure or other beneficial experiences, on the one hand, and for reason, rational agency, or autonomy, on the other. In either case, moral relations seem distorted and

---

[3] 'Persons, Character, and Morality', in *Moral Luck* (Cambridge, MA: Harvard University Press, 1982), p. 18.

[4] Nel Noddings, *Caring: A Feminine Approach to Ethics and Moral Education* (Berkeley, CA: University of California Press, 1984).

[5] *In a Different Voice*, p. 11. Gilligan sometimes calls this latter the 'ethics of rights', but this seems misleading since writers in her tradition generally also contrast utilitarianism with the ethics of care in precisely these terms.

[6] *Ibid*. This term comes originally from G. H. Mead.

[7] Iris Murdoch, 'The Sublime and the Good', in *Existentialists and Mystics*, ed. Peter Conrad (New York: Penguin Books, 1999), p. 215.

alienated, since genuine relationship is always between individuals relating to one another as such.

1. Individual-regarding Rationales for Utilitarianism and Kantianism

Now I think there is an important grain of truth to this line of criticism, but also that both utilitarianism and Kantian ethics have things to say in response. It is unquestionably true that genuine care and respect, at least of the kinds having the greatest importance to ethics, are individual-regarding. But I also think it is possible to go some way toward providing fundamental motivations for utilitarianism and Kantian deontology while fully appreciating that fact.

Let me acknowledge up front, however, that there are ways of holding either moral theory that are genuinely vulnerable to this critique. G. E. Moore's 'ideal utilitarianism' might be an example, since Moore denies even the intelligibility of welfare or of something's being 'good for' someone except as the intrinsic value of something someone might have or experience, like pleasure, or of their having or experiencing it. If I attend to others in thought and deed only in so far as doing so can realize such intrinsic values, it would seem that I am not doing so out of any genuine concern for them. And there are ways of being a welfarist utilitarian that might be criticized along these lines also. One might think it is a good thing intrinsically for people to be happy and want their happiness for its own sake without wanting this for *their* sake, that is, out of any concern for *them*. For example, one might be led from an intuition of the rationality of pursuing one's own interest to the rationality of pursuing the greatest interest of all by the Sidgwickian thought that others' welfare is no less good from 'the point of view of the universe', without being led thereby to caring for *them*.[8] The perspective of the universe is not necessarily one of genuinely benevolent concern. We might well imagine the possibility, for example, of someone's being convinced by such an argument, hearing of some individual's premature terminal illness, and thinking that something objectively undesirable had occurred without having thereby any disposition to sadness or concern on that individual's behalf. Despite thinking that the individual's premature demise would be intrinsically undesirable, and wishing for its own sake that it would not occur, this person might not wish this *for the individual's sake*, that is, out of genuine caring or benevolent concern for her.

---

[8] Henry Sidgwick, *The Methods of Ethics*, 7th edn (London: Macmillan, 1967), p. 382.

Similarly, there are strains of thought in Kant's ethics and in some moral philosophy that derives from him in which respect for persons can seem more like esteem for the moral virtue that persons can achieve or for the status that rational agents occupy in the great chain of being by virtue of their capacity to regulate appetites by reason than a recognition of any claim that is made on us by any individual person.[9] Relations between persons that are governed by respect of this kind seems appropriately criticized in Murdochian terms. What one seems to be respecting is not the individual to whom one is relating or any claim that he himself makes on one, so much as some feature in him.[10]

By the same token, however, it seems possible to think one's way into either utilitarianism or Kantianism while fully appreciating the individual-regarding character of care and respect, respectively. When we are moved to sympathetic concern for someone by a vivid depiction of her plight, say for the child that Mencius describes who is about to fall into a well, the object of our concern is an individual, this particular child.[11] We take an interest in and feel concern for *her*. And, in so doing, we see her as valuable, as mattering, and her welfare as valuable because *she* is.[12] It is this individual child whom we see to have value. But, of course, we can be moved to feel similarly about other children, in principle, each and every child, or, let us suppose, about any human being, or even any sentient being. And reflection on this fact and, consequently, on the fact that all are worthy of our concern, can lead to a genuine concern for all children, all human beings, or all sentient beings. But as universal as this concern may be, it need be no less individual-regarding than is the concern for an individual child. It involves not just a desire for the welfare of all as a state of the world that matters intrinsically (as one might think as a result of the Sidgwickian exercise of taking the 'point of view of the universe'). It involves rather a desire for that state of affairs for *their* sake, that is, an intrinsic desire for this state for the sake of all those for whom one cares (all individual children, or human beings, or sentient beings). Its object is not some abstraction (the

[9] I discuss some of these strains, but also respect for persons as respect for equal second-personal authority that I discuss below, in Kant in my 'Kant on Respect, Dignity, and the Duty of Respect', in *Kant's Virtue Ethics*, ed. Monika Betzler (Berlin: Walter de Gruyter, 2008), pp. 175–200.

[10] For a very interesting argument along these lines that respect for autonomy in people can come apart from respect for *them*, see Sarah Buss, 'Value Autonomy and Respecting Persons: Manipulation, Seduction, and the Basis of Moral Constraints', *Ethics* 115 (2005), pp. 195–235. Buss argues that Kierkegaard's *Diary of the Seducer* can be read as a case in which Johannes precisely does respect autonomy *in* Cordelia without really respecting Cordelia.

[11] *Mencius*, trans. D. C. Lau (London: Penguin Classics, 1970), p. 82.

[12] This is an important theme of Elizabeth Anderson's *Value in Ethics and Economics* (Cambridge, MA: Harvard University Press, 1993). I attempt to develop it systematically into an account of welfare and its significance in *Welfare and Rational Care* (Princeton, NJ: Princeton University Press, 2002).

'generalized other'); it is concrete: each and every human or sentient being. Consider God's concern for his creatures. Is that not individual-regarding in the same way that ours is when we feel concern for Mencius's child? If, consequently, we are attracted to the principle of utility out of universal benevolence, understood as an equal concern for each individual human or sentient being, then it would seem that we will have thought ourselves into utilitarianism in a way that respects the individual-regarding character of care.[13]

An analogous movement of thought is possible within Kantian ethics, only this time with respect rather than care. Kant speaks of respect as the 'strik[ing] down' or 'humiliating' of self-conceit by our awareness of the moral law as this might be represented to us in the conduct of a 'common humble man'.[14] The idea is that we are prone to a kind of self-importance that involves not just an inclination innocently to reckon values and reasons from our own point of view, but to see our point of view as exclusively reason-giving, as the source of all reasons. This is far from innocent because we know on some level that it is a fantasy, that we cannot have an authority to be a source of reasons that others do not have. And we can be brought vividly to this recognition by an encounter with another person that inspires respect for that person and his equal authority.

Sarah Buss describes one way this can happen when we experience shame in recognizing another's view of us as shameful in some respect.[15] Shame is not the fear of being seen as shameful; neither is it an awareness of actually being so seen. It is, rather, feeling as if a(n imagined) view of oneself as shameful is to be credited. It is the experience of seeming to be correctly thus seen, as recognizing the view of oneself one gets from an (perhaps imaginary) other's perspective. This is why Buss says that shame felt through an actual encounter with another involves respect. Shame feels as if the other can see one as one really is—as if she has a competence and authority to judge one that one's shame implicitly recognizes. And this respect is for the individual herself, we see *her* as having this authority.

But so far the relevant authority seems only epistemic, that the other is in a position to judge or assess us, not that *she* makes any claim on our conduct. The other might have the authority we credit in shame even if the

---

[13] We may, of course, not be attracted to the principle of utility from this standpoint, since we may think it makes unacceptable tradeoffs between individuals' welfare (just as we might not be attracted to it as a principle for how to distribute benefits and burdens within a family when we consider the principle from the perspective of equal concern for all members of the family).

[14] Immanuel Kant, *The Critique of Practical Reason* [1788], in *Practical Philosophy*, ed. and trans. Mary Gregor (Cambridge, MA: Cambridge University Press, 1998), 5: 77.

[15] Sarah Buss, 'Respect for Persons', *Canadian Journal of Philosophy* 29 (1999), pp. 517–50.

values or reasons we also implicitly credit have nothing to do with the dignity of persons, that is, with any claim on our conduct that individuals have an authority to make just by virtue of being persons. We might well imagine, for example, shame being felt by a Nietzschean who has what she regards as a weakness for showing Kantian respect for members of the herd and so is the object of her fellow Nietzscheans' disdain. She might see herself as appropriately disdained, and so respect her fellows' authority to disdain her, precisely in terms of values that heap scorn on the very idea that persons have equal dignity.

A more promising case for launching a line of reflection that might conclude with individual-regarding respect for all persons is the experience of guilt. Suppose someone says something that reveals to you that you have hurt him terribly in ways you could easily have been aware of but had avoided or evaded thinking about. You feel guilt about the harm you have done, about your culpable inattention, and about your failure to take responsibility in relating to him. As with shame, guilt involves a felt recognition of an authority, but in this case it is not just, or perhaps not even, an authority the other has to evaluate one in some way. Suppose that the person you have hurt does not charge you with wronging him or express any blame; he just says things that make it clear to you that you have injured and wronged him and that you are to blame. In feeling that you have wronged him, you are, as Adam Smith put it, 'sensible that the person whom [you] injured did not deserve to be treated in that manner' and that he has and had the authority to expect or demand better of you.[16] This authority shows itself in his having, as it seems to you now, the standing to reproach, but also to forgive, you for what you have done.

In such a case, you implicitly respect the particular other person in recognizing his authority to claim better treatment and to hold you responsible, and, therefore, to make claims and demands of you at all. The object of this respect is *he*, the specific person you have wronged. But as with the line of thought involving care, reflection on what underlies and grounds one's response in this case can lead to a broader and, in the end, to a universal attitude. If one sees the other's legitimate claims as those that any individual person would have in his place, then this can give rise to a universal respect for the dignity of all persons. And just as universal benevolence can be individual-regarding, so also can universal respect. It can be a respect for each and every individual person that, while no doubt is for them in light of their having features that

---

[16] Adam Smith, *The Theory of Moral Sentiments* [1759], ed. D. D. Raphael and A. L. MacFie (Indianapolis, IN: Liberty Classics, 1982), pp. 95–6.

make them persons, say rational agency of some form, is not thereby respect for these features and so not really for them.

2. Particular Personal Relationships

I take it, then, that there are forms of universal benevolence and respect that are genuinely individual-regarding and that this goes some way to answering the kinds of worries about universal moral theories like utilitarianism and Kantianism that I mentioned at the outset. But only some way. There is also a sense in much of the writing I am referring to that many important ethical questions are, in their nature, internal to particular personal *relationships* and that, for questions of this kind, universal ethical theories like utilitarianism and Kantianism are at best unhelpful and at worst utterly beside the point. When it comes to personal relations, the thought seems to be, how you and I should treat and relate to one another is a question that is essentially different from any question concerning how people should treat one another in general or even how they should treat each other in a relationship like ours. In the relevant sense, there is no such thing as a relationship *like ours*. There is just our particular relationship, and any 'fracture' of that relationship must, as Gilligan puts it, 'be mended with its own thread'.[17] Appeals to universalist considerations are at best one thought too many, and at worst, they depersonalize and distort the relationship.

Now it is no doubt true that many of the issues we encounter in personal relations are too dependent on contingencies of shared history, idiosyncratic personality, special circumstances, and so on for universal moral theories to provide much useful specific guidance. And it is true as well that explicitly appealing to such considerations can sometimes depersonalize and distort. Moreover, much ethical thinking within relationships is best done by the parties collaboratively rather than unilaterally, especially when the latter risks presuming a mantle of superior authority. But I am sceptical that the kinds of considerations that universalist moral theories bring to bear are of no help or that they are irrelevant to issues that arise within personal relations. And I am especially sceptical of the idea, sometimes suggested in some of this writing, that personal relationships occupy a kind of morality-free zone, in which universal concerns of weal and woe and the dignity of persons either do not apply or distort otherwise healthy personal relations.

[17] *In a Different Voice*, p. 31.

Indeed, I think that we cannot adequately understand the distinctive ways in which we are ethically connected to one another within mature personal relationships unless we appreciate how an aspect of our equal dignity as persons—what I shall call our *second-personal authority*, our standing to make claims and demands and have expectations of each other and hold one another accountable—must always be in the background. I shall argue in what follows that what makes it possible for us to enter into and develop many forms of human personal relationship is our capacity to recognize a shared authority we have as beings who have this capacity—an equal second-personal authority we have by virtue of our shared second-personal competence.[18]

I need to make two preliminary remarks before I begin. First, I shall be discussing personal *relationships*, that is, *relatings* between individuals, and not relations of other kinds, like fellow citizen. Second, I shall restrict myself to relationships between adults that are substantially voluntary in the sense that both parties recognize some significant freedom in whether, or at least in how, to relate to one another. Although significant attention is often given within the literature I am concerned with to other relationships, for example those between parents and children, it is hard to see how anything in the particularist critique specifically depends upon it. I take it that the critique is meant to apply as much to mature personal relations as it is to paternal relations. Mature relationships between consenting adults seem no less particularistic and individual-regarding by virtue of being substantially voluntary.

3. Equal Dignity as the Requisite Background for Personal Relationships

Once we make these restrictions, however, there will already be a sense in which the relationships we are concerned with must involve joint acknowledgement of a standing or authority that both individuals have just by virtue of being persons. This can be brought out by considering Margaret Gilbert's account of genuinely collective action and intention.[19] On Gilbert's analysis, two individuals can take a walk *together* only if their collective intention was formed in a certain way, and only if they regard themselves as having some

---

[18] I shall be able to develop this idea only in broad outline here. I attempt to do more in *The Second-person Standpoint: Morality, Respect, and Accountability* (Cambridge, MA: Harvard University Press, 2006).

[19] Margaret Gilbert, 'Walking Together: a Paradigmatic Social Phenomenon', *Midwest Studies in Philosophy* 15 (1990), pp. 1–14.

resulting obligation or responsibility *to* each other not to defect unilaterally. Two individuals are not really walking *together* in this sense if they are striding along in tandem by chance, or even when they mutually coordinate their movements but without any implicit invitation or uptake.[20] In the latter case, if, when one stops, the other says, 'Hey, I thought we were taking a walk together', it is open to the other to reply, 'What do you mean "we"?' In a genuine 'walk together' the individuals have explicitly or implicitly *agreed* to take a walk, and, by virtue of that agreement, they come to be in a relation of responsibility or answerability *to* one another. By virtue of this second-personal moral relation to one another, neither may simply defect from the agreement unilaterally. Some kind of release, or due notice, or *something*, to or from the other seems necessary and, without it, the other would seem to have some standing to reproach, but also perhaps to forgive, and so on. If someone were simply to forego the agreed activity unilaterally without saying anything about it to the other at all, then the other would seem to be entitled to conclude, either that he had forgotten, or that, if he hadn't, he didn't really understand the idea of doing something together in the relevant sense, or that, if he did, he had failed to respect the other's claim and their mutual standing in relation to one another by virtue of their agreement.

Obviously, personal relationships involve many explicit and implicit agreements and actions taken and activities engaged in together in Gilbert's sense. But more importantly, there is a sense in which the kind of personal relationship we are considering is *itself* a Gilbertian joint activity. Having a relationship is something that you and I do together. I think it is this central aspect of personal relationships that leads Gilligan sometimes to refer to the ethic she associates with the 'different voice' as a 'morality of responsibility'.[21] As Gilbert's analysis brings out, it is part of the very idea of a personal relationship of the kind we are considering that the parties have responsibilities *to* one another they otherwise would not have had, that they have a standing that makes them answerable to each other with an authority to have expectations of or claims on one another.

But this has an important consequence. It is possible for individuals to come to have such assumed special responsibilities to one another only if they already regard themselves as having the authority to assume them in

---

[20] No doubt we can meaningfully speak of shared intentions in some such cases. On this point, see Michael Bratman, 'Shared Cooperative Activity', *The Philosophical Review* 101 (1992), pp. 327–41; and Michael Bratman, 'Shared Intention', *Ethics* 104 (1993), pp. 97–113. I take it though that relationships of the kind we are discussing involve Gilbertian agreements in addition to Bratmanian shared intentions.

[21] See, e.g., *In a Different Voice*, p. 19.

the first place. In order to make such an agreement freely, the parties must regard themselves as already having the authority to make demands of each other, for example that they not simply be subjected to the other's will unilaterally. The capacity of individuals to relate to one another and form plural subjects depends upon their already presupposing one another's second-personal authority in seriously addressing each other in the first place. Any resulting special obligation or responsibility that is internal to their resulting relationship thus depends both on what they presuppose in such mutual address, namely, that they both have the requisite authority to decide freely to relate together in some mutually agreeable way, and on their addressing one another on terms that presuppose this authority. It is the terms of this standing as mutually accountable persons in general that give them the authority to obligate themselves especially to one another through their agreement.[22]

Writers in the tradition we have been discussing stress the role of care or sympathetic concern in personal relationships, and this is indeed an essential aspect. We care for our friends and loved ones and desire their welfare for their sake. Indeed, part of what we come warrantedly to expect from them and have a special responsibility to provide for them is just such sympathetic concern. But the reflections we have just been involved in show that mature personal relationships also involve mutual respect, most obviously, of the special standing that friends and loved ones have with respect to each other, but also of the (universal) authority that persons have to enter freely into such relations in the first place.

The standing to be obligated by agreements at all is a second-personal authority that presupposes mutual accountability. It is impossible for agreement-generated responsibilities and obligations to come from agreements all the way down. Unless you and I already have the authority to bind ourselves by a free agreement and to object to brute coercion, we cannot create a resulting obligation. Before you and I consummate an agreement to do something together, then, we are already obligated to one another as equal free and rational persons (as we presuppose in any serious conversation about whether to agree), although not yet specially obligated as we would come to be by a consummated agreement.

So far, this just gets the parties into the space of mutual accountability; it is insufficient to establish a binding agreement. However, some demand of good faith has to be built into the very idea of second-personal authority, since that concerns representing ourselves to and addressing one another by its very

[22] For further argument, see *The Second-person Standpoint*, pp. 198–203.

nature.[23] Responsibility or answerability *to* one another and the authority to have expectations and make claims of each other to which it is conceptually tied essentially involve second-personal *address*. The very existence of the category depends on there being a distinction between serious representations or undertakings, on the one hand, and those that are not serious, on the other. But for that distinction to be in place, individuals must be accountable to one another for the seriousness of their representations and undertakings, they must have a claim against one another that they not present themselves as making serious representations and undertakings when they are not serious (with, of course, the usual escape clauses about play, humour, irony, and so on). So if two parties present themselves to one another as having a serious conversation about whether to enter into a relationship of some specific kind, then both must have *some* resulting claim that the agreement be kept. Both already had a claim that any address on the matter of whether to agree be in good faith. And since it is a presupposition of a serious conversation about whether to agree that the parties will be bound if they agree, then some claim actually to the agreement's being kept must follow also from their common authority to demand good faith.

The rhetoric of honesty, good faith, seriousness, not trifling, and so on is not just found in Jane Austen's novels or *The Vicar of Wakefield*. These concerns seem an essential aspect of any relationship of the kind we are considering. The reason, I think, is that implicit and explicit agreements are part of the stuff of which personal relationships are made and so some mutually recognized authority to demand straightforwardness seems built in. Of course, we shouldn't get too Victorian about it—or, at least, we need not respect Victorian rhetoric. Some mutually acknowledged space for silence, indirection, misdirection, and so on may be part of a relation that you and I freely undertake. Nonetheless, even here we will presume some background authority to claim honesty, if only in conversations about what direction and shape our relationship is to take.

4. Equal Dignity and Second-personal Authority

I have been arguing that a respect for the equal dignity of persons in the form of mutual accountability and shared second-personal authority to make claims and demands of one another at all, including, on that basis, a claim

---

[23] Along similar lines, one might say that a warranted demand for honest dealing is built into the very idea of relating accountably to others.

not to be coerced or treated falsely, is presupposed as part of the background for voluntary adult personal relationships, so that, although problems within such relations must normally 'be mended with [the relationship's] own thread', this must nonetheless be within a commonly presupposed second-personal framework.[24] But what, exactly, is this second-personal authority of which I have been speaking? One way into this subject is to consider Strawson's influential critique of consequentialist accounts of moral responsibility in 'Freedom and Resentment'.[25] Against approaches that seek to justify practices of holding people responsible by their 'efficacy . . . in regulating behaviour in socially desirable ways', Strawson argued that social desirability cannot provide a justification of 'the right *sort*' for practices of moral responsibility 'as we understand them'.[26] When we seek to hold people accountable, what matters is not whether doing so is desirable, either in a particular case or in general, but whether a person's conduct is culpable and we have the authority to bring him to account. Desirability is a reason *of the wrong kind* to warrant the attitudes and actions in which holding someone responsible consists in their own terms.

To be a reason of the right kind, a consideration must speak directly to the 'reactive attitudes' that, Strawson so influentially argued, are distinctively involved in holding people responsible and blaming them. Just as the desirable concerns norms and reasons for desire, so the *culpable* concerns norms and reasons for reactive attitudes, for what is warrantedly blamed, resented, and so on. The desirability—whether moral, social, personal, or otherwise—of holding people responsible or blaming them is a reason of the wrong kind to warrant doing so in the sense that is relevant to whether they *are* morally responsible or blameworthy.

Strawson pointed out that what is common to reactivate attitudes like indignation, resentment, guilt, blame, and so on is that they implicitly address claims and demands. They invariably involve 'an expectation of, and demand for' certain conduct from one another.[27] So, in our terms, they implicitly presuppose second-personal authority. They assume the authority to demand

---

[24] For a more systematic development, see my *The Second-person Standpoint*.

[25] P. F. Strawson, 'Freedom and Resentment', in *Studies in the Philosophy of Thought and Action* (London: Oxford University Press, 1968).

[26] *Ibid.*, pp. 72, 74.

[27] 'Freedom and Resentment', p. 95. Gary Watson stresses this also in 'Responsibility and the Limits of Evil: Variations on a Strawsonian Theme', in *Responsibility, Character, and the Emotions: New Essays in Moral Psychology*, ed. F. D. Schoeman (Cambridge: Cambridge University Press, 1987), pp. 263, 264. Note also R. Jay Wallace: 'there is an essential connection between the reactive attitudes and a distinctive form of evaluation . . . that I refer to as holding a person to an expectation (or demand)' (*Responsibility and the Moral Sentiments* (Cambridge, MA: Harvard University Press, 1994), p. 19).

and hold one another responsible for compliance with moral obligations (which just are the standards to which we can warrantedly hold each other). But they also presuppose that those we hold accountable have that standing also. They address another in a way that 'continu[es] to view him as a member of the moral community; only as one who has offended against its demands'.[28] As Strawson analysed it, therefore, holding people responsible with reactive attitudes presupposes a shared second-personal authority to make demands of one another as equal members of the moral community. We can express the same thing by saying that we are equally accountable to one another for complying with moral demands.

Consider guilt, again. To feel guilty is to feel as if one is appropriately blamed and held responsible for something one has done. Guilt feels like the appropriate (second-personal) response to blame: an *acknowledgement* of one's blameworthiness that recognizes both the grounds of blame as well as the *authority* to level it. To feel guilt is to feel as if one has the requisite capacity and standing to be addressed as responsible. So it involves an implicit recognition of others' second-personal authority, those with the authority to make the demand one has violated, as well as one's own. And guilt's natural expressions are also second-personal—confession, apology, making amends, giving future assurances, self-addressed reproach, and so on.

When I say, therefore, that you and I must presuppose a common second-personal authority when we initiate or shape a personal relationship of some kind together because we must already assume that we are mutually accountable as a presupposition even of any Gilbertian invitation and uptake, however implicit, I mean to draw on Strawson's point that holding one another responsible always presupposes an authority to make claims and demands of one another as equal members of the moral community. This is an important aspect of the dignity of persons, in my view, which Kant captures when he says that 'a human being regarded as a *person*, that is as the subject of a morally practical reason, . . . possesses a dignity . . . by which he exacts *respect* . . . from all other rational beings in the world'.[29] By 'exact' Kant means claim or 'demand', as he explicitly then says. The dignity of persons thus includes the second-personal authority to make claims and demands of one another, including to claim respect for this very authority. Rawls makes essentially the same point when he says that persons are 'self-originating sources of valid claims'.[30]

---

[28] 'Freedom and Resentment', p. 93.

[29] Immanuel Kant, *Metaphysics of Morals* [1797], in Kant, *Practical Philosophy*, trans. and ed. Mary J. Gregor, intro. Allen Wood (Cambridge: Cambridge University Press, 1996), 6: 435.

[30] John Rawls, 'Kantian Constructivism in Moral Theory', *Journal of Philosophy* 77 (1980), p. 546.

Moreover, claiming respect for this equal second-personal authority is what we are fundamentally aiming to do, according to Strawson, when we hold one another responsible: we address a demand and claim respect for our authority to do so. Adam Smith makes the same point, again, when he says that what resentment is 'chiefly intent upon, is not so much to make our enemy feel pain in his turn, as . . . to make him sensible that the person whom he injured did not deserve to be treated in that manner'.[31] The implicit aim of reactive attitudes is to make others feel respect for our dignity (and, less obviously, their own), including our authority to claim this respect.

So far, I have been discussing a shared second-personal authority as persons that you and I must presuppose in common for us to have a personal relationship. What I wish to consider now are the special responsibilities that arise within personal relationships. These also have a fundamentally second-personal structure: they are responsibilities that the parties have *to* one another within the relationship, and they therefore involve a special second-personal authority. People sometimes talk about a responsibility *to* a relationship, but this seems to me to risk a kind of reification. It can be a quite unobjectionable way of referring to distinctive values that a relationship might involve and to reasons that are associated with those values. But there can't be a responsibility to a relationship in any literal sense. The special responsibilities that parties to a personal relationship have are responsibilities to one another. And like any responsibility *to*, these relationship-specific responsibilities involve second-personal authority; they involve the parties' relationship-specific authorities to have expectations of each other and to hold one another to them. Indeed, I believe that these special second-personal authorities partly constitute what personal relationships of the kind we are considering themselves are.

5. Special Responsibilities within Special Relationships

Now it may seem clear enough that personal relationships involve the idea of standing in some sense. Friends and loved ones clearly have a special standing in our affections and attentions, a place in our hearts, devotions, and lives, that others do not have. But what does any of that have to do with any kind of authority? Even if we could have an authority to demand love and attention from friends and loved ones, isn't what we want that their love and attention

[31] *Theory of Moral Sentiments*, pp. 95–6.

be freely given and not that it be given out of respect for such an authority? These, as they say, are delicate matters. And it will take some care (and maybe some respect?) to sort them out.

First, let me just note some important general differences between care, in the sense of benevolent or sympathetic concern, and respect. When we care for someone in this sense, we want what is for her good. In caring for someone, we see her as a being with a welfare, just as, in respecting someone, we see her as a being with a dignity.[32] There is, however, a fundamental difference in the perspectives from which we have or feel these different attitudes. Respect for persons' dignity, at least for their second-personal authority, is, I have argued elsewhere, also fundamentally second-personal.[33] It is an acknowledgement of this authority that we realize in how we relate to another second-personally, holding ourselves accountable to her, taking her will and point of view seriously in deciding how to act, and so on. Sympathetic concern, on the other hand, views the other third-personally and shows itself in a desire that she flourish quite independently of how we conduct ourselves toward her. Benevolent concern is a source of motivation, of course, but the point is that it moves us to act in whatever way we believe will help realize its object's welfare. The desire that such a concern gives rise to, first and foremost, is for the state of the world in which the cared-for flourishes, and secondly, for whatever actions one take that would help bring that about. The object of the desire that springs from respect for someone's dignity, by contrast, is, first and foremost, one's conduct in relating to that person. One desires to regulate one's conduct towards her by the legitimate demands her dignity gives her standing to make, including by acknowledging this authority in relating to her second-personally.

The important point for our purposes is that, although respect inherently involves a second-personal acknowledgement of the authority of the other's point of view, benevolent concern, taken in itself, does not. This is the deep thought that underlies criticism of paternalism in the pejorative sense. When someone seeks, against our wishes, to restrain or otherwise direct us for our own benefit or to prevent us from harm, what is objectionable need not be that his benevolent concern for us is somehow mistaken or defective. He may really be right that we would be better off with his direction. The failure is rather one of respect. In failing to be guided by our wishes, he fails to respect our authority to do as we wish even at some risk to ourselves. I don't mean

[32] Here I am referring to *recognition respect* rather than *appraisal respect*, which is a form of esteem for merit. On this distinction, see my 'Two Kinds of Respect', *Ethics* 88 (1977), pp. 36–49.
[33] 'Respect and the Second-person Standpoint', *Proceedings and Addresses of the American Philosophical Association* 78 (2004), pp. 43–60.

that this authority is absolute, of course. It is enough for the point I am making here if it has any weight whatsoever, since any weight it has will be registered exclusively by respect; it will come onto the radar screen of care (in the sense of benevolent concern) only to the extent that it finds representation in the person's welfare as, of course, it no doubt will to some extent. But even if it does, the point will remain that what has intrinsic normative relevance for care is not the other person's point of view as such, but reasons that one can grasp from the third-person perspective of 'one-caring'. Respect of the kind we are considering involves second-personal engagement with the other's point of view essentially; care does not.

Personal relationships of the kind we are discussing involve both care and respect. Friends are not simply a mutual benevolence association, but neither are they bound just by mutual respect. They want what is best for each other, but they also respect one another's authority to give shape and meaning to their own lives. Indeed, friends actively *support* each other in pursuing valued projects or activities even when concern for their friend's welfare might move them otherwise.[34]

Responsibilities to one another in personal relationship bring second-personal authority into the relationship itself. I argued earlier that voluntary relationships are possible only on the assumption that the parties share a basic second-personal authority as persons. Now I want to consider the special forms of second-personal authority that arise within and partly structure any personal relationship. Any such special responsibility *to* each other that parties within a particular relationship have must partly consist in a special second-personal authority. Otherwise the responsibility will simply be with respect to each other and not really *to* each other; it won't involve accountability or answerability *to them*. So if the parties are responsible to each other for providing support of some kind, then they must in some sense be answerable to each other for this. The idea that they have the authority to demand it may seem too heavily freighted, but they clearly have *some* claim on each other they otherwise would not have. Even where it would be out of place to say something like, 'Hey, I thought we were friends', it will clearly be appropriate to feel something one might thus express in an internal dialogue. Such a feeling is a reactive attitude; it implicitly lodges a complaint and so assumes the authority to make it.

It is significant that among the reactive attitudes Strawson lists is 'hurt feelings'.[35] Feelings are hurt when people act in ways one supposes contrary to

---

[34] For this point, see Joseph Raz, 'Darwall on Rational Care', *Utilitas* 18 (2006), p. 411.
[35] 'Freedom and Resentment', p. 75.

expected personal regard, which expectations one takes the other reciprocally to have recognized or takes it that he should have recognized. One need not see oneself as having a claim to the other's regard that would warrant resentment.[36] But one feels as if some issue of rejection and mutual trust has been raised that puts the relationship in some question.

Reflection on the difference between jealousy and envy is relevant here. Envy is not particularly tied to relationships in the way that jealousy is. We can feel envy just by being aware of someone else's 'superior advantages', as the OED puts it. Jealousy, on the other hand, is tied to fear or suspicion of being supplanted in some relationship to someone. The idea of a relational standing is thus essential to jealousy in a way it is not to envy. Moreover, it seems clear that jealousy has a natural, and depressingly familiar, psychic connection to reactive attitudes that envy does not. Indeed, according to the OED, 'jealousy''s original meaning, now obsolete, was identical with 'wrath, indignation, or anger'. Novels and newspapers are replete with accounts of jealous, jilted partners who take out their wrath on would-be or would-have-been lovers. Although the saying from Congreve's play had it that 'hell hath no fury like a woman scorned', statistics show that male violence on women is the significantly more likely pattern. In any case, my point here is that even this grotesque form of 'holding responsible' honours in a distorted way the idea of second-personal authority. Batterers don't just beat up their partners; they tend to do so while indulging in the fantasy that their partners 'have it coming'.

Finally, it is worth considering in this context some fascinating research on sources of marital discord and failure. As reported in Malcolm Gladwell's *Blink*, the psychologist John Gottman has studied videotapes of conversations between married couples and has developed a way of analysing expressed emotions that enables him and his colleagues to predict with 90 per cent accuracy whether the couple will be married fifteen years later on the basis of a fifteen-minute tape. (Gottman can increase his accuracy to 95 per cent if he looks at a one-hour interview.)[37]

---

[36] Although this obviously can happen also, as with Medea's response to Jason's leaving her for the Princess of Corinth or, as in the lyrics of Alanis Morisette's 'You Oughta Know': 'And I'm here to remind you, Of the mess you left when you went away. It's not fair to deny me, Of the cross I bear that you gave to me, You, you, you . . . oughta know.' Or Bob Dylan's 'Desolation Row': 'Yes, I received your letter yesterday/(About the time the door knob broke)/When you asked how I was doing/Was that some kind of joke?/ . . . /Don't send me no more letters no/Not unless you mail them/From Desolation Row' (Dylan 1965).

[37] Malcolm Gladwell, *Blink* (New York: Little, Brown, and Co., 2005), pp. 21–2. Gottman's findings are presented in John Gottman et al., *The Mathematics of Marriage: Dynamic Nonlinear Models* (Cambridge, MA: MIT Press, 2002).

Gottman believes that far and away the greatest predictor of marital discord and break-up are expressions of contempt. Gladwell notes that Gottman has discovered 'that the presence of contempt in a marriage can even predict such things as how many colds a husband or wife gets'. As Gladwell puts it, 'having someone you love express contempt toward you is so stressful that it begins to affect the function of your immune system'.[38]

Gottman describes contempt as 'speak[ing] from a higher plane' and as 'closely related to disgust'. 'What disgust and contempt are about', he says, 'is completely rejecting and excluding someone from the community.'[39] A familiar behavioural manifestation of contempt is rolling one's eyes. In Gottman's view, 'contempt is qualitatively different from' and 'far more damaging' than criticism. It is, he says, the 'sulphuric acid of love'.[40]

As I analyse this phenomenon, contempt is the attitude or feeling of being justified in not according someone second-personal authority as an equal, that another does not deserve this respect. Unlike reactive attitudes such as resentment or even anger, contempt refuses to engage its object second-personally and so to recognize the other's authority to hold the contemner answerable. It is essential to reactive attitudes, however, that they are expressed second-personally, even if only in imagination. They are addressed to and seek acknowledgement from their object. They come with an RSVP and engage their object, as Strawson points out, on equal terms. Contemptuously rolling one's eyes is as likely to be addressed, however, to oneself or to an imagined audience off stage as it is to the object of one's contempt. (After all, if someone is worthy of contempt, he isn't going to appreciate what makes him contemptible and an appropriate object of rolled eyes in the first place.) And contempt decidedly does not come with an RSVP. If it calls for any response from its object, the response it calls for is more like disappearance or shrinking away in shame or humiliation.

Contempt is not usually, therefore, a form of holding responsible. To the contrary, as Gottman says, it reads its object out of the community of mutually accountable persons or, in the case of personal relations, reads him out of a mutually answerable relationship. The reason that contempt is the sulphuric acid of relationship is that it undermines the very second-personal relations and responsibility to one another that personal relationships partly consist in.

I take this to be strong evidence that respect for the second-personal authority that, in my view, is essential to the equal dignity of persons is not

[38] *Blink*, p. 33.   [39] *Ibid.*
[40] Jim Giles, 'Maths Predict Chances of Divorce', *Nature@nature.com* 14 February 2004, http://www.nature.com/news/2004/040209/pf/040209-18-pf.html

just something we have to assume in order to form personal relationships in the first place; it is also part and parcel of what we want and need *within* such relationships. We make ourselves vulnerable to and reveal ourselves to friends and lovers in ways that we typically do not to strangers. They come to know us in ways that others do not, including in some of our most unrespectable moments, not just when we are less than presentable, but also when we have subjected them to injuries and betrayals, petty and grave. I think this is partly what makes respect from them so important to us and contempt so significant.

The upshot is that while it is certainly true, as particularist critics of universalist moral theories have argued, that we are emotionally connected and invested in personal relationships in ways that resist adequate universalist formulation and, as well, that what we want in personal relations is love, attention, concern, interest, acceptance, and the like that are freely given and not the product of a further thought about what we are owed as equal moral persons, part of what we need in such relations is also this further affirmation from those who know us best. And as the words to an old song say: 'You can't always get what you want/ . . . But if you try sometimes, you just might find, . . ., you get what you need.'[41]

---

[41] 'You Can't Always Get What You Want', Mick Jagger and Keith Richard.

8

Which Relationships Justify Partiality? General Considerations and Problem Cases*

NIKO KOLODNY

We have, or at least we take ourselves to have, reason for patterns of action and emotion towards our parents, siblings, friends, spouses, children, and others with whom we have significant ties.[1] This *partiality* involves seeing to it that both these *relatives* and our relationships to them fare well, as well as respecting both in our decisions. It also involves feeling certain positive emotions (e.g. joy, relief, gratitude) when they fare well or are properly regarded, and feeling certain negative emotions (e.g. grief, anxiety, resentment) when they fare poorly or are not properly regarded. Famously, these reasons for partiality are *agent-relative*. I have reason to be partial to my relatives, whereas you do not, and you have reason to be partial to your relatives, whereas I do not. Less often noted, these reasons support requirements that are *owed* to our relatives. When we breach these requirements, we wrong our relatives, if not morally, then in some other sense. We give them claim, which others lack, to privileged kinds of complaints, such as resentment.

* Since this essay, and its companion, 'Which Relationships Justify Partiality? Parents and Children', *Philosophy & Public Affairs* 38 (2010), pp. 37–75, began as a chapter of my 2003 University of California, Berkeley Ph.D. thesis, 'Relationships as Reasons', I owe thanks first to Sam Scheffler, Jay Wallace, Chris Kutz, and Seana Shiffrin for their comments on that thesis. Descendants of that chapter were presented at the conference on Partiality and Impartiality in Ethics, at the University of Reading in the autumn of 2005, and at Sam Scheffler and Eric Rakowski's Workshop on Law, Philosophy, and Political Theory, at the Boalt School of Law of the University of California, Berkeley, in the winter of 2008. I am very grateful for comments from participants at those events, as well as for correspondence from Josh Glasgow, Francesco Orsi, and two anonymous referees for Oxford University Press.

[1] Throughout, I make certain claims about what 'we' take to be true of ourselves. I don't mean to presume somehow that every reasonable or decent reader will agree with every such claim. The hope is only that enough readers will agree with enough of these claims for the attempt to make sense of them to be of interest.

This presents a puzzle, however. Although we have countless interpersonal relationships, we have reason for partiality only in some. Why is this? Why is there reason for friendship and love of family, but not for racism or *omertà*?[2] Without an answer, without a principled distinction between the relationships that support partiality and the relationships that don't, a creeping scepticism sets in about partiality as a whole.

My hope is to make some progress towards a principled distinction, or set of distinctions. In Section 1, I clarify the challenge. The challenge would be easy to meet, I observe, if reasons for partiality were not, in a certain sense, 'basic'. The problem is that some reasons for partiality are basic, in that sense. In Section 2, I discuss a neglected form of normative explanation, 'resonance', which might help us to meet analogous challenges about other domains, such as the moral emotions. In Section 3, I apply resonance to our challenge, suggesting how it might explain why some relationships—friendship and cultural membership are the examples—support partiality. (In a companion essay, 'Which Relationships Justify Partiality? Parents and Children', I distinguish various reasons for familial partiality, focusing on the relationships between parents and children.) In Section 4, I suggest how resonance might explain why other relationships do not support partiality, paying special attention to the case of racism. In Section 5, I end with some reflections on the implications of this account for other relationships, such as co-citizenship; for the defence of partiality in general; and for the difficult relations between partiality and other norms, most notably those of impartial morality.

1. A Request for Explanation

Think of the challenge this way. Imagine the exhaustive *List of partiality principles*, of all of the true normative claims of the form:

---

[2] Compare John Cottingham, 'Partiality, Favouritism, and Morality', *Philosophical Quarterly* 36 (1986), pp. 357–73; Simon Keller, 'Making Nonsense of Loyalty to Country', in Boudewijn de Bruin and Christopher S. Zurn (eds), *New Waves in Political Philosophy* (Basingstoke: Palgrave Macmillan, 2009), pp. 87–104; Katja Vogt, 'Freundschaft, Unparteilichkeit und Feindschaft', *Deutsche Zeitschrift für Philosophie* 40 (2001), pp. 517–32; Christopher Heath Wellman, 'Relational Facts in Liberal Political Theory: Is There Magic in the Pronoun "My"?' *Ethics* 110 (2000), pp. 537–62; and Nick Zangwill, 'Against Analytic Moral Functionalism', *Ratio* 13 (2000), pp. 275–86, at p. 280. Zangwill writes:

A lot of ethical theorists are happy to notice the friends, family and community cases, but they do not see the problem of where it might end . . . . How about my colleague, my tribesman, my countryman, my gender, my patient, my co-religionist or my species? These are all controversial and disputed. We need to ask the question: *which* loyalties are okay and which are not? . . . *When* do indexical considerations contribute to determining a moral property? This is a fundamental moral question—perhaps even *the* fundamental moral question.

one has reason for parental partiality toward one's children,
one has reason for spousal partiality toward one's spouse,

and so on. We need not imagine the List fully enumerated. It is enough to imagine it including relatively uncontroversial cases, like parental and spousal partiality, and excluding relatively uncontroversial cases, like prison-gang and blood-type partiality. Our challenge is then to *explain* the List: to explain why all and only the partiality principles that it contains are true.

To be clear, the challenge is not to provide *reasons to believe* the List.[3] This latter challenge might be met with abductive arguments to the effect that the List best explains our particular judgements about reasons for partiality. But the challenge to *explain* the List cannot be met in this way. Nor is the challenge to explain how *any* partiality principle could be true. Such a challenge might be issued, for example, by philosophers who find agent-relative reasons, in general, inexplicable. Rather, granting (at least for the sake of argument) that partiality principles are *not otherwise problematic*, the challenge is to explain why only those partiality principles on the List, and no others, are true.

I assume that all *normative claims*, which, by stipulation, are of the form 'One has reason . . .', are explained only by other normative claims and claims with no normative or evaluative content.[4] Given this assumption, it may seem that the explanation of any normative claim must take one of two forms. The first, *deduction*, shows how one normative claim follows from a more fundamental normative claim (and perhaps further nonnormative premises) by rules of inference familiar outside of the normative domain. For example, the explanation of the claim that I have reason to admire Mark Twain may be, first, that if someone is a great author, then everyone has reason to admire that person, second, that Mark Twain is a great author, and, finally, universal instantiation, twice applied. The second kind of explanation, *facilitation*, shows how one normative claim follows from a more fundamental normative claim and a transmission principle of the rough form: if one has reason for something, then one has reason for the (causal or constitutive) means to it. For example, the explanation for why I have reason to travel to New York consists, first, of the normative claim that I have reason to be in New York, second, of the nonnormative claim that my travelling there is a means to my being there, and, finally, of the transmission principle that if one has reason for something, then one has reason for the means to it.[5]

---

[3] Christopher Heath Wellman, 'Relational Facts', in particular, seems to confuse the challenge to *explain* the List with this latter challenge to provide *reasons for believing* it.

[4] I relax this assumption in n. 9, below.

[5] See Joseph Raz, 'The Myth of Instrumental Rationality', *Journal of Ethics and Social Philosophy* 1 (2005), pp. 2–28.

Can we explain the List by appeal to just deduction and facilitation? Yes, say *reductionists*. They hold that no partiality principle is, in a certain sense, basic: more precisely, that every partiality principle:

one has reason to be partial in ways *P* to people with whom one has an interpersonal relationship of type *R*,

can be explained, by deduction or facilitation, from normative principles that are not partiality principles.[6] Most often, reductionism appeals to a normative principle of the form:

one has reason to *phi* (or to feel *E*)

and a non-normative *response equivalence* of the form:

being partial in way *P* to people with whom one has *R* is an instance of, or facilitates, *phi*-ing (or feeling *E*).

For example, the reductionist might seek to explain the partiality principle:

one has reason to be parentally partial to one's children,

by appeal to the normative principle that:

one has reason to maximize well-being,

and the non normative claim that:

being parentally partial to one's children is an instance of, or facilitates, maximizing well-being (because, e.g., one knows their needs better than others do).

Or the reductionist might seek to explain the partiality principle:

one has reason to be spousally partial to one's spouse,

---

[6] This discussion of reductionism is indebted to Samuel Scheffler, 'Relationships and Responsibilities', *Philosophy & Public Affairs* 26 (1997), pp. 189–209. However, Scheffler defines reductionism as the position that reasons for partiality 'actually arise out of discrete interactions that occur in the context of . . . relationships' (p. 190). For present purposes, this definition is, in one way, too narrow, and, in another way, potentially misleading. Too narrow, because some reductionist explanations (such as the one below that appeals to well-being) need not appeal to any discrete interactions between relatives. Potentially misleading, because a non-reductionist might hold that although reasons for partiality arise from relationships and not from discrete interactions, some of the relevant relationships (such as the histories of encounter discussed below) are *constituted* by discrete interactions. The whole provides reasons that the parts do not.

by appeal to the normative principle that:

one has reason to fulfil expectations, that one has voluntarily and intentionally, or voluntarily and negligently, led others to form, that one would perform morally permissible actions

and the response equivalence that:

being spousally partial is an instance of, or facilitates, fulfilling such expectations.

Reductionists thus have at least a clear *strategy* for explaining the List. They can claim that there are relevant response equivalences for all and only the partiality principles on the List. For example, they can claim that being gang-partial to one's fellow Aryan Brothers, or being blood-type-partial to fellow O positives is not an instance of, and does not facilitate, maximizing well-being, or fulfilling expectations of morally permissible actions.

Yet, setting aside whether it explains why the List *excludes* what it does, I doubt that reductionism explains why the List *includes* what it does. First, consideration of some familiar proposals suggests that reductionism does not explain reasons for many of the partial *actions* that we take ourselves to have reason to perform. For one thing, I may be no more efficient than strangers at promoting my relatives' well-being. If my mother became senile, it might not matter to her whether I or a stranger cared for her, and it might be clear enough to a stranger what her care required. For another, I may be no more efficient at promoting my relatives' well-being than strangers' well-being. Some children are much worse off materially than my daughter, and a deranged stalker might be no less emotionally vulnerable to me than my wife. Some reductionists may reply that the difference is that I did not voluntarily and intentionally (or negligently) lead the stalker to become vulnerable to me. But a voluntary act cannot be necessary, since I have reason for partiality to family members, such as my parents and siblings, regardless of any such act. And voluntarily and intentionally (or negligently) leading someone to become vulnerable to my failing to be partial to her cannot be sufficient, as the familiar phenomenon of 'leading someone on' confirms. Someone might voluntarily and intentionally encourage me to form the mistaken belief that she has the attitudes constitutive of being my friend or lover, thereby leading me to become vulnerable to her not treating me as her friend or lover. We would all agree that she has reason to 'let me down gently'.

But no one believes that she has reason to treat me as a friend or lover, precisely because there is no relationship that would make sense of such partiality.[7]

Next, even if reductionism explained *some* reasons for partial actions, these are not *the* reasons on which people, in being partial, act. When moved to do something for my daughter or my wife, for example, it would be oddly estranged to view her claim on me as merely that of a stranger whose well-being I could promote, or whose expectations I have raised. Finally, reductionism does not explain reason for partial *emotion*. Even if, on occasion, I have reason to do the same for a stranger's daughter as for my own, I do not have reason to feel the same way about the stranger's daughter.

It is natural to react to these last two points with the thought that the motivations and emotions distinctive of partiality have nothing do with reasons. 'Those motivations and emotions are simply *love* itself, and love is not a response to reasons. Indeed, it cannot be: love is focused on a particular, e.g. *Jane*, and something's being the very particular that it is is not a reason for anything.' To take this view, however, is to misunderstand ourselves. As I have tried to argue elsewhere, it is false to the lived experience of love, rendering it an unintelligible urge; it is contradicted by our reflective judgements that love is called for by some objects (such as our own children) and not by others (strangers' children); and it fails to explain a variety of other facts about love, such as the prediction that I would cease to love my wife if I lost all memory of our history together, even if I retained memories of what preceded that history that allowed me to recognize her as the very particular she is (whatever that comes to). To love someone, I think, just is, in part, to see one's relationship with her as providing reason for partiality to her.[8]

My aim here is not to make a conclusive case against reductionism, which the foregoing no doubt fails to do. It is only to say enough about the apparent limitations of reductionism to motivate interest in the alternative, *non-reductionism*. This is the view that some partiality principles are *not* explained via deduction and facilitation from normative principles that are not partiality principles: that some partiality principles are, in this sense, basic. If so, then our question is how non-reductionism can explain the List. Clearly it cannot explain the List as reductionism does: by showing that all and only the partiality principles on the List follow by deduction or facilitation from normative principles none of which are partiality principles. What alternative is there?

---

[7] Compare Talbot Brewer, 'Two Kinds of Commitments (And Two Kinds of Social Groups)', *Philosophy and Phenomenological Research* 66 (2003), pp. 554–83, at p. 557.

[8] See my 'Love as Valuing a Relationship', *Philosophical Review* 112 (2003), pp. 135–89.

Non-reductionists might propose, with reductionists, that all and only the partiality principles on the List follow by deduction or facilitation from other normative principles, but, against reductionists, that some of these principles are partiality principles. In particular, they might appeal to a Generic Partiality Principle:

One has reason for Generic Partiality toward people with whom one has a relationship of the Generic Type.

And they might seek to derive all other partiality principles on the List, by deduction or facilitation, using response equivalences of the form:

being parentally partial to one's children is an instance of, or facilitates, being Generically Partial to people with whom one has a relationship of the Generic Type,

being fraternally partial to one's siblings is an instance of, or facilitates, being Generically Partial to people with whom one has a relationship of the Generic Type.

The explanation of List would then be that relevant response equivalences obtain for all and only its entries. But this approach seems hopeless. There seems no way to specify the Generic Type, other than by a disjunction of all the relationships on the List, which would hardly meet the challenge. Moreover, there is no one kind of Generic Partiality. Parental partiality, for example, is quite different from fraternal partiality.[9]

---

[9] We have been assuming that the explanation of the List would appeal solely to facts of the form: 'One has reason . . . '. However, some might think that facts of the form 'One has reason . . . ' are explained by facts of the form: 'Such and such is of value . . . ' or 'Such and such "provides" (or is a "source" of) reason . . . '.

While this is plausible, it does not help with our problem. Again, there will appear to be two kinds of explanation. *Promotion* explains the fact that X has reason to *phi*, or to feel E, by showing that the fact that X's *phi*-ing, or feeling E, would *bring about* something of value, or *prevent* something of disvalue. *Recognition* explains the fact that X has reason to *phi*, or to feel E, by showing that X's *phi*-ing, or feeling E, would properly *respect* or *acknowledge* or *be for the sake of* something of value, or disvalue. To say that something 'provides' or 'is a source of' reason, I think, is just to say that it plays the role of the thing of value (or of disvalue) in an explanation of that reason.

Now, non-reductionists might well explain each entry on the List by appealing to facts of this kind. The explanation would presumably appeal to recognition and would take the relationship mentioned in the entry as the relevant value, or source of reason. For example, non-reductionists might explain why:

one has reason to be parentally partial to one's children

by saying that:

At this point, one might well ask why we should *expect* an explanation of the List. 'Consider an analogy. Why should we be troubled that we cannot explain, by appeal to further normative principles, why the principles:

one has reason to seek knowledge,
one has reason to cause pleasure,

belong on the list of true normative principles, whereas the principles:

one has reason to cause pain,
one has reason to count blades of grass,

do not? Perhaps we should be troubled if we accepted monism: that all normative claims follow by deduction or facilitation from a single normative principle. But we should not be monists.'

We need not be monists, however, to expect an explanation of the List. Granted, we may not expect a common explanation of why knowledge and pleasure provide reasons. But this is because knowledge and pleasure are so manifestly different, both in themselves and in the responses they call for. By contrast, friendship and marriage are remarkably similar, both in themselves

one's parental relationship to one's children is something of value, and being parentally partial to one's children properly respects this value,

or:

one's parental relationship to one's children provides, or is a source of, reason to be parentally partial to one's children.

And non-reductionists might then propose to explain the List by claiming that all and only the relationships mentioned by partiality principles on the List are valuable, or reason-providing, in the relevant way. (Compare the suggestion of Scheffler, 'Relationships and Responsibilities', that the relationships provide reasons for partiality are just those that we have 'reason to value noninstrumentally'.) This is why all and only the partiality principles on the List are true.

The problem is that this seems only to postpone the challenge. Why, one now wants to know, are all and only the relationships mentioned by the partiality principles on the List valuable, or reason-providing, in the relevant way?

This is why it is unhelpful to suggest that the partiality principles on the List involve relationships of just those kinds that contribute to their participants' well-being, or the meaning of their lives. The suggestion would be not the reductionist claim that one's reason for partiality is to enhance one's own well-being overall, but instead that relationships of kinds that contribute to one's well-being other things equal are associated with the partiality principles on the List, principles that are not explained via deduction or facilitation from other normative principles. (In a given case, such a relationship might not enhance one's well-being overall, because of the sacrifices it requires.) This connection to well-being or meaning is plausible, and it may even be useful in identifying, or justifying belief in, the principles on the List. But it does not help to explain *why* those and only those principles are on the List. On the most plausible views, when activities and experiences contribute to well-being and meaning, they do so because they are independently valuable. So the challenge recurs: why are these relationships, and no others, independently valuable?

and in the responses they call for. And where there are similar phenomena, we expect a common explanation. There ought, it seems, to be something that we can say about the partiality principles on the List that explains why they, and only they, are true.

So the challenge to explain the List remains. All that we have settled so far is that if we are to meet it, we need to find another kind of normative explanation, beyond those that we have already discussed.[10]

2. Resonance

To illustrate what this kind of normative explanation might look like, consider a similar request for explanation about the *reactive emotions*: responses—most notably, guilt, resentment, gratitude, and indignation—to attitudes, expressed in decisions, towards certain people and things. Why do I have reason to feel a given reactive emotion toward *some* decisions, but not *others*? For example, why do I have reason to *resent* it when, say, a paediatrician expresses in his decisions a lack of concern for my *child*, but not when he expresses a lack of concern for the *parasite* that threatens her health?

'Because', one will say, 'you have reason to *care* about your child, whereas you do not have reason to care about the parasite. That is, you have reason to feel certain *non-reactive emotions* in response to how she fares: positive non-reactive emotions (e.g. hope, relief, joy) when she fares well, and negative non-reactive emotions (e.g. anxiety, fear, grief) when she fares poorly.' But what is the nature of this 'because'? This answer, namely that:

> I have reason to *feel negative non-reactive emotions* at my child's faring poorly, but not at the parasite's faring poorly,

does not explain by *deduction* or *facilitation* why:

> I have reason to *resent* lack of concern for my child, but not lack of concern for the parasite.

---

[10] The problem can look easier than it is. Keller, 'Making Nonsense of Loyalty to Country', writes (p. 91):

There are some loyalties that you should not have . . . It is easy to explain why each of these loyalties is objectionable. Loyalty to the Nazi Party is immoral . . . [L]oyalty to a bank is imprudent. You should not be a loyal fan of Bon Jovi, because the object of that loyalty is aesthetically unappealing.

But, first, one might think whether loyalty is immoral depends, in part, on whether or not there are reasons for that loyalty. If so, then we cannot appeal to its immorality to explain why there are no reasons for it. Second, if my wife remained loyal to me although I became ruined, incapacitated, or ostracized, her loyalty would be imprudent. Finally, the object of her loyalty is aesthetically unappealing (looking something like a cross between a monkey and a squirrel).

The necessary response equivalence:

> resenting lack of concern for my child is an instance of, or facilitates, feeling a negative non-reactive emotion at her faring poorly,

does not obtain. First, the *responses* themselves differ. The negative non-reactive emotions—such as anxiety, fear, grief, loss—lack resentment's distinctively communicative register. Because resentment concerns how another person regards what we care about, it lays claim to responses from that person: apology, acknowledgement, respect, and so on. Because non-reactive emotions concern simply what happens to what we care about, by contrast, they do not demand anything from anyone. They merely celebrate or lament the course that events take. Second, they are responses to different *things*. If some malevolent no longer has the power to harm my child, then I have reason for resentment, but not for anxiety. And if good intentions, or mindless nature, harm her, then I have reason for grief, but not for resentment. One might put the point this way: the non-reactive emotions and the reactive emotions are addressed to different *dimensions* of importance.[11] It matters to us not only that certain people and things *fare well in nature*: that they escape harm, flourish, and so on. It matters to us also that they be *properly regarded by others*.

Why, then, do we take the fact that I have reason to care about my child, but not about the parasite, to explain why I have reason to *resent* lack of concern for my child, but not lack of concern for the parasite?[12] Because, it seems, we accept the more general principle that:

> one has reason to *resent* decisions that aim at, or fail to prevent, events or conditions about which one would have reason to feel *negative non-reactive* emotions.[13]

---

[11] 'Importance' is meant here as a broad covering term. Something is important if it is something of value or disvalue, or if it affects reasons for positive or negative responses.

[12] I am trying to state the question neutrally, although it could be stated in terms of the contractualism of T. M. Scanlon, *What We Owe to Each Other* (Cambridge: Harvard University Press, 1998), to which I am sympathetic. Why do I have reason to *resent*, rather than feel *grateful* for, a willingness to act in such a way that a principle permitting such actions could be reasonably rejected on the basis of what people in my position would have reason to *want* (where wanting, when fully spelled out, might simply consist in a disposition to experience such emotions)?

[13] There is more to it than this, of course. First, the action must lack a certain kind of justification. Second, the events and conditions must involve things that are specially related to oneself: things that one has *agent-relative* reason, which others lack, to feel certain non-reactive emotions about. Otherwise, one would have reason to feel indignation, not resentment. Finally, one can also have reason to resent decisions that do not aim at any natural event or condition, such as decisions to treat one unfairly. The point is only that, where there *is* a corresponding natural event or condition, it is one about which one has reason to feel *negative* non-reactive emotions.

But what explains this principle? Why shouldn't one have reason to resent decisions that aim at events about which one would have reason to feel *positive* non-reactive emotions? The underlying thought, as I shall put it, is that reactive emotions should *resonate* with non-reactive emotions.

> *Resonance of reactive emotions*: one has reason to respond to a *decision* by which someone expresses an intention (or a lack of concern to prevent) that X fare a certain way with a *reactive* emotion that is similar to the *non-reactive* emotions with which one has reason to respond to X's *actually faring that way*, but that reflects the distinctive importance of how *others regard* what one cares about.

Reactive emotions should be 'similar' to non-reactive emotions at very least by sharing their 'valence'.[14] For example, since I have reason for *negative non-reactive* emotions, such as grief, when something *bad* happens to my child, I likewise have reason for *negative reactive* emotions, such as resentment, when *someone's decision* aims for that bad thing to happen (or does not take care to prevent its happening). Since I have no reason for negative non-reactive emotions when something bad happens to the parasite, I have no reason for negative reactive emotions when someone's decision aims for it to happen.

Here is another example of resonance. Certain aims are *agent-neutrally* important. That is to say that everyone has reason to respond to them in certain ways: reason not to impede their advancement, reason to hope that they progress, or simply reason not to deny or disparage their worth.[15] However, when one has a *personal history* with a particular aim, when it has been, say, one's life's work to advance it, then that aim takes on a further dimension of *agent-relative* importance. One has reason, which others lack, to care specially whether *that* aim is advanced: to care more about it than one does about other, equally worthy, aims with which one shares no history. And one may also have reason, which others lack, to care specially whether one advances the aim *oneself*: reason, for example, to care whether someone else, even if equally qualified, replaces one in one's life's work.[16]

---

[14] I do not have a general account of the difference between 'positive' and 'negative' responses to offer. I am here just relying on our shared intuitive grasp of the difference. The similarity is not restricted to valence. For example, n. 19. and the preceding text describe more substantive ways in which the responses called for by a discrete encounter are similar to the responses called for by a shared history of encounter.

[15] Compare the reasons for respect discussed by Joseph Raz, *Value, Respect, and Attachment* (Cambridge: Cambridge University Press, 2001).

[16] This may be the phenomenon that Harry Frankfurt, 'On Caring', in *Necessity, Volition, and Love* (Cambridge: Cambridge University Press, 1999), pp. 155–80, has in mind when he writes, 'certain

Here a similar request for explanation arises: why do some personal histories provide these agent-relative reasons whereas others do not? Why has a researcher who has spent years pursuing a cure for some disease reason to care whether he succeeds, whereas a lunatic who has spent years counting blades of grass on the asylum grounds has not? The explanation has something to do with the fact that the cure is agent-neutrally important, whereas knowledge of the sum is not. But again the explanation cannot proceed by deduction or facilitation from a response equivalence. There is no response equivalence, since the agent-relative importance that finding a cure has for the researcher goes beyond its agent-neutral importance for the rest of us. Again, I think, the explanation is to be found in resonance.

> *Resonance of personal aims:* one has reason to respond to a *history* of pursuing some aim with a concern for that aim, and one's pursuit of it, that is similar to the responses that one has reason to give that *aim apart from such a history*, but that reflects the distinctive importance of a personal history.

The aim of finding a cure is agent-neutrally important for anyone—everyone has reason, say, to hope that it is achieved—and so the aim is agent-relatively important for the researcher—she has reason to feel elated when her work moves forward and defeated when it is set back. The aim of counting blades of grass is agent-neutrally pointless—no one has reason to care whether it is achieved—and so the aim is also agent-relatively pointless for the lunatic—he has no reason to care whether he fills another tally sheet.

The point can be generalized. Many things of agent-neutral importance, not only aims, can come to have agent-relative importance for us when we are personally related to them: when they are specially 'ours', in some sense.[17] The personal relation is often that of having a *history* of a certain kind with the thing: the history of *pursuing* an agent-neutrally important *aim*, the history of *engaging* with an agent-neutrally important *culture* or *institution*, or the history of experiencing some agent-neutrally important *adversity* or *loss*. But the personal relation might also be some ahistorical *situation* involving the thing. One might

---

kinds of activity—such as productive work—are inherently valuable not simply *in addition to* being instrumentally valuable but *precisely because of* their instrumental value' (p. 178). See also his 'On the Usefulness of Final Ends', in *Necessity, Volition, and Love*, pp. 82–94; and the ditch diggers described by David Wiggins, 'Truth, Invention, and the Meaning of Life', in *Needs, Values, Truth, Second Edition* (Oxford: Blackwell, 1991), pp. 87–137, at pp. 132–4.

[17] This is not to say that agent-relative importance is always explained by appeal to something of corresponding agent-neutral importance.

be *exposed* to some agent-neutrally important *adversity*, whether or not one has experienced it, or one might *have* some agent-neutrally important *trait* or *capacity*, whether or not one has manifested or exercised it. In all of these cases, the suggestion goes, the agent-relative importance of the thing for oneself resonates with its agent-neutral importance for anyone.

We have seen, then, several instances of the general phenomenon of:

> *Resonance*: one has reason to respond to X in a way that is similar to the way that one has reason to respond to its counterpart in another dimension of importance, but that reflects the distinctive importance of the dimension to which X belongs.[18]

A deeper explanation of resonance is elusive. One might suggest that if natural emotions were not to resonate with moral emotions, or if our responses to things with which we have a personal history were not to resonate with our responses to those things whether or not we have such a history, then our normative outlook would be, in a certain way, incoherent. We would thank those who deliberately sought to destroy what we most cherished, while resenting those who came to our aid. We would attach great meaning to our history of pursuing aims that we otherwise saw as trivial, while attaching no meaning to our history of pursuing aims that we otherwise saw as important. However, I wonder whether appealing to 'coherence' in this way gives us any deeper explanation. Our sense that such a normative outlook would be 'in a certain way incoherent' may simply be our expectation of resonance under another description.

3. Resonance and Relationships

In any event, our aim is not to explain why there is resonance, but to appeal to it to explain the List: why we have reasons for partiality in some relationships, but not in others. To do this, we first need a clearer view of what 'relationships'—that is, relationships of the sort with which the debate about partiality is concerned—are.

---

[18] A further instance of resonance may be the relation, explored by Thomas Hurka, *Virtue, Vice, and Value* (Oxford: Oxford University Press, 2001), between virtues and 'base-level' goods, such as pleasure, knowledge, and achievement. Although virtues are no less 'intrinsic values' than base-level goods, Hurka suggests, they stand in a systematic relation to base-level goods: roughly, virtues consist in 'loving' base-level goods for themselves. (Somewhat more precisely, virtues are defined recursively as love of what is intrinsically valuable (including base-level goods and virtues) for itself and hatred of what is intrinsically disvaluable (including base-level evils and virtues) for itself.)

3.1. Shared Histories of Encounter

Consider first *histories of encounter*. One person has an *encounter* with another person when the actions, attitudes, or reasons of one affect, or are about, the other. *Histories* of encounter are temporally extended patterns of encounter involving the same people. Such histories of encounter include, for example, the relationships between spouses, friends, and siblings.

The suggestion, then, is that the proper responses to a *history of encounter* should resonate with the proper responses to the *discrete encounters* of which it is composed. Take friendship. I share a friendship with someone when we share a history of encounters of certain kinds: aiding one another, confiding in one another, pursuing common interests, and so on. A discrete encounter of one of these kinds might occur outside the context of a friendship. For example, a stranger might aid me, intentionally, disinterestedly, and respecting my autonomy. This encounter would give me reason for gratitude, consisting in reciprocating, or in expressing my thanks, in some way proportional to the help received, with like disinterest and respect. Friendship is a history of, *inter alia*, encounters of aid. And friendship calls for, *inter alia*, feelings and actions that might naturally be seen as resonant with, *inter alia*, the gratitude that discrete encounters of aid call for.[19]

The natural worry is that this is really a reductionist explanation, by deduction, from a normative principle that is not itself a partiality principle. 'Friendship is just a series of encounters of mutual aid, and the partiality of friends is just the discharge of the sum of the debts of gratitude thereby incurred. In other words, the partiality principle:

one has reason for friendship toward one's friends,

is derived, by deduction, from the normative principle:

one has reason for gratitude toward people who have helped one,

and the fact that

one's friends are people who have helped one many times, and friendship is gratitude many times over.'

---

[19] I have focused on encounters of aid, but friendship is, of course, also constituted by encounters of other kinds, such as sharing confidences and pursuing joint interests. Discrete episodes of sharing confidences elicit trust, albeit limited. Discrete episodes of pursuing a joint interest elicit cooperation, albeit instrumental. According to resonance, therefore, friendship should provide reason for more open-ended trust and non-instrumental cooperation.

This is false to the phenomenon, I think, in ways that at first may seem overly subtle, but on reflection appear fundamental. Imagine a lone traveller, of a bygone age, making his way west. Along the way, he helps and is helped by the people dwelling in the places he passes through, creating and incurring various debts. Contrast him with a different traveller who helps and is helped in the same ways, but by one and the same companion throughout. The companioned traveller has reason for responses that are not simply the sum of the responses for which the companionless traveller has reason, but just re-focused, as it were, on a single person. The companionless traveller has accumulated a series of debts that he might repay and then move on. But things are not like that for the companioned traveller. He has reason for a concern for his friend's interests that is open-ended: that keeps no ledger and that asks only that like concern be reciprocated. And he has reason not to move on, but instead to sustain his friendship going forward. Their history together roots an expansive loyalty, in a way in which no string of encounters with a changing cast could. Such is the distinctive kind of importance that only a shared history with another person can have.

Our present proposal, generalizing a bit, is:

> *Resonance of histories of encounter*: one has reason to respond to a *history* of encounter in a way that is similar to the way that one has reason to respond to the *discrete* encounters of which it is composed, but that reflects the distinctive importance of a history shared with another person.[20]

It is hard to say, in general terms, what 'reflecting the distinctive importance of a shared history' is, because in any particular case it will depend on the responses called for by the particular discrete encounters of which the particular shared history is composed. In some cases, as we have seen, it takes the form of love or loyalty, because the relevant discrete encounters call for resonant responses, such as gratitude, trust, and cooperation. However, in other cases, as we shall see, reflecting the distinctive importance of a shared history cannot

[20] 'Suppose that someone benefits me time and again, without any reciprocation', one might worry. 'If these discrete encounters give me debts of gratitude, then why should not the shared history of these encounters give me reason for friendship, or something like it, toward this benefactor?' If one is troubled by the suggestion that a friendship might be imposed on one unilaterally in this way, it is probably because one imagines that these discrete benefactions are either invasive or servile—as they most probably would be. But if they are invasive or servile, then they do not give one reason for gratitude. So resonance would not imply that a history of such encounters gives one reason for friendship, or something like it. Things might be different, say, when one castaway nurses another back to health after being shipwrecked on a desert isle. But in this case it does not seem so troubling that this shared history gives the beneficiary reason for partiality.

take this form, because it resonates with discrete encounters that call for no responses at all, or for responses of rejection.[21]

3.2. *Common Personal Histories and Situations*

Another important class of relationships is constituted by personal histories or situations of the kind discussed in Section 2: for example, the personal history of pursuing an aim, or enduring some trial. I share a *personal history or situation* with someone just when she and I each have a personal history or situation of the same kind, involving the same thing. We may share this personal history or situation even if we have never had any encounter. For example, I may have a personal history of engaging with a particular culture, having been initiated into its traditions and lived its way of life. This personal history gives me reason to continue engaging with, and seeking to preserve, the culture. By facilitation, I may already have reason to care whether others have a personal history of the same kind. It will be easier for me to engage with, and preserve, the culture if others do as well. But the fact that we share this history, it is ordinarily thought, provides us with reason for a partiality that goes beyond this. It gives me reason for a kind of solidarity with them. If I were to betray the culture, for example, I would have reason to feel not only that I had betrayed it, but also that I had betrayed them.

> *Resonance of common personal history or situation*: one has reason to respond to a *common personal history* with, or *situation* involving, a thing in a way that is similar to the way one has reason to respond to the *personal history* or *situation* itself, but that reflects the distinctive importance of sharing a personal history or situation with another person.

As before, what 'reflecting the distinctive importance of sharing a personal history or situation with another person' comes to in any particular case depends on the personal history or situation in question. In some cases, as we have seen, it takes the form of a *solidarity* that is specially focused on the thing with which one has that history or situation. If what one shares is a history of engagement with an institution, for example, then the solidarity is focused on the survival and functioning of the institution. For example, one owes it to the others to close ranks in defence of the institution, but not necessarily to see to it that their lives go well in other ways. If the personal relation is of

---

[21] Strictly speaking, it resonates with the responses, not the encounters. But putting it this way makes the sentence almost unparsable.

experiencing, or being exposed to, adversity—to take an example that will be important for what follows—then the solidarity is tied to efforts to recognize, alleviate, or overcome the effects of that particular adversity. As we shall now see, however, in other cases, reflecting the distinctive importance of a common personal history or situation cannot take this form, because it must resonate with a personal history or situation that calls either for no responses at all, or for responses of rejection.

4. Relationships that do not Provide Reasons for Partiality

Our question, again, is whether resonance explains why there is reason for certain kinds of partiality, but not for others. So far we have seen how it might explain why certain partiality principles are *on* the List. Now we need to ask whether resonance can explain why certain other (possible) partiality principles are *off* the List.

4.1. Trivial Relationships

The easiest cases are the countless trivial interpersonal relationships that no one imagines provide reasons for partiality. The fact that someone always gets off the train at the station where I get on, or that I have a kidney of the same weight as his, do not provide reasons for partiality. Resonance explains this straightforwardly. Neither the discrete encounter of boarding a train that another is leaving, nor the personal situation of having a kidney of a specific weight, matters. One has no reason to respond to this encounter, or to this personal situation, in any particular way. Thus, according to resonance, one has no reason to respond in any particular way to the corresponding history of encounter, or common personal situation. There is, so to speak, nothing for partiality to resonate with.[22]

---

[22] Keller, 'Making Nonsense of Loyalty to Country', asks why loyalty to a coffee mug, or to a group of people whose names start with 'P', involves a kind of error. Because, he answers, it involves mistaking 'the object of loyalty to be something with which you could share a relationship of mutual recognition and care'. The same error, he provocatively suggests, is involved in loyalty to country. In contrast, I think that one can have reason for partiality to persons (such as an autistic child) or things (such as one's life's work) with whom or which one cannot share a relationship of mutual recognition and care. So I prefer the explanation in the text: the encounters one has with one's coffee mug, and the situation one shares with other people whose names start with 'P', are trivial.

4.2. Externally and Internally Negative Relationships

The same cannot be said of what we might call *negative* relationships, however. Consider, first, *externally* negative relationships, which are either (i) shared histories of encounter in which relatives jointly wrong some non-relative, or unjustifiably disrespect or harm some thing of value, or (ii) common personal histories in which relatives have individually wronged some non-relative, or unjustifiably disrespected or harmed something of value. Examples are the relationships between members of the same prison gang, secret police, fascist party, military *junta*, terrorist cell, concentration-camp detail, polluting industrial concern, or iconoclastic cult (these last two being examples of harming things, rather than necessarily wronging people). Consider, second, *internally* negative relationships, which are composed of discrete encounters in which one relative wrongs the other. Examples are the relationships between master and slave, pimp and prostitute, abusive husband and abused wife, exploitative boss and exploited worker, or enemy and enemy. One surely has reason to respond to the discrete encounters and personal histories that constitute these relationships. So, according to resonance, one should have reason to respond to the relationships themselves. Yet this may seem like precisely the result that we sought to avoid: that these relationships do provide reasons.

While resonance may imply that *externally* negative relationships provide reasons, however, these are not reasons for *partiality*. One does not have reason to respond to discrete encounters, or a personal history, of wronging others, or harming something of value, by continuing to do so. Instead, one has reason to feel guilt, to repair the damage, and so on. According to resonance, one has reason to respond to an externally negative relationship with responses that are similar to these, but that reflect the distinctive importance of a shared history with another person. Perhaps this means seeing to it that one's relatives make amends. Or perhaps it means distancing oneself from them, just as one might have reason to distance oneself from one's own past history of wrongdoing. Either way, it means not sustaining, but rather undoing, these relationships (at least *as* externally negative relationships). Of course, a *particular* relationship may belong to more than one *type* of relationship, or may share constituents with another particular that belongs to a different type. Thus two people who share an externally negative relationship may also share a friendship, or some other kind of camaraderie or collegiality. In such cases, they would have conflicting reasons arising from both types of relationship.

There is a more basic problem with the idea that *internally* negative relationships might provide reason for partiality. It seems to offend against a generalization of the principle of ought implies can: that it be possible, at least in principle, for every participant in a relationship to respond to the reasons that that relationship gives them. This is not possible when the relationship is internally negative and the putative reasons are reasons of partiality. If the *wrongdoer* responds to his (putative) reason of partiality to *care* about his relative, then he *ends* the internally negative relationship, thereby failing to respond to his (putative) reason of partiality to *sustain* that relationship.

The worry about internally negative relationships, I take it, is not that they provide reason for partiality, but instead that they provide reason for, as it were, partiality's negative image. The worry is that the master–slave relationship, say, gives slave reason to submit to master, and master to exploit slave. As Katja Vogt puts it: 'Have we just as much reason to harm our enemies as we have to help our friends?'[23]

A discrete encounter of wrongdoing, again, gives the wrongdoer reason to feel guilt, to make reparations, and to seek forgiveness. It gives the wronged victim reason to feel resentment, to seek reparations, and to demand apology. It may also give the victim reason for other hostile or distancing responses, such as ceasing to wish the wrongdoer well, or refusing to trust and cooperate with him. I assume, however, that it does not give the victim reason for retribution, or reason of any other kind to *harm* the wrongdoer. Therefore, whatever resonance implies, it is not that an internally negative relationship gives the wrongdoer reason to *continue* wronging the victim, or the victim either reason to *submit* to it, or, alternatively, reason to *seek vengeance*. If anything, resonance implies the opposite: that the wrongdoer has reason to make amends, and that the victim has reason to stand up for herself, but not to pursue retribution. For wrongdoer and victim to respond to these reasons just is for them to end the relationship.[24]

I have been trying to dispel the worry that resonance implies that negative relationships provide reasons for certain objectionable responses. In doing so, I have made some assumptions about the responses called for by the discrete

[23] 'Haben wir ebenso viel Grund, dem Feind zu schaden, wie wir Grund haben, dem Freund zu helfen?' 'Freundschaft, Unparteilichkeit und Feindschaft', p. 525. Vogt reminds us that this view was commonplace in antiquity, referring, in particular, to the exchange between Socrates and Polemarchus in *Republic*, Book I. I am also indebted to Hans Sluga, who put the same question to me, referring to the same text, after a talk some years ago.

[24] Some relationships may involve conflict or opposition, but no wrongdoing. Consider competitors in sports or adversaries at law (such as an assistant DA and public defender who confront one another regularly in court), who have long played by the rules of a permissible contest. Discrete encounters of this kind provide no reason for reparation or resentment. Perhaps they are really instances of an abstract form of collaboration, in which cooperation at one level makes possible competition at another. Resonance might therefore imply that a shared history of such encounters provides reason for respect and fair dealing. But this consequence does not seem objectionable.

encounters, or personal histories, of which these negative relationships are composed. All that matters for the dialectic is that those who find these responses objectionable also find these assumptions plausible. No doubt, other assumptions can be made. Imagine a warrior code according to which a raid on a neighbouring tribe gives the raiders no reason to make amends, but gives their neighbours reason to take revenge. When applied to such a code, resonance might well imply that enmity—the history of blood debts issued and collected—gives one reason to harm one's enemy. But this is no objection to resonance. For no one who is troubled by the implication, namely that enmity gives one reason to harm one's enemy, subscribes to such a code.[25]

4.3. Racism and Racial Partiality

The challenge that we have been considering is often dramatized in the following way: unless we explain why partiality to members of the same race belongs off the List, we commit ourselves to racism.[26] As it stands, however, this a category mistake. Racism is, in one way or another, organized around the belief that one race is superior to others.[27] The belief that one race is

---

[25] Among extant treatments of the subject, the one closest to the view discussed here is Thomas Hurka, 'The Justification of National Partiality', in Robert McKim and Jeff McMahan, *The Morality of Nationalism* (Oxford: Oxford University Press, 1997), pp. 139–57; at p. 152:

Some activities and states of people, most notably their doing good or suffering evil, call for a positive, caring, or associative response. Others, such as their doing evil, call for a negative or dissociative response. Partiality between people is appropriate when they have shared history of doing good, either reciprocally or to others, partiality between them in the present is a way of honouring that good fact about their past. (This is why partiality among former SS colleagues is troubling; it seems to honour a past that properly calls for dishonour.)

See also Thomas Hurka, *Virtue, Vice, and Value*, pp. 200–4. The suggestion that the relevant shared histories are either of 'suffering evil' together, or of 'doing good' together, however, is too restrictive. For example, parents need not do good together, or suffer evil together, with their young children.

[26] Compare Cottingham, 'Partiality, Favouritism, and Morality'; Andrew Oldenquist, 'Loyalties', *Journal of Philosophy* 79 (1982), pp. 173–93, at pp. 176–7; Wellman, 'Relational Facts'; and Zangwill, 'Against Analytic Moral Functionalism'. Kwame Anthony Appiah, 'Racisms', in *Anatomy of Racism*, ed. David Theo Goldberg (Minneapolis, MN: University of Minnesota Press, 1990) also tends to confuse racism (at least of the 'intrinsic' form) with the belief that there is reason for partiality to members of the same race, as does Paul Gomberg, 'Patriotism is Like Racism', *Ethics* 101 (1990), pp. 144–50.

Some of the discussion of this section applies similarly to other forms of group chauvinism, such as sexism.

[27] A standard dictionary definition of 'racism', for example, is: 'a doctrine or teaching, without scientific support, that claims to find racial differences in character, intelligence, etc., that asserts the superiority of one race over another or others'. *Webster's New World Dictionary, Third College Edition* (New York: Webster's, 1988), s.v. 'racism'. No doubt this is too narrow a definition, since racism is not limited to explicit doctrines or teachings. As the phrase 'in one way or another, organized around the belief' is meant to acknowledge, racist attitudes and practices are often far less directly connected to

superior neither implies, nor is implied by, the belief that there is reason for partiality to members of one's race. When agent and beneficiary belong to the allegedly superior race, it may be hard to see the practical difference between these beliefs. But the difference is evident in other contexts. If there is reason for partiality to members of one's race, then members of the allegedly inferior race do *not* have reason for partiality to members of the allegedly superior race, but they *do* have reason for partiality to one another. According to the racist, by contrast, members of the inferior race *do* have reason for deference, submission, etc. to members of the superior race, but they do *not* have reason to do anything for one another. (For example, in so far as the antebellum slave owner thought that there was a rationale for slavery, and did not turn a deaf ear to questions of justification, he did not believe that this rationale gave slaves reason to assist one another in resisting him. Instead, he thought that slaves ought to recognize their inferiority in the eyes of God or the order of Nature, and acquiesce in what, given that inferiority, was a justified social arrangement.) Since the claim that there is reason for partiality to members of one's race is not racism, to claim that there is reason for partiality to relatives of certain kinds is not to incur some special burden to explain why racism is false. At any rate, the burden is easily discharged. No race is superior to others.

The challenge must be restated. Even if *racists* do not believe that there is reason for partiality to members of one's race, *someone* might believe this. Does resonance vindicate this belief? Since I share a race with many people whom I have never encountered, relationships of shared race are not histories of encounter. However, sharing a race might consist in sharing a personal history or situation. But *which* personal history or situation? I take it that members of the same race share no biologically interesting essence. And I take it that the manifest ethnic and cultural diversity within familiar racial classifications shows that members of the same race do not share a personal history with some common ethnic or cultural heritage. Two possibilities seem to remain. On the *somatic basis* view, the personal history or situation is that of having (or, following the 'one-drop rule', being the genetic descendant of people who

the belief in racial superiority: a fact that helps to explain their resilience. For discussion, see Tommie Shelby, 'Ideology, Racism, and Critical Social Theory', *The Philosophical Forum* 34 (2003), pp. 153–88. The claim is only *that* some connection to such a belief is constitutive. For criticism of even this weaker claim, see the work of Jorge Garcia—his 'Racism and Racial Discourse', *The Philosophical Forum* 32 (2001), pp. 125–45, gives a succinct summary—and Josh Glasgow, 'Racism as Disrespect' (unpublished). For a response to Garcia, to which I am sympathetic, see Tommie Shelby, 'Is Racism in the "Heart"?' *Journal of Social Philosophy* 33 (2002), pp. 411–20. At any rate, even on Garcia's and Glasgow's alternative conceptions, racism is not distinguished by a belief that everyone has reasons to be partial to members of his or her own race. So their criticism does not affect the main point that I am making here.

had) the superficial, physiognomic traits by which members of a given race are classified. On the *social consequence* view, the personal history or situation is that of experiencing, or at least of being exposed to,[28] the social consequences of that racial classification.

Having the somatic basis associated with a certain racial classification is, in itself, of no significance. Like having attached earlobes, or a widow's peak, it provides no distinctive reasons. So, according to resonance, sharing this personal situation with another provides no distinctive reasons. The social consequences of racial classification, by contrast, are far from trivial. Since different racial classifications have different social consequences, members of different races have different kinds of personal histories and situations. American blacks, for example, share a personal experience of, or exposure to, a specific kind of adversity, namely, that of being mistreated because of their racial classification.[29] In general, a personal history of adversity gives one reason to honour what the adversity destroyed and to repair what it harmed. To the extent that some part of oneself was harmed, then one's efforts at repair will be focused, to that extent, on oneself. According to resonance, therefore, a common history of adversity provides reasons to work with, or minister to, other people who faced adversity of the same kind, in order to honour, repair, and preserve the things at which it struck, including aspects of those other people themselves. This does not seem an implausible conclusion, at least if the widespread acceptance of organizations such as the NAACP and of the sense of solidarity that they embody is any guide.

Why, then, does the relationship of shared *whiteness* not likewise give whites reason to minister specially to the needs of other whites? Why should we not welcome equally an NAA*W*P? Because whites do not share, as whites, a personal experience of, or exposure to, mistreatment on the basis of their classification as whites. If they share a personal history or situation as whites, it is that of fostering, acquiescing in, or at very least benefiting from, the practice of mistreating blacks (and others) on the basis of their racial classification. While such a personal history or situation might provide some reasons, they would be reasons to repudiate benefits received and to ameliorate harm done. So the common personal history or situation of whites would not provide reasons for the same sort of responses as the common personal history or situation of blacks.[30]

---

[28] As noted earlier, one can be exposed to adverse social consequences without yet having experienced them.

[29] This understanding of the relevant relationship is heavily indebted to Tommie Shelby, *We Who Are Dark: Philosophical Foundations of Black Solidarity* (Cambridge, MA: Harvard University Press, 2005).

[30] Compare Hurka, 'The Justification of National Partiality', p. 152. Of course, racist organizations often appeal to the rhetoric of adversity (e.g. 'Too long have whites sat back while their rights have

One might object that this explanation is circular. 'How have blacks been mistreated? By being excluded from the partiality that whites show other whites. But to call this "mistreatment" is already to assume that whites have no reason for partiality to other whites. And this is precisely what you set out to explain.' The reply is that blacks have been mistreated in ways (e.g. slavery, disenfranchisement, their enduring effects) that went, and go, far beyond merely being excluded from favours that whites may have done one another. Moreover, this mistreatment was born of, and still is largely sustained by, the doctrine, objectionable in itself, that blacks are inferior.

'But indulge in a fantasy that unburdens us of our past,' the objector will counter.

> Those who would be classified as white have lived together, with peace and justice, as political and economic equals, with those would be classified as blacks. Suppose that, in this world, whites were partial to other whites. To claim that whites had no reason for this partiality, you would have to claim that they were mistreating blacks. But in order to call it mistreatment, you would have already to have assumed that they have no reason for this partiality.

The reply here is that we do not need to claim that whites would be mistreating blacks in order to explain why whites would not have reason for such partiality. Once we strip away the social consequences that our collective past attaches to whiteness, shared whiteness is just a shared somatic basis, which, as we saw earlier, provides no reasons.

5. Implications

I end with a few words about what this account implies about the broader debate about partiality.

5.1. Partiality in Other Relationships

Thus far, I have tested the account by considering relationships that relatively uncontroversially belong on the List, or off it. One hopes, however, that once calibrated against less controversial cases, the account might then provide guidance about more controversial ones. Among these more controversial

---

been taken from them'). Perhaps this betrays some dim recognition of the justificatory power of a common history of adversity.

relationships, co-citizenship has attracted perhaps the most interest recently, no doubt because of the profound differences in the actual treatment of co-citizens and non-citizens. In the present framework, co-citizenship might be understood as a common personal history of involvement with the institutions of the state. The responses for which this common personal history gives reason should resonate with the responses for which the personal histories give reason. And these responses should resonate, in turn, with the responses for which the institutions provide reason, apart from any history. It would take another chapter to explore what this would imply in any detail. In broad outline, though, it would seem to suggest that the responses that co-citizenship calls for will depend on an independent appraisal of the value or disvalue, justice or injustice, of the state in question—and, indeed, of states in general.

5.2. Other Objections to Non-reductionism

I have aimed to defend non-reductionism against only one objection: that it cannot explain the List. While other objections are possible, this defence suggests that these objections are not available to certain philosophers, namely, those who accept that there are reasons for reactive emotions, or reasons to respond to personal histories or situations. There is something unstable, or at least unmotivated, about accepting that discrete encounters can give us reasons for reactive emotions while denying that the histories that those encounters compose can give us reason for partiality, or in accepting that personal histories or situations can give us reason while denying that sharing them can. To accept that there are reasons for resentment, guilt, and gratitude, or that personal histories or situations can have agent-relative importance, is to accept that there are agent-relative reasons. And to accept that there are reasons for the reactive emotions, which are keyed to reasons for the non-reactive emotions, or to accept that there are reasons to respond to personal histories and situations, which are informed by the agent-neutral importance of the aims, institutions, or sufferings that they involve, is to accept the phenomenon of resonance. Provided there is intuitive support for the claim that relationships of these kinds provide reason for partiality, therefore, it is obscure what theoretical basis for denying it might remain.

5.3. Partiality and Other Norms

Finally, this account may shed some light on the troubled relationship between partiality and other norms. Most important among these are the norms of impartial morality: what we owe to others whether or not we share any special relationship with them. But partiality can also come into competition with other norms, which do not reflect what we owe anyone, but instead govern how we are to relate to things of impersonal value, such as cultural achievements and the natural environment. Proper responses to shared histories of encounter, I have suggested, resonate with proper responses to discrete encounters. And the proper responses to discrete encounters are largely the province of impartial morality. Similarly, proper responses to common personal histories and situations resonate with proper responses to personal histories and situations. And proper responses to personal histories and situations are informed by other norms: by the importance, moral or otherwise, of the aims, institutions, experiences, etc. that they involve. This does not mean that reasons for partiality cannot conflict, in particular cases, with other norms. But it does mean that partiality does not represent an outlook somehow divorced from, or incompatible with, them.[31] On the contrary, it draws its content from other norms.

A consequence of this, which I end by noting, is to raise the stakes of a much-discussed complaint: that certain conceptions of impartial morality, such as consequentialism, are overly demanding, because they would morally prohibit responding to reasons of partiality, such as those of friendship.[32] If consequentialism is true, then departures from maximizing the agent-neutral good are instances of wrongdoing. So, if consequentialism is true, the discrete encounters of which friendship is composed are, in all but rare cases, instances of wrongdoing. So, if consequentialism is true, friendship is an externally negative relationship, which provides no reason for partiality. So, if consequentialism is true, there *are no* reasons of friendship in the first place. However, the point cuts both ways. If there *are* reasons of friendship, then it follows immediately that consequentialism is false.

---

[31] Contrast Alasdair MacIntyre, 'Is Patriotism a Virtue?', *Lindley Lecture* (University of Kansas, 1984).

[32] Arguably, this complaint cannot be brought against indirect forms of consequentialism, such as those explored by Derek Parfit, *Reasons and Persons* (Oxford: Oxford University Press, 1984), pt 1; and Peter Railton, 'Alienation, Consequentialism, and the Demands of Morality', *Philosophy & Public Affairs* 13 (1984), pp. 134–71. If so, then the discussion that follows does not apply to such forms of consequentialism.

9

Fairness and Non-Compliance*

MICHAEL RIDGE

In some contexts, moral obligations are plausibly understood in the first-person plural—as owed by *us*.[1] For example, if my spouse and I together promise our son to take him to his friend's house on Mondays then *we* incur an obligation to him. Equally plausible is the idea that if obligations are held in common, then the burdens of discharging them should be fairly divided. Just what constitutes a fair division of such burdens is a good question in what John Rawls called 'ideal theory', the relevant idealization being that everyone does their fair share.[2] For present purposes, I remain neutral about the difficult question of what constitutes a fair division of burdens in conditions of full compliance. Some philosophers have argued that fairness should not really be understood as a substantive value that is fundamentally distinct from the values of consistent and impartial application of rules, fidelity, and proportionality.[3] While I do here assume that fairness can matter morally in its own right, this is compatible with taking fairness in these contexts to consist primarily in some sort of proportionality (of welfare to required sacrifice, e.g.). So my argument may be compatible with such deflationist accounts of the nature of fairness. Rather than rely on a particular conception of fairness and its importance, I instead rely on what I take to be commonly held moral intuitions about which outcomes would be fair. These first-order intuitions are, I hope, compatible with a wide range of background theories about the fundamental nature and value of fairness.

* Thanks to the participants of the University of Edinburgh Work In Progress Series, the participants in the York Political Theory Group, the participants of the Reading workshop on Impartiality at which a version of this chapter was presented, Brad Hooker, Keith Horton, Liam Murphy, Bill Pollard, Sean McKeever, Hannah Wildman, and two anonymous referees for helpful discussion.

[1] For further discussion of the importance of the first-person plural for moral deliberation, see Gerald Postema, 'Morality in the First Person Plural', *Law and Philosophy* 14 (1995), pp. 35–64.

[2] See John Rawls, *A Theory of Justice* (Cambridge, MA: Belknap Division of the Harvard University Press, 1971).

[3] See especially Brad Hooker, *Ideal Code, Real World* (Oxford: Oxford University Press, 2000), pp. 45–55.

Sadly, on any plausible conception of fairness, people all too often do not do their fair share. The non-compliance of others can leave the conscientious moral agent with the moral conundrum of what to do when those with whom he jointly holds a moral obligation fail to do their fair share. The question is of very general interest, but is perhaps especially urgent in the case of the jointly held obligation of those in the affluent West to provide much-needed and highly cost-effective assistance to those in less fortunate circumstances suffering in what Robert McNamara characterizes as 'absolute poverty'.[4] In McNamara's terms, such people lead lives 'so characterized by malnutrition, illiteracy, disease, squalid surroundings, high infant mortality and low life expectancy as to be beneath any reasonable definition of human decency'.[5] When hundreds of millions of people must live on less than the equivalent of $1.00 per day and unsurprisingly lead lives that are nasty, brutish, and short, it is very plausible to suppose that the citizens of the industrialized West, who are grotesquely wealthy by global standards, have a collective obligation to help the less fortunate. The philosophical case for this conclusion has been made at length, and I shall not repeat the main moves of that dialectic here.[6] The point here is that this obligation is very plausibly understood as one that is owed by *us*, yet one that many (most) of us do not do our fair share to discharge. It therefore offers a useful and morally important test case for the view I shall develop.

Ideally, the burdens of fulfilling this obligation to the poor would be divided fairly, with very wealthy people devoting a higher percentage of their income and wealth to meeting the obligation than average middle-class citizens of industrialized nations of the West. Given full compliance, the burden on any one person certainly would not require giving virtually everything to charity, and on some accounts the burdens on each individual would actually be quite small. However, our actual conditions are in this sense very far from ideal. Most affluent people give nothing or next to nothing to help those in absolute poverty, and hence fall far short of doing their fair share to meet this jointly held obligation. This puts the problem of how an individual should act in conditions of partial compliance in stark relief. Philosophers like Peter Unger and Peter Singer argue that in these circumstances the morally decent agent must give away virtually everything to help those in such great need, simply because the needs of the less fortunate are so much greater and more urgent than the needs of the relatively affluent.

---

[4] See Robert McNamara, *Annual Meeting of the World Bank, IFC/IDA* (1976), p. 14, and Peter Singer, *Practical Ethics* (Cambridge: Cambridge University Press, 1979), ch. 8.

[5] See Robert McNamara, *World Development Report* (Washington, DC: World Bank, 1978), p. iii.

[6] See, e.g., Singer, *Practical Ethics*, ch. 8, and Peter Unger, *Living High and Letting Die: Our Illusion of Innocence* (New York: Oxford University Press, 1996).

As compelling as these arguments are, they seem simply to ignore the issue of fairness, an issue that after all seems so obviously relevant when we are thinking about our obligations in conditions of full compliance.[7] Yet if how much I should do in circumstances of full compliance is a function of what would be my fair share, then surely considerations of fairness should play *some* role in determining my obligations in conditions of partial compliance too, or so one might reasonably suppose, anyway. Why, the conscientious agent might well ask, should I be expected to pick up the enormous slack left by the non-compliance of others? Surely the most one could reasonably demand is that I do my fair share, where fair shares are defined in terms of full compliance. If others do not do their fair share, then they, and not I, am to blame for that. Doing their fair share as well as my own might be morally virtuous, but it can hardly be my duty. These intuitions are powerful, and Liam Murphy has recently defended a set of moral principles that are meant to vindicate those intuitions. Very roughly, Murphy argues that in conditions of partial compliance a person is never morally required to sacrifice so much that he would thereby end up less well off than he would have been under full compliance from then onwards.[8] Murphy calls his principle the 'collective principle', since it emphasizes the idea that our obligations are held in common, and I shall here follow his terminology.

However, the collective principle's interpretation of the role of fairness itself seems problematic. For just as a conscientious agent in the affluent West can reasonably complain about the unfairness of being forced to do more than his fair share, those living in absolute poverty can reasonably complain that it is unfair for them to be forced to bear the entire brunt of the non-compliance of those who shirk their duties. Why should those who are already so much worse

[7] Of course, Singer and Unger could acknowledge the value of fairness and argue that the demands of beneficence trump considerations of fairness in some way, and some of their examples might well be deployed to bolster this idea. Still, so far as I know, they do not confront the issue of unfair demands directly. Furthermore, even if this trumping suggestion is right (and I do not at this stage mean to suggest that it is), it remains important to get the overall map of the overall moral terrain correct, including even moral reasons that are trumped by other considerations in the particular case of duties of beneficence to those in absolute poverty. Moreover, in other situations in which the stakes are not nearly so high as in the case of absolute poverty, it will not be nearly so plausible to suppose that other reasons trump considerations of fairness, which gives us a more general reason to become clear about how fairness functions in these contexts. Thanks very much to Keith Horton for prompting me to discuss this point in more detail.

[8] See Liam Murphy, *Moral Demands in Nonideal Theory* (Oxford: Oxford University Press, 2000). The characterization given in the text roughly paraphrases Murphy; see Murphy, *Moral Demands*, p. 87. Murphy takes Parfit's discussion of these issues in *Reasons and Persons* as his starting point, although Parfit himself does not endorse Murphy's conclusion. See Derek Parfit, *Reasons and Persons* (Oxford: Oxford University Press, 1984). Thanks to Brad Hooker for helpfully reminding me of the etiology of Murphy's views in Parfit's work.

off be forced to bear all of the negative consequences of the non-compliance of those who do not do their fair share, particularly when others who are much better off could in effect absorb some of those negative consequences by giving more? While the moral principles advocated by Singer and Unger seem to ignore the arguably unfair burdens imposed on the conscientious moral agent, the collective principle seems to ignore the arguably unfair burdens imposed on the poor.[9]

The upshot seems to be that in conditions of partial compliance, unfair burdens are simply inevitable; the question is just whether and to what extent they fall on moral agents or moral patients. What is not inevitable is any particular distribution of those unfair burdens. Unfairly imposed burdens can in general themselves be more or less fairly distributed. For example, a cruel teacher may always and quite unfairly single out two particular children to bear the burden of cleaning the blackboard while the other children head off to recess. This burden is unfair, in that these two children have done nothing to warrant being singled out. It does not follow, however, that this unfair burden cannot be more or less fairly distributed between them. All else being equal, if one child regularly did 90 per cent of the work while the other child idly daydreamt, then this would be a paradigmatically unfair division of the *already* unfairly imposed burdens shared by the two children.

My suggestion here is that this is how we should approach the issue of fairness in conditions of partial compliance. I agree with Murphy that fairness should supply an upper limit on an individual's obligation in conditions of partial compliance, at least all else being equal (fairness is, after all, plausibly only one value among many). However, that limit should not correspond to the burden the agent would be forced to bear under conditions of full compliance. Instead, fairness dictates that in conditions of partial compliance no agent can be required to do so much to make up for the non-compliance of others that he thereby bears more than his fair share *of the burdens of non-compliance*, or so I shall argue. In other words, we conceptualize the moral problem of partial compliance to provide a set of unfair burdens that are taken to be roughly analogous to the unfair burden imposed on the two children in my toy example. We can then decide how those admittedly unfair burdens should be divided, and fairness can be relevant here, just as it plausibly is in the case of the two children. Again, the point is that unfair burdens can themselves be more or less fairly distributed.

[9] Keith Horton, in an unpublished manuscript, very helpfully refers to this as the 'tu quoque' reply to Murphy. The basic point against Murphy is also made in passing in Susan Hurley, 'Fairness and Beneficence', *Ethics* 113 (2003), pp. 841–64.

The approach advocated here is a kind of compromise between uncon-strained beneficence (Singer and Unger) on the one hand, and beneficence as strictly constrained in conditions of partial compliance by fair shares under full compliance (Murphy) on the other. Like Murphy's account and unlike Singer's and Unger's account, the account offered here does take considerations of fairness seriously. However, like Singer's and Unger's account, and unlike Murphy's account, the account given here also insists that we may nonetheless sometimes have a moral duty to pick up at least some of the slack of those who do not fully comply. To put the point another way, on Singer's and Unger's account the perspective of those in absolute poverty seems to be complete-ly dominant in determining our duties in conditions of partial compliance, while on Murphy's account the perspective of the affluent seems much more dominant.[10] The account developed here attempts to give due weight to both of these perspectives. Ultimately, our actual moral obligations in the case of assistance to those in absolute poverty may turn out on the account offered here to be much closer to the extreme demands advocated by Unger and Singer than to the more moderate demands advocated by Murphy, although I shall not try to settle this difficult (and in large part empirical) issue here. Nonetheless, the account on offer is still in an important conceptual sense a compromise between the two positions, and the accounts certainly will diverge in their recommendations in a wide range of other cases of partial compliance. It is important to remember that the scope of the account developed here extends well beyond the particular case of helping those in absolute poverty. The account on offer addresses the more general issue of how to think about the obligations of any given individual who finds him- or herself in conditions of partial compliance with regard to some jointly held moral obligation. I focus on the case of absolute poverty simply because it is of enormous moral importance.

I

The idea that we can never be morally obligated to do more than our fair share in discharging our collectively held moral duties has a lot of intuitive support. To reject this idea seems to put the morally decent at the mercy of the morally lazy and irresponsible. Furthermore, the idea that we are never obligated to do

---

[10] Murphy himself no doubt would not characterize his position in such stark terms, and presumably would emphasize the importance of recognizing the agency of others. Nonetheless, this perspective does seem to give greater weight to considerations that do in fact work to the advantage of the affluent and that presumably would naturally seem more salient to the affluent for that reason.

more than our fair share in such cases is compatible with the idea that it would be morally virtuous but 'above and beyond the call of duty' to do more. In spite of its initial plausibility, though, this idea cannot be sustained. Before explaining why this idea is indefensible, it is important to be clear about the dialectic. The suggestion is *not* that considerations of fairness provide moral reasons for us not to do more than our fair share. The idea is rather that considerations of fairness limit our other obligations by somehow functioning to transform what would otherwise be a moral reason underwriting an obligation into a moral reason that merely underwrites supererogation (roughly, going 'above and beyond the call of duty'). In the example of helping those in absolute poverty, the moral reason to give more is that it would help those in grave need—a reason of beneficence. The fact that giving more would constitute my giving more than my fair share is meant not to entirely defeat that moral reason of beneficence, so that it no longer functions as a reason at all. Rather, the fact about fairness is instead meant to transform my reason into the sort of reason that generates only supererogation rather than an obligation. Exactly how we should understand the distinction between reasons that ground obligations and reasons that ground supererogation is itself a very difficult topic, which for present purposes must be set to one side. The main point is that the issue here is whether considerations of fairness can transform moral reasons in this way in conditions of non-compliance. Different moral theories will provide different accounts of how fairness might function in this way.

Since this idea that considerations of fairness could somehow 'transform a reason' from one that grounds an obligation into one that grounds only supererogation might seem strange or obscure, so it is worth pausing to help put the idea in perspective. One theory (though certainly not the only one) that makes this sort of transformative role intelligible is contractualism of the sort defended by T. M. Scanlon.[11] On Scanlon's account, an action is morally required if and only if it would be required by principles for the general regulation of behaviour that nobody could reasonably reject. Scanlon allows that moral considerations like fairness can themselves provide reasonable grounds for rejection of principles. Within the contractualist framework, we might interpret the proposed role of fairness as providing those who would have to do more than their fair share with grounds on which they could reasonably reject any moral principle requiring them to do more—the fact that such principles would themselves be unfair to them would provide the basis for reasonably rejecting them. On this account, considerations of fairness provide a moral reason after all, but *not* a moral reason not to do more than

[11] *What We Owe to Each Other* (Cambridge, MA: Harvard University Press, 1998).

one's fair share. Rather, considerations of fairness provide a moral reason to reject a principle that would *require* one to do more. Such considerations might not, however, ground the reasonable rejection of moral principles that merely encourage one to do more in conditions of partial compliance. This idea of principles *encouraging* but not requiring actions would be one way in which Scanlon might extend his theory to handle the idea of supererogation. So far as I know, neither Scanlon nor Scanlonians have explicitly taken up this approach to supererogation, but it is natural enough once we think of moral principles as socially embodied. After all, socially embodied principles can provide 'carrots' for good behaviour as well as 'sticks' for violations of strict rules. I mention this Scanlonian approach to supererogation here only *en passant* to help fill out the idea of 'transforming' a reason from one of duty into one of supererogation, although I would like to develop the idea itself in more detail at some stage.

Having illustrated and clarified the role of fairness here in transforming reasons in this way, I now return to the main line of argument. When others default on their fair share of a collectively held moral obligation, some unfair burdens are inevitable—I here put to one side the lucky case in which fulfilling one's obligation is no burden at all. In particular, either one of two forms of unfairness will result. First, some of the other people who hold this collectively owed moral duty might pick up the slack of those who default. As Murphy's discussion emphasizes, this is unfair to those who pick up the slack. Second, though, if others do not pick up the slack of those who default on their fair shares, then a burden will be imposed on those to whom the collective duty is owed, and it is hard to resist the conclusion that this burden is unfairly imposed. In conditions in which some unfairness is inevitable, we should aim for the lesser of the evils. How, though, might we reasonably determine the lesser of the evils here?

The relevant evil is unfairly imposed burdens, and this evil is inevitable because of the non-compliance of some. Of course, we presumably should do our best to encourage or even (in some cases) force those who would otherwise not comply to do so. However, let us here focus on cases in which forcing compliance is either impossible, unduly costly, or objectionable on other moral grounds. When partial compliance is inevitable, we are faced with the problem that an unfair burden inevitably will be imposed upon someone—either those to whom the duty is owed or those who pick up the slack of those who default (the 'or' is inclusive). Our question, then, is how we should deal with a situation in which the imposition of unfair burdens is inevitable. One of the examples briefly discussed in the introduction provides a clue as to how we should deal with such situations.

Recall the case of the teacher who unfairly singles out two children from the rest of the class to clean the blackboard. These children have by hypothesis done nothing to deserve this burden, but there is no feasible way for them to avoid it either; parental intervention, we may assume, is unavailable. The case is one in which the non-compliance of one party (the teacher) makes the imposition of an unfair burden on others (the two children) inevitable. The only relevant difference between this case and the ones that are the focus of our discussion is that the teacher's obligation is not a collectively held one in which she fails to do her fair share, but rather an individually held one that she flouts altogether. As I suggested in the introduction, it seems obvious that the children should fairly distribute the unfair burdens imposed on them by the teacher. All else being equal, the children should divide the task evenly. The moral of this story seems to be that when unfair burdens are inevitable, those burdens should (all else being equal) be fairly distributed, and that is the principle I shall defend here. Call this the 'fair shares principle'.

Return now to cases in which some people fail to do their fair share in discharging a collectively held moral duty. We have seen that in most cases their non-compliance makes it inevitable that others bear unfair burdens. We might therefore call these unfairly imposed burdens the 'burdens of non-compliance'. Once we see the situation in this light, the analogy with the blackboard example should be obvious. Just as the unfair burdens imposed by the teacher should be fairly distributed (all else being equal), so should the unfairly imposed burdens of non-compliance. In which case, considerations of fairness do not seem to support the idea that under conditions of partial compliance an individual agent can never be morally required to do more than what would be his fair share under conditions of full compliance. For that would simply be to allow those to whom the duty is owed to absorb *all* of the unfair burdens imposed by those who do not comply. This would be analogous to one child doing all of the work to clean the blackboard while the other child daydreams, which hardly seems like a fair distribution of their unfairly imposed burden. Moreover, this approach seems *especially* unfair in the case of our obligations to those in absolute poverty, since those to whom the obligation is owed are already so much worse off than those who owe the obligation. For if only one side or the other should be forced to bear the full brunt of the burdens of non-compliance, it seems only decent that it should be the affluent rather than the destitute.

It will be helpful now to see how the fair shares principle works in a range of cases. First, consider again the example very briefly mentioned in the introduction in which two parents have promised their son to take him to visit his friend on Mondays. Suppose the father is a kind of 'deadbeat dad' who refuses ever to take the child to his friend's house with no excuse or justification. Moreover, we might add that the father is shameless about this and his unwillingness to do his fair share has damaged his relationship with his son. This addition to the story means that the mother will not be able to 'cover' for the father for the sake of their son. The father's unwillingness to take the son to his friend's house in effect imposes a burden of non-compliance on the mother and son. The natural extension of Murphy's collective principle to this case suggests that the mother can be morally required to do her fair share but no more, which in this case would be taking her son to his friend's house twice per month.

This seems implausible on a number of grounds. For a start, consider the implications in terms of pressuring the father to do more. Suppose that the mother finds it very burdensome to pressure the father to do his fair share—he becomes aggressive, belligerent, and very unpleasant, though (let us suppose) not dangerous—he is a deadbeat dad, but not a wife-beater. Moreover, the mother is very unsure whether the pressure will lead anywhere; she rationally thinks that the odds of success are not great. On the natural extension of the collective principle to this case it seems that the mother cannot even be morally required to pressure the father to do his fair share in addition to doing her own fair share.[12] For by hypothesis her pressuring the father would itself be burdensome, in which case her both pressuring the father to do more and taking the son to visit his friend twice per month would already impose a burden on her that is greater than the burden she would face under conditions of full compliance. Surely the son could reasonably complain that it is unfair for him to absorb all of the burdens of his father's unreasonable behaviour. At a minimum, his mother should do her best to get him to do his fair share while still doing her own fair share as well.

By contrast, the fair shares principle defended here can vindicate these intuitions. For the fairest of the available outcomes (keeping the father's non-compliance fixed, which precludes maximal fairness) would be for the burdens imposed by the father to be fairly distributed between the mother and son in so far as those burdens really are inevitable. This means that the mother has a moral obligation to do more to help get her son to his friend's house

---

[12] The point against Murphy must be cast in terms of the 'natural extension of Murphy's account' rather than in terms of Murphy's own account, for Murphy explicitly limits his account to jointly held obligations of beneficence, and the obligation in question here is an obligation of fidelity. However, Murphy's reason for restricting his account to obligations of beneficence is that only in the case of beneficence do we have a jointly held moral obligation. As he puts it, 'We could say, somewhat tendentiously, that a principle of beneficence is directed to agents as a group, whereas other moral principles are directed to agents individually' (Murphy, *Moral Demands*, p. 73).

than simply taking him twice a month, which would be her fair share given full compliance. Whether this is best done by pressuring the father or taking the child more frequently herself or some combination will depend on the details of the case. Nor on the account proposed here is there no limit imposed by fairness on how much the mother can be morally required to do. Once the mother has sacrificed so much that any further sacrifice would mean she is bearing more of the burdens of non-compliance than her son, no further sacrifice may be imposed as a matter of duty. For that would be to require the mother to bear more than her fair share of the burdens of non-compliance imposed on the father. Perhaps a reasonable compromise would be for the mother to take the child three times a month and pressure the father to do his fair share. Doing more than that might, in a given case, impose a burden on the mother that would be greater than the burden imposed on the child. The account developed here seems to strike a principled and reasonable compromise between the mother and son in terms of dealing with the fallout of the father's poor behaviour.[13]

To be clear, the moral reason for the mother to take the son to his friend's house the extra time each month is on this account *not* that this best promotes the value of fairness. The moral reason to take the son to his friend's house is instead that they promised to take him, or some such reason of fidelity. The point is that considerations of fairness do not limit the scope of this obligation to no more than the mother's fair share in circumstances of full compliance. In Scanlonian terms, the son could reasonably reject any principle that did not require the mother to do more than she would in conditions of full compliance, and his reason for rejection would be that such a principle does not distribute the burdens of non-compliance fairly. However, a more suitable principle that did distribute those burdens more fairly and that therefore could not be reasonably rejected would not itself be a principle of fairness. Rather, the principle will still be a principle of fidelity, but the content of that principle will be partly fixed by what could be rejected on grounds of fairness. It is important to see that the positive reason to do more than one's fair share in these cases is not itself a reason of fairness. Rather, the reason to do more remains the original reason that grounded the collectively held moral obligation in the first reason—that they promised, or some such.

Finally, whether the mother really should, all things considered, take the child to visit his friend an extra time per month will also depend on various

---

[13] Of course, it is perfectly legitimate to impose burdens on the father in this case as well, but for him the limits of fairness do not apply. For it is the father's failure to do his fair share that generated the problem in the first place.

further facts. Perhaps most notably this will depend on whether doing so would serve to legitimize the father's non-compliance in his mind on the grounds that the mother will pick up most of the slack anyway. Such effects are also morally relevant to what the mother should do, all things considered, and may negate her obligation to take the child to his friend's house more frequently than would be her fair share if her doing so would simply encourage still more non-compliance by the father in other arenas. The point here is that these incentive-based limits on our obligations in conditions of non-compliance are not themselves limits of fairness. I return to questions of incentives in Section II.

One possible complication in this case is that there is a child involved, and one might argue that because children are uniquely vulnerable, they should not be forced to bear what would otherwise be their fair share of the burdens of non-compliance. Moreover, children are often not well suited to dealing with risk, particularly the risks of abandonment or neglect by their own parents. These points are well taken, but do not suggest that the mother should bear more than her fair share of the burdens of non-compliance. Rather, they suggest that in this particular case her fair share may well be more than an equal share of the burden, but this may still fall short of absorbing all of those burdens. It might instead be insisted that the mother should fulfil the promise in its entirety in order to teach the child the value of honesty. However, the child might just as easily infer from his mother's behaviour that if someone (a man, in particular, perhaps) does not do his fair share, then someone else (a woman, perhaps) will pick up the slack. The child might infer that women should be servile. Such a lesson in patriarchal values might, all things considered, be problematic enough to outweigh the fact that the mother's behaviour would emphasize the importance of honesty.

I do not take the fact that there are a number of complex variables involved in this last case to invalidate the approach on offer. Realistic cases will typically involve many variables, and the power of the proposal on offer is in how it structures our thinking about such cases rather than in its ability to make it easy to determine the right course of action, all things considered. However, it is useful to imagine a structurally similar case in which the specific complexities associated with childrearing are absent. Suppose now that a married couple together promise their neighbour that they will feed his dog each day while he is out of town. Once the neighbour has left, however, the husband refuses ever to feed the dog so that he can spend more time on some leisure activity. If the wife then feeds the dog only every other day, as would be her fair share in conditions of full compliance, then the neighbour would have a reasonable complaint that she did nothing to absorb the costs of her husband's non-compliance and instead let the burden fall entirely on the neighbour and his dog. In this particular case we might even think that the wife is obligated to feed the dog every day even though this would involve her absorbing all of the costs of non-compliance. However, this might be for reasons that do not undermine the account on offer here. For one reason we might think this is simply that the dog's basic need for food trumps the wife's interest in convenience and even trumps considerations of fairness as such. Although my aim here is to discern what fairness implies in these sorts of cases, unlike Murphy I do not assume that once we have settled the issue of what fairness implies we have thereby settled the issue of what our moral requirements are. Sometimes the adage that 'life isn't fair' is apt, in that sometimes we morally must do more than our fair share.

The main point here is that the neighbour has at least two complaints against the wife if she feeds the dog only every other day. First, he can complain that she did not *even* absorb her fair share of the burdens of non-compliance, for on any plausible view that would at least involve feeding the dog a few extra times. Second, he can perhaps also reasonably complain that she did not appreciate the stringency of a moral requirement generated by another sentient creature's basic needs and that she really should have fed his dog every day even though this would arguably have been somewhat more than her fair share of the burdens of non-compliance. So long as each of these complaints is cogent and reasonable in its own right, we have some further confirmation for the account on offer here.

The first of the previous two examples involved complexities associated with childrearing, while the second involved complexities associated with arguably incommensurable considerations (convenience of the wife versus the basic need for food of the dog). Again, I make no apologies for this, as it is useful to consider how the proposal on offer would structure our thinking about realistic cases that often involve further complications. However, it will be useful to consider an even more straightforward case in which neither of these sorts of further complexities is present, and in which fairness might plausibly be taken to decide the matter. Here I offer an example taken from *Reservoir Dogs*, a film by the infrequently cited moral philosopher, Quentin Tarantino. Eight men are finishing breakfast in a diner. They are gangsters about to do a big job and using fake names (they do not know each other's real names) so that if only some of them are caught they will not be able to tell the police the names of the others involved.

EDDIE: All right. Everybody cough up some green for the little lady. Come on. Throw in a buck.

MR PINK: Uh-uh. I don't tip.

After Mr Pink has clarified his stance, the dialogue continues as follows:

MR PINK: Hey look, I ordered coffee, right? Now we've been here a long fuckin' time, and she's only filled my cup three times. When I order coffee, I want it filled six times.

MR BLONDE: Six times? Well, you know, what if she's too fucking busy?

MR PINK: Words 'too fucking busy' shouldn't be in a waitress' vocabulary.

EDDIE: Excuse me, Mr Pink—the last fucking thing you need's another cup of coffee.

MR PINK: Jesus Christ—I mean these ladies aren't starving to death. They make minimum wage. You know, I used to work minimum wage. And when I did, I wasn't lucky enough to have a job society deemed tip-worthy.

MR BLUE: You don't care they're counting on your tips to live?

(*Mr Pink rubs two of his fingers together.*)

MR PINK: You know what this is? It's the world's smallest violin playing just for the waitresses.

MR WHITE: You don't have any idea what you're talking about. These people bust their ass. This is a hard job.

MR PINK: So's working at McDonald's, but you don't feel the need to tip them, do you? Why not? They're servin ya food. But no, society says don't tip these guys over here, but tip these guys over here. That's bullshit.

MR WHITE: Waitressing is the number one occupation for female non-college graduates in this country. It's the one job basically any woman can get and make a living on. The reason is because of their tips.

MR PINK: (*pauses*) Fuck all that.

(*They all laugh.*)

After some further banter, the gang's leader, Joe, returns.

JOE: All right, ramblers, let's get ramblin'. Wait a minute. Who didn't throw in?

MR ORANGE: Mr Pink.

JOE: Mr Pink? Why not?

MR ORANGE: He don't tip.

JOE: He don't tip? What do you mean you don't tip?

MR ORANGE: He don't believe in it.

JOE:	Shut up. What do you mean you don't believe in it? Come on, you, cough up a buck, you cheap bastard. I paid for your goddamn breakfast.
MR PINK:	Alright—since you paid for the breakfast, I'll put in, but normally I would never do this.

I have quoted this dialogue not only for the inherent comic value of a group of ruthless killers discussing the morality of tipping in such earnest, although that might be reason enough. It is also important to the force of this example that one appreciates the plausibility of the idea that tipping in certain kinds of circumstances is morally obligatory and not merely a discretionary perk. In my opinion, Mr White makes a forceful case for this view. I assume here that the obligation to tip is owed by the table to the server for the service given to the table, and that it is a conventionally recognized way of expressing gratitude for service. In the end, Mr Pink does contribute his fair share to the tip, but only as an expression of gratitude to Joe, who paid for his breakfast, and not as an expression of gratitude to the waitress. Suppose, though, that Mr Pink remained unmoved; just modify the scenario so that Mr Pink paid for his own breakfast and therefore felt no gratitude to Joe. In that case, in spite of Mr White's best efforts, Mr Pink will be imposing burdens of non-compliance on the waitress or Mr White and the rest of those having breakfast. Again, on the most natural extension of Murphy's account it seems that the most everyone else can be morally required to do in this case is simply to give their $1.00 and leave it at that.

Indeed, in so far as arguing with Mr Pink is burdensome (and Mr White certainly seems to find it so!), the most natural extension of Murphy's account seems to imply that arguing with Mr Pink or leaving an additional tip would be above and beyond the call of duty. This, however, seems wrong. The rest of the group should bear their fair share of the burdens of non-compliance. If Mr Pink does not tip then the waitress will be short $1.00. Now perhaps simply arguing at length with Mr Pink is already enough of a burden, so that the rest of the party cannot reasonably be expected to bear any more of the burdens of non-compliance. Still, this would already be more than the most natural extension of Murphy's account would have morally required them to do, and their pressuring Mr Pink might after all work and generate full compliance, as it did in the film. To be clear, my suggestion is not that there is an obligation to argue with Mr Pink in this case, but rather that (all else being equal) there is a duty *either* to argue with Mr Pink or give a greater tip (the 'or' is inclusive). Suppose, though, that the rest of the party know that Mr Pink cannot be convinced (they have had this frustrating conversation on many different occasions now) and this time he paid for his own breakfast and so will not be moved by gratitude to one of his fellow gangsters. In that case, there seems to be little or no reason to argue with Mr Pink. However, it still seems inadequate for the rest of the party simply to shrug their shoulders and leave their $1.00 each and not a cent more. Suppose the waitress really is owed a minimum of $8.00 in tips. Remember, she depends on tips for a living, and we can stipulate that in this modified version of the case that the service was truly excellent—Mr Pink even got his coffee refilled seven times and not just six, for example. In that case, it seems that the rest of the party should absorb their fair share of the burdens of non-compliance. Again, a good baseline for fairness would be an equal division. Putting to one side the possibility that a dollar might mean more to the waitress than it would to a successful gangster, this would imply that the other seven men should each give a tip of around $1.13, which would give the waitress $7.91. The waitress would then be nine cents short, but each of the diners would be contributing an extra thirteen cents, which is as close to equality as is possible given the impossibility of giving fractions of a cent!

Of course, there is something absurd about this level of precision in determining tips, but this is in part because we are working from a conventionally and hence to some extent arbitrarily fixed percentage. Moreover, a morally virtuous person would probably round up in such cases anyway, particularly if the service were especially good; working out precise figures here seems miserly and shameless. The main point, though, is that it is very plausible to suppose in such cases that the upper limit on how much the rest of the party can be obligated to give is not merely their fair share of $1.00, but rather a bit more than that, so that they along with the waitress bear their fair share of the burdens of non-compliance imposed by Mr Pink. Once again, the account proposed here seems to fit well with our moral intuitions in such cases, since most people who really think the waitress is morally owed $8.00 in tips would find it far too miserly for the rest of the party not to pick up any of the slack generated by Mr Pink's non-compliance, yet might also be sympathetic to the idea that they should not have to pick up all of his slack. Again, fairness does impose some limits on what we can be obligated to do in conditions of non-compliance, but those limits are not so severe as Murphy's account would suggest. The burdens of non-compliance must themselves be fairly divided. No doubt Mr White would just shoot Mr Pink before paying more, but this is not the place for a discussion of gangster morality.

A variation on the *Reservoir Dogs* example may be helpful, since the money involved in the original example might seem too insignificant to raise a genuine moral issue. Suppose you are at a fancy dinner with a party of ten, and your waiter has worked extremely hard all night, providing good service in spite of having too many tables to work. Nonetheless, for bogus reasons the other people in your party refuse to tip. In your view, the party owes this waiter the standard 10 per cent, which for this dinner would be £100 (it is a fancy dinner, £100 per head). It seems in this case far too miserly for you to just leave your £10, even though £10 is your fair share. Intuitively, you ought to give more in this case, putting worries about bad incentives to one side—it might help in this regard to assume you could leave more after the rest of the party had left so that they would not get the message that they can morally free-ride on your generosity or just add that they don't care one way or the other about that. The point is that the most you could fairly be asked to provide, on the account on offer, is £55. For in that case you and the waiter would have fairly divided the burdens of non-compliance—each of you is out by £45 more than you would be given full compliance. Here to simplify, I again stipulate that your pounds are equally valuable to you and to the waiter—no differential diminishing marginal utility, etc. To be clear, the account developed here does *not* itself entail that you morally must give the £55 tip, *all things considered*. There may be good moral arguments having nothing to do with fairness, but instead having to do with the way gratitude functions in such cases, or features unique to conventional morality, which show that you are not obligated to give anything like that much (or perhaps that you ought to give even more). The point here is simply that, so far as fairness goes, the limit on how much you might have to give is more than your fair share (£10) but also less than what the waiter is owed from the group (£100).

Finally, the fair shares principle seems to have interesting consequences in cases of iterated failures to do one's fair share.[14] Return to the previous example of the expensive dinner. Now modify the example, so that while eight of your companions refuse to tip at all, one of your companions, call him 'Liam', does provide a tip of £10 but offers no more than this. It seems now that in addition to the burdens of non-compliance imposed by the eight companions who default altogether, there is a further albeit smaller burden of non-compliance imposed by Liam. For now, given our account, Liam is failing in his secondary duty of absorbing his fair share of the burdens of the non-compliance of the others. So far as fairness goes, it seems that keeping the non-compliance of the other eight fixed, you and Liam and the waiter should fairly divide the burdens of the non-compliance of the remaining eight. In this

---

[14] Thanks very much to Keith Horton for bringing the importance and interest of these cases to my attention.

case, a tip that would involve taking on your fair share of the burden for each of you would (assuming that fairness is equality here just to keep things simple) amount to £26.66 each, as that would involve the same level of departure from the sacrifices each would need to make in ideal theory as the sacrifice thereby imposed upon the waiter. However, we are now keeping it fixed that Liam gives only £10. This means that while he is doing his fair share of the original collective obligation to tip, he is not taking on any of the burdens of non-compliance. If we conclude that he does have an obligation to bear his fair share of those burdens (if no considerations other than fairness block this conclusion, that is), then he is defaulting on doing his fair share of that further moral obligation, which itself is usefully understood as one owed by an 'us'—in this case the us being you and Liam. This means that in addition to bearing your fair share of the burdens of the non-compliance of the eight, you must also bear your fair share of the non-compliance of Liam. Presumably this means that you must give £50, so far as considerations of fairness go. For when combined with Liam's £10, this would provide a tip of £60 in total, leaving the waiter short by £40 of what he deserves and also leaving you short by £40 of what you should have had (since you really only should have had to pay £10). Again, I do not contend that you actually owe £50 all things considered, but maintain only that the fairness-based ceiling on what you could be held to owe is £50. There may be other reasons for thinking you do not actually owe this much that have nothing to do with fairness, although I shall not explore the specifics of the morality of tipping in enough detail to explore these nuances.

This slightly unusual example also illustrates an important point about the proposal offered here.[15] To apply the fair shares principle, we must first stipulate to whom we are applying it and then keep fixed the behaviour of everyone else. If we try to figure out what I should do without first fixing what the other members of the collective are going to do (or at least fixing the probabilities of the various actions they might perform—we can do the relevant calculations in terms of expected utility or expected pounds rather than actual utility or pounds), then there is no way to determine what my fair share would be. For without that information there is no way to assess the extent of the burdens of non-compliance and hence no way to determine what would count as a fair share. So to apply the fair shares principle, we must in effect take the principle around with us to each of the different moral agents involved. Obviously, the facts we keep fixed as we move from one agent to the next in applying the principle must shift. For while in determining what you should do we must

---

[15] Thanks to Bill Pollard for prompting me to be more explicit about this feature of my view.

keep what I shall actually do fixed, we certainly cannot keep fixed what I shall do in determining what I shall do and instead we shall now need to keep fixed what you will do.

One important implication of this approach is that those who do not do their fair share in the first place are not thereby 'off the hook' when it comes to doing their fair share to absorb the burdens of non-compliance. For to determine what a free-rider should do, we would *not* keep his free-riding as fixed, but rather fix the behaviour of everyone else involved. If everyone else does their fair share, then the free-rider's duty is only to do his fair share. If, however, some of the other people involved default while others do only their fair share, then our free-rider would actually have a moral duty to do more than what would be his fair share under full compliance. A failure to appreciate this aspect of the application of the fair shares principle could easily lead one to think it is vulnerable to the objection that the free-rider is implausibly exempted from any obligation to bear the burdens of non-compliance. Properly understood, free-riders have just as much of an obligation to do their fair share in bearing the burdens of the non-compliance of other free-riders as the rest of us. While this particular objection rests on a seductive misunderstanding of the fair shares principle, other objections are not quite so easily disarmed. In the following section I explore what I take to be the most important objections to the fair shares principle.

II

I now consider two objections to my approach.

'It is the Non-Compliers, and not the Principle, Which is at Fault.'

In the spirit of one of the National Rifle Association's notorious slogans, this reply seems to amount to the claim that moral principles don't impose unfair burdens; people impose unfair burdens. There does seem to be something plausible about this reply. If we personify a moral principle, we could imagine the collective principle complaining that it is not his fault that some people do not do their fair share, since he requires them to do so. So while the outcome is perhaps less fair if some people do only their fair share when others do not than if others did more than their fair share, this is supposed in no way to reflect poorly on the moral principle which holds that nobody is ever required to do more than their fair share. The responsibility for this unfair outcome, rather, rests squarely on the shoulders of those who choose not to do their fair share and is not a problem for a moral principle that enjoins everyone to do his or her fair share.

At first blush, this simply seems like a false dichotomy. Why could it not instead be the case that both the non-compliance of the villains of the piece and the moral principle that sanctions the failure of others to pick up any of the moral slack *both* be rightly seen as responsible for the unfair outcome? Indeed, Murphy's own account is committed to thinking that moral principles are in some cases responsible for unfair distributions of burdens, for that is in his view what makes act-utilitarian principles of beneficence objectionable. However, the charge of a false dichotomy is too quick. For we can distinguish two ways in which a moral principle might be responsible for the imposition of an unfair burden. First, the moral principle might actually *require* the imposition of that burden, and that seems to be what Murphy finds objectionable about act-utilitarian principles of beneficence. Second, and in contrast, a moral principle might merely *permit* the imposition of an unfair burden. In that case, one might argue, the collective principle is not itself really morally responsible in any way for the unfair outcome that results from people not picking up the slack of those who do not comply. For the principle still allows people to do more than their fair share, and indeed is compatible with its being morally virtuous to do so. It is the discretionary choices of those who fail to do more than their fair share that is responsible for the unfair outcome, and not a moral principle that merely permits but does not require this omission. In effect, this seems to be Murphy's considered reply to the objection that his own account gives insufficient weight to the unfair burdens imposed on those in absolute poverty:

And though the victims of non-compliance with the optimizing principle are worse off than they would be under full compliance, this is not unfair to them in the sense of fairness embodied in the compliance condition. The compliance effect is worse than it would be under full compliance, not because of the *requirements* the optimizing principle makes of people under partial compliance—not because of a sacrifice the victims are *required* to make *or because a loss has been imposed on them by others complying* with the principle.[16]

The crucial distinction here seems to be between costs imposed by the requirements of a principle and costs imposed by people permissibly acting in ways neither required nor forbidden by a principle. It would be different, on this account, if the moral principle in question either directly required the relevant unfair sacrifices or required people to do things that imposed those unfair sacrifices on others (if complying with the principle was sufficient

---

[16] Murphy, *Moral Demands*, p. 92, emphasis mine.

for the imposition of such costs). Since neither of these points is true of the collective principle, it is, Murphy insists, innocent of the charge of unfairness.

In effect, Murphy's reply relies on something broadly akin to the act/omission distinction. Although we must personify moral principles to put the point in this way, it seems apt to suggest that the point of the reply is that while the collective principle may allow people to fail to do more than their fair share, it does not actively require them to do so. If we think the distinction between acts and omissions is morally important in the right way, this might bolster the plausibility of Murphy's suggestion. Of course, the flip side of this point is that if we are antecedently very wary of the moral significance of the distinction between acts and omissions, then we should be suspicious of the distinction Murphy draws. Plausibly, the most this line of argument really establishes is a comparative thesis—that the collective principle is not *as* objectionable as a principle that actually required people not to do more than their fair share even when this would do much good. Indeed, this seems absolutely right: the collective principle is much less objectionable than this rather absurd moral constraint. It would, however, be a big jump to go from that reasonable inference to the much stronger conclusion that the collective principle is not objectionable *at all* in virtue of its connection to the imposition of unfair burdens.

Consider an analogy. A legal system might well permit racial discrimination in hiring, and such legal systems have been sadly common in human history. Libertarian arguments notwithstanding, such legal systems are objectionable because they allow people to impose unfair burdens on people by refusing to hire them simply because of the colour of their skin. It would be very implausible to try to defend such a legal code on the grounds that it does not actually require racial discrimination. For while that it is true, it does not yet establish that the state has done enough to prevent such discrimination. Intuitively, the state's failure to prohibit racial discrimination makes it vulnerable to an objection from fairness. The same point seems to apply to a moral code that permits but does not actively require the imposition of an unfair distribution of burdens when an alternative moral code (like the one proposed here) could reasonably require that these burdens be more fairly distributed.

Indeed, one of Murphy's own examples underscores the point. Murphy gives the example of the government of Norway deciding to tax its citizens for the sake of development assistance, and to tax them at enormous rates that would be optimal given the non-compliance of other nations.[17] Murphy plausibly

---

[17] See Murphy, *Moral Demands*, p. 78.

argues that *if* we think that the citizens of Norway are not morally obligated to give more than their fair share under conditions of full compliance, then we should also think that the government of Norway is not morally obligated to tax its citizens so that they must contribute more than their fair share. However, Murphy implausibly does not follow this moral intuition through to its natural conclusion. For anyone who shares Murphy's intuition in this case will think not only that Norway is not morally required not to impose such enormous taxes on its citizens, but furthermore will think that Norway is morally forbidden from doing so. For a moral code that even *permitted* but did not require the Norwegian government to impose such taxes would intuitively be objectionable for the same basic reason (but to an admittedly lesser extent) that a moral code that actually required such a tax scheme would be objectionable. The fact that this seems to follow so naturally from the intuitions Murphy himself mobilizes serves only to reinforce the idea that moral principles can be objectionable on grounds of fairness for failing to forbid certain forms of behaviour that will in turn impose unfair distributions in just the same way in which principles that actually require the imposition of such distributions are objectionable.

Murphy tries to deflect this line of argument by suggesting that the further intuition that it would be wrong to impose such a tax scheme stems from the completely independent intuition that it is wrong to impose sacrifices that are not morally required.[18] This seems to draw an overly sharp boundary between these two sets of issues. For the reason we think it is wrong to impose such a sacrifice in this case is precisely that to do so would be unfair. Moreover, it is not even obvious that the intuition that it is in general wrong to impose sacrifices that are not morally required can adequately explain our intuitions in these cases. People who share the intuition canvassed in the Norway case may well think with perfect consistency that other impositions of morally unrequired sacrifices are permissible. For example, I may not be morally required not to walk on the grass, since my doing so will make no difference whatsoever in the case at hand, and we might be sufficiently sympathetic to act–utilitarianism to think that this makes all the difference here. Nonetheless, it might well be reasonable for the state to forbid people from walking on the grass quite generally because such a general law is the only feasible way to keep the frequency of people walking on the grass low enough to preserve the grass. The argument deployed here is consistent with the soundness of this line of thought.

So it seems reasonable to conclude that the fact that the collective principle does not actively require but merely permits an unfair distribution of the

---

[18] See Murphy, *Moral Demands*, pp. 83–4.

burdens of non-compliance does not save it from reasonable rejection. The distinction between requirements and omissions cannot bear the philosophical weight needed for this reply to succeed. Of course, this is not to say that the imposition of an unfair distribution of the burdens of non-compliance may not sometimes be appropriate, all things considered. The point here is simply that considerations of fairness as such would if anything support a fair distribution of the burdens of non-compliance. In which case, fairness as such cannot support the conclusion that nobody is ever required to do more than their fair share under conditions of full compliance. Still, fairness is just one value among many and the account developed here does not presuppose that considerations of fairness as such might not be overridden by still other considerations. Fairness as such might be a very weak moral reason on the account developed here. This is why the most salient positive moral reason to do more than one's fair share in situations of non-compliance will not be fairness as such but rather the original reason of beneficence or fidelity or gratitude or whatever. The point here remains that a proper understanding of fairness will not limit the force of those original reasons as obligation-generating reasons to doing one's fair share but no more.

'Requiring People to do More than their Fair Share would Produce Perverse Incentives.'

We have already encountered this concern in discussing the example of the mother's reaction to the husband who refuses to ever take their son to his friend's house in spite of their promise. The more general worry is that a moral principle that required the rest of us to do more than our fair share when others fail to comply would soothe the consciences of those who are antecedently inclined not to comply, thereby increasing the total amount of non-compliance. Returning to Scanlon's framework, this might itself give us reasonable grounds to reject the principle, since, all else being equal, we should prefer a moral code that does not encourage non-compliance. A rule-utilitarian could make much the same point, since a set of rules that would encourage non-compliance with principles aimed at promoting human happiness is, *ceteris paribus*, less valuable than a set of rules that does not have this effect. Another perverse incentive worth considering is that those who are morally virtuous may be less inclined to engage in collective activities of the relevant kinds because of the risk of being left with enormous moral obligations due to the non-compliance of others.[19] Of course, these putative perverse incentives

---

[19] Many thanks to Hannah Wildman for bringing this point to my attention.

would then have to be weighed against the advantages of having people do more than their fair share in situations in which others are not doing their fair share, but the balance of reasons could come out against such a principle.

The first and most central point about this line of argument is that even if it works, it does not actually undermine the main point of my argument. For my aim has been to explore to what extent considerations of fairness as such impose limits on how much people can be expected to do in conditions of non-compliance. Murphy's account seemed in this regard to be on to something important even if his interpretation of the idea turns out not to have been the most plausible one. A consideration of exactly what limits fairness as such imposes on our duties in such situations is important, and that is my aim here. Whatever else we may think about the objection from perverse incentives, it is not an argument that appeals to fairness as such. Rather, it appeals to considerations of expedience. This is not to downplay such considerations, but simply to point out that the force of such considerations in limiting our obligations would not, even if successful, vindicate the idea that fairness as such limits those obligations in any particular way. Second, even if the objection from incentives succeeds in the actual world, it should also be very clear that its success is contingent on peculiarities of human motivation. So these limits on our obligations in conditions of non-compliance will not be as deep or necessary as limits stemming from the idea of fairness as such might be.

Third, the extent of the perverse incentives can easily be exaggerated. For one thing, other people will in many cases not be required by the proposed account to pick up *all* of the slack of those who do not comply. In the *Reservoir Dogs* case, for example, the waitress will still not get the tip she really deserves even if everyone other than Mr Pink bears their fair share of the burdens of non-compliance. In the example of the son being taken to his friend's house, the son will still not get everything he deserves even if the mother bears her fair share of the burdens of non-compliance. The point generalizes, and suggests that it would be irrational for one's conscience to be soothed by the fact that others are picking up some of the slack left by one's moral negligence. For they will still not be picking up all of that slack, and that in itself should be enough to produce some guilt and shame in those non-compliers who are potentially subject to such emotions in any substantial way to begin with.

Of course, human beings are notoriously good at rationalizing their behaviour, so they may well find ways of thinking that others really are picking up all of the moral slack when in fact they are not. This is not obvious, though, and suitable empirical evidence would need to be marshalled to show it is true. Furthermore, even if such empirical evidence were forthcoming, it might well prove too much, in that it might show that those who tend not to comply are so good at rationalizing their behaviour that they will do so even if others do nothing to pick up the moral slack they leave. In the example of the deadbeat dad, he might well convince himself that his son spends too much time with his friends and not enough time on his studies anyway, so that he might feel no guilt even if the mother did absolutely nothing to pick up the moral slack created by his negligence. This propensity to rationalization by those who tend not to do their fair share might be pervasive. In that case, the appeal to incentives does nothing to favour an account like Murphy's over my own proposal. So for the objection to work against my proposal, those who do not do their fair share must be disposed to rationalize their behaviour, but not *too* disposed to do so. This already suggests that the objection's soundness depends on delicate empirical questions to which we do not know the answers, and indeed requires that the answers to those questions fall into a particular narrow band. *Ex ante* this does not seem terribly likely.

The preceding arguments do not yet directly address the other main perverse incentive worth considering—that the fair shares principle would discourage the virtuous from engaging in collective projects in the first place for fear of being caught out by non-compliers and morally forced to do more than they would have had to do under conditions of full compliance. However, this does not yet seem to be an accurate characterization of the incentive that would be generated. For the morally virtuous agent should have no qualms about engaging in collective activities *with those who are likely to do their fair share*. The incentive generated by the fair shares principle would simply be to avoid engaging in collective agency with those who are likely not to do their fair share. Presumably this is a motivation most people have already, at least to some extent. Perhaps more importantly, it is not obviously a perverse incentive. For the more people avoid potentially mutually advantageous cooperation with those who will not do their fair share, the greater the pressure is on the potential free-riders to change their ways and start doing their fair share after all. So in fact the account on offer provides a positive incentive for moral agents to do their fair share under full compliance in the first place, for not doing so would put them at risk of being seen as undesirable partners in otherwise mutually beneficial joint pursuits.

Finally, the account developed here provides a powerful *counter-incentive* that should put more pressure on moral non-compliers like the deadbeat dad. We have already seen how on the account developed here the rest of us might have a strong moral reason to pressure those who are inclined not to comply to do so. For pressuring them to do so would be one way in which we could productively (assuming we often succeed in getting the villains to act) bear some of the burdens of non-compliance, whereas on an account like Murphy's we are in any event not morally required to impose such pressure on those who fail to comply. Furthermore, on the account proposed here, when some people do not do their fair share, the burdens imposed on the rest of us increase. When someone else does not comply, then, as a morally decent agent, I must choose between sacrificing my moral integrity by not doing more than my fair share or sacrificing some of my welfare by doing more than my fair share. This could in itself provide us with considerable *additional* motivation to pressure those inclined not to comply to do so. For now, so long as the rest of us keep our commitment to doing our moral duty fixed, our own welfare is at stake—given a commitment to moral decency, the more others do not do their fair share the more I must sacrifice. Self-interest is typically a very powerful source of human motivation, so this additional motivation might dramatically increase the extent to which the rest of us pressure those inclined not to do their fair share to do so after all. Mr White's argument with Mr Pink seemed to be motivated primarily by moral concerns because the stakes were so low, but if the amount of money involved was much greater, then considerations of self-interest (in conjunction with a commitment to do the right thing) might well increase the motivation to argue in this vein. Assuming that interpersonal pressure can effectively motivate people to do their fair share (and this seems a reasonable empirical assumption), this means that the account developed here provides an important incentive to get people to do their fair share.

Since the perverse incentives attributed to the account on offer are themselves dubious, for reasons discussed above, it seems that an appeal to incentives actually on balance favours the account developed here as superior to an account like Murphy's. For the positive incentives it would generate seem more certain, reliable, and powerfully motivating than the speculative perverse incentives that are supposedly associated with it but not with an account like Murphy's. On an account like Murphy's no such choice between integrity and our own welfare is forced upon us when others do not comply, so this additional motive to pressure others to do their fair share is absent from such accounts.

Interestingly, Brad Hooker's recent rule-utilitarian account of duties of beneficence also fails to produce these kinds of incentives to get others to do more. On Hooker's account, each of us must help others to the point at which our aggregate sacrifice (over the course of a whole life) for others is 'significant'. The key idea is that the level of sacrifice be fixed aggregately, so that the sacrifices I have already made on other occasions may well be relevant to how much I must sacrifice now; in effect, the principle gives moral authority to something like the 'I gave at the office' defence, though one must, so to speak, have given enough at the office to constitute a significant cost from the point of view of one's whole life. The basic idea is that inculcating a moral code which demanded more than this from us to help others would be incredibly difficult and costly, given the limits of natural human sympathy and benevolence. The notion of significance in play in Hooker's formulation is admittedly vague, but that is not my concern. Indeed, some vagueness may well be unavoidable in these matters, as Aristotle famously suggested. Rather, my concern is that if this were the only limit on our obligations to help others, then my obligation to help others in need in conditions of mere partial compliance would not necessarily be a function of how much others are helping. My overall duty might often indirectly be a function of how much others are helping, in that if others help enough then there will simply be no need for me to do more than my fair share.

Nonetheless, the account developed here provides an additional incentive to get others to help more even when this will still fall *far* short of getting them to do their fair shares. Getting others to help more will still reduce my fair share of the burdens of non-compliance even when many more people remain in need in spite of my best efforts. The contrast here is between an upper limit fixed in absolute terms (which is roughly Hooker's idea) by a concern to avoid being overly demanding, and a limit of fairness that is not a fixed value antecedently set by our theory, but instead varies inversely with the extent to which others are helping. This does not mean that the account developed here will not impose costs on agents that are in Hooker's sense significant; I explore this issue below. The point, rather, is that the account developed here provides an additional and important incentive of self-interest for people who want to do the right thing to get others to do their fair share. Nor, I hasten to add, does any of this mean that the account developed here is incompatible with rule-utilitarianism. Indeed, Hooker's own version of rule-utilitarianism could easily be modified to accept this point. In other words, the account developed here could be understood as a supplement rather than a substitute to Hooker's account. For a rule-utilitarian like Hooker could allow that our obligation to help those in need in conditions of partial compliance is a function not only of demandingness and limits of human psychology (which the aggregative personal cost criterion is meant to capture), but is also a function of fairness. Such a hybrid theory would have the virtues of Hooker's own account while at the same time capturing widely held moral intuitions about fairness in these cases and providing important further motives for people to encourage others to do more to help those in need. The provision of such positive incentives might be particularly important in a rule-utilitarian framework, assuming that I am right that these positive incentives outweigh the negative incentives emphasized by critics.

Conclusion

I have argued that, when others fail to do their fair share to discharge a collectively owed moral obligation, considerations of fairness do not imply that the rest of us can be required to do absolutely no more than our fair share. Rather, we should reconceptualize the situation as one in which those who do not do their fair share impose an unfair burden on the rest of us. Assuming this burden is unavoidable (assuming, that is, that we cannot convince or permissibly force the moral offender to do his or her fair share), considerations of fairness would counsel in favour of our doing enough to bear our fair share of the burdens of non-compliance imposed by the shirker(s). I have not yet returned to the morally urgent question of how much each of us should do to help those in absolute poverty while knowing that most other people do virtually nothing to see how the proposed account might apply in that case. I therefore briefly conclude with a few comments on this important but difficult question.

Fully working out a detailed answer to this question would require an account of how we should measure our sacrifices in a way that would allow us to commensurate them with the burdens facing those in absolute poverty. This may not be easy to do, since many of the sacrifices we might make will pale in comparison to those facing people in absolute poverty. Moreover, some of the sacrifices they face seem deeply incommensurable with almost anything we could imagine sacrificing for their sakes. Even fairly large financial sacrifices by those of us fortunate to live in the industrialized West pale in comparison with the misery, destitution, and grossly premature death associated with absolute poverty. Still, perhaps we could in some way commensurate our sacrifices with theirs in terms of something like expected Quality Adjusted Life Years (QALYs). Premature deaths can then be commensurated in terms of the QALYs thereby lost in contrast with the person's expected QALYs if we did more to help. This measure is itself rather conservative since we have more to lose than those in absolute poverty simply because our quality of life is so much higher than theirs.

Even so, it seems very likely that on a QALY-based account, for me to bear my fair share of the enormous burdens of non-compliance imposed by the hundreds of millions of people who give nothing or virtually nothing to Oxfam and similar organizations would be very demanding. Since I am so much better off than those in absolute poverty, it is plausible to assume that I should bear more than an equal share of those burdens, but even if I were merely to accept an equal share of the burdens imposed, that would involve a huge sacrifice. For those in absolute poverty are so badly off that the gap between their actual expected QALYs and their expected QALYs if everyone did their fair share to help them must itself be enormous. For me to bear my fair share of these burdens would involve making a comparable sacrifice in my own QALYs, discounting of course for the difference my contribution makes to the expected QALYs of those living in absolute poverty. The examples discussed above illustrate the importance of this discount rate. Because the mother's taking the son to his friend's house an extra time reduces the burdens of non-compliance on him, it also reduces the further amount she must do in order to bear as much of the burden as her son. However, in the case of helping those in absolute poverty this discount will be pitifully small unless I am as wealthy as someone like Bill Gates, simply because even if my donations saved several hundred lives this would be a very small drop in the bucket when one considers the millions of people living in absolute poverty. If the difference my contribution makes in expected QALYs to everyone in absolute poverty is computed as the expected chance any particular person in absolute poverty be helped by my contribution multiplied by the amount my contribution actually helps those relatively few it does help, then the increase in expected QALYs for those in absolute poverty will be very small indeed even though it may make all the difference in the world to the relatively few people it does help (which is why the positive reasons of beneficence to help remain so strong). A one in a billion chance of getting even a truly enormous benefit is still a miniscule expected benefit. It seems, therefore, that considerations of fairness would not do much to block reasons of beneficence from requiring me to give to the point that I have sacrificed as many expected QALYs as those living in absolute poverty are forced to sacrifice by the non-compliance of most other people living in absolute affluence.

This may still not force me to sacrifice as much as Unger and Singer argue I should—virtually to the point at which I am as badly off as those whom I am helping. Whether this is true in turn depends on just how robust our duties are when everyone does do their fair share. If our duty is simply to ensure that those in absolute poverty have their basic needs met in some intuitive sense of 'basic need', then the gap between their actual welfare and their expected welfare under full compliance, while large, may not be so large relative when measured in QALYs and relative to the much higher quality of life I am likely to have. This means that for me to sacrifice as much as them would not require me to become close to as badly off as them, simply because I am so much better off to begin with. This may itself seem objectionably conservative, but here I am simply assuming for ease of exposition that a fair division here would be an equal division. The worries of those concerned about the conservatism of taking my much greater initial welfare as a normatively laden baseline could perhaps be met if we instead insisted that a fair distribution would, in the spirit of John Rawls's famous 'difference principle', be more skewed in the direction of helping those who are worst off. These are substantive questions about what constitutes a fair division in the first place, which are of course very important but which also go beyond the scope of my discussion. As I noted in the introduction, I am not offering a full theory of the nature of fairness as such here.

Finally, I should note that the account developed here would still not entail that we have such heavy obligations. For all I have done here is show that considerations of fairness do not, when properly understood, seem likely to do much to limit our obligations in conditions of non-compliance in the particular case of helping those in absolute poverty, although those considerations may well limit our obligations in interesting ways in other cases (like the two examples discussed in Section II). The fact that considerations of fairness do very little to limit our obligations does not yet mean that our obligations are incredibly demanding. For there may yet be other reasons to reject such obligations. Perhaps, for example, as Bernard Williams has argued, such stringent demands are deeply alienating. Alternatively, a rule-utilitarian account like Hooker's might plausibly argue that the costs of inculcating such a demanding morality may outweigh its benefits, in which case ideal rules for the real world would include an upper limit on the aggregative personal costs which morality can impose for the sake of beneficence.[20] My aim here has not been to consider all of the myriad different grounds on which one might argue that moral obligations of various kinds might be limited in conditions in which some people fail to do their fair share. Rather, my aim has been the more modest one of getting a clearer sense of how considerations of fairness might serve to limit our obligations in such circumstances. More generally, the aim has been to get clear on what role fairness should play in structuring our thinking about cases of partial compliance quite generally. The fact that getting clear on this does not provide us with all the answers about what to do in cases of partial compliance is no objection to the account developed here. Rather, it simply reflects the complexity of the moral landscape, which on any plausible view is not limited to considerations of fairness.

[20] See Brad Hooker, *Ideal Code*, ch. 8.

10

I Will If You Will: Leveraged Enhancements and Distributive Justice*

DAVID ESTLUND

The maintenance of economic equality can easily seem to depend on participants caring more for impartial values such as distributive justice than they are morally required to do. A liberal morality in which partial concerns for the interests of oneself or one's loved ones are given some scope might seem to permit people to refrain from doing what is impartially best unless they are compensated in ways that produce inequality. In this way, Thomas Nagel writes, 'individual choices and efforts and personal attachments which are themselves unexceptionable combine on a large scale and over time to produce effects that are beyond individual control and grossly unequal'.[1]

This tension between liberal morality and egalitarianism is often exaggerated by a failure to consider the limits of permissible partiality even in a liberal, or partiality-friendly, morality. Partial concerns will often be overruled morally if some burdensome work would be good enough from an impartial standpoint. For example, if the agent's burden is either not very great, or is reduced by compensation, it may not be permissible for her to refuse to do the work. However, such compensation would often be ruled out because it would produce inequality. If, instead of reducing the agent's burden, we intentionally enhance the impartial value of the work, her option to refrain might again

* I am grateful for useful criticisms and suggestions from Arthur Applbaum, Richard Arneson, G. A. Cohen, Robert Goodin, Alon Harel, Thomas Hurka, Erin Kelly, Amy Lara, Andrew Levine, Sharon Lloyd, Geoff Sayre-McCord, David Stevens, Larry Temkin, John Tomasi, Peter Vallentyne, Martin Wilkinson, the students in my graduate seminar at Brown in fall 1999, and participants in the conference on 'Impartiality and Partiality in Ethics' at the University of Reading in December 2006.

[1] Nagel, *Equality and Partiality* (Oxford: Oxford University Press, 1991), p. 120. The same point applies to a wider range of distributive principles and I concentrate on equality only for simplicity.

be cancelled, but this time without producing any inequality. This idea, of intentionally enhancing the agent-neutral value of work that would otherwise be optional, has important normative consequences both for personal morality and for the design of social institutions with an eye to distributive justice. I begin by exploring the idea in a relatively non-political context, then turn to its significance at a more institutional level.

1. The Tension between Liberal Morality and Egalitarian Justice

I was recently on a very long flight, and overheard a flight attendant ask one passenger to trade places with another. It seems there was a tall gentleman whose legs would be pressed against the seat in front of him for twelve hours unless he could sit in one of the front seats (still in 'economy') that afforded ample leg room. One of the passengers in the front seats was travelling alone, which would make switching places easy. Despite the flight attendant's most persuasive efforts, this passenger declined to move, and no one had the authority to compel him.

The inconvenience in moving would have been smaller than the substantial suffering of the taller passenger, but that isn't enough to settle whether the shorter man was wrong to refuse. It is common to think that each of us is entitled to prefer our own interests to those of others to some extent. Even the shorter man was not short, and the extra leg room was certainly an advantage even to him. If we adjusted his height just right, it could easily turn out that he was morally permitted to stay put even though things would be better from an impartial point of view if he chose to switch.

If you are this passenger you are permitted not to move, perhaps on the grounds that it would be a burden to you. That, by itself, is not a great obstacle, since the airline, or perhaps the tall passenger, could compensate you for your trouble. On the other hand, it may be that the goods they would have to give you to compensate would leave them with a net loss even after your performance, and so it is not worth it. Even if compensating you would be worth it, there is another possible problem: it may be that the compensation would upset a just distribution. If, to take a simple example,[2] justice requires equal income per person and this equality would otherwise obtain, then paying you to relinquish your seat would upset this equality and produce injustice.

---

[2] The point applies to a wider range of principles and circumstances, as I argue in Section 3.

There appears to be a difficulty for normative theory: either we must relax the distributive principle—say, equality—that gets violated by your extra wealth, or stick to it. If we stick to it, then the extra value that could be obtained by inducing you to perform must simply be forgone unless we think you are required to move even without compensation. To maintain distributive justice we must refrain from paying you the money that would be required to compensate your burden, leaving you morally free to stay put while the tall man suffers transatlantically. All this, even though you could have switched with no net burden if only we were allowed to compensate you.[3]

Liberal morality, as I use the term, is, putting it roughly first, the view that a certain range of individual choice is insulated from the judgement of morality. It is similar in structure to liberal political philosophy in which a certain range of choice is insulated from legitimate legal interference, although neither entails the other. (It is not to be confused with whatever characteristic morality might be thought to accompany liberal political philosophy or liberal culture.)[4] Here is a tension, then, between *liberal morality*—understood more specifically now as a morality that grants certain agent-centred exceptions from an imperative to maximize agent-neutral value—and *egalitarian justice*: if we accept the agent-centred permission or obligation to refrain from maximizing agent-neutral value in certain cases, and also stick with an egalitarian conception of distributive justice, we may be forced in certain cases to forgo substantial gains in agent-neutral value. Call this tension *the problem of forgone value*. It is no surprise that agent-centred exceptions interfere with maximization of agent-neutral value.[5] The point I concentrate on here is that while exceptions could often be cancelled by compensation, this in turn raises problems for distributive justice. If and when justice precludes using compensation in this way, then there is value that must be forgone.[6] The same challenge applies

---

[3] There would be a cost to the compensator, of course. But, not affecting the compensator's income, this cost would not bear on justice of the kind in view in this example. In other cases the compensation might be drawn from a public fund so that no individual's holdings suffer when the funds are spent. Similar points apply in many other cases, although on some views the cost of compensation might itself bring about injustice. Throughout, I assume for simplicity that it does not.

[4] MacIntyre uses the term in this way in 'Is Patriotism a Virtue?', *Lindley Lecture* (University of Kansas, 1984).

[5] The fact is related to Nozick's argument that 'liberty upsets patterns' (*Anarchy, State, and Utopia* (New York: Basic Books, 1974), esp. pp. 160–4). In Nozick, though, the liberty is freedom from interference rather than, as here, freedom from certain moral obligations.

[6] Value is forgone, but only in a special sense: in some circumstances inequality-producing compensation could induce extra value if only the compensation were permitted. Even if it were permitted, though, it might not be required, and in any case it might not be actually offered. Furthermore, the case only arises if the person who could produce the extra value exercises an option not to produce it without compensation. So it is not as if there is a quantity of value that certainly

to certain non-egalitarian conceptions of distributive justice, but I shall not attempt to determine which ones here for reasons of space.

Does the problem of forgone value make it implausible for egalitarianism to admit prerogatives? Put the other way around: if we insist on liberal morality, does the problem of forgone value make egalitarianism (and certain other conceptions of distributive justice) implausible? Can egalitarians allow prerogatives?

2. Leveraged Enhancements

Having emphasized this tension, the next goal is to relax it to some extent, to show that this problem of forgone value is not as great as might be thought due to a neglected structural feature of liberal morality, a feature that is of interest even apart from questions of distributive justice.

We said that you are permitted not to trade seats even supposing the move would be better from an agent-neutral perspective. But we can't compensate you in order to remove your burden and reinstate your duty to promote the collective good, because this would upset the just distribution. Of course, the amount of good you could do by moving is pretty modest. If the amount of good you could do were enormous, then you would indeed be obligated to do it. For example, if one of the passengers took the others hostage and threatened their lives, and your giving him a better seat could placate the perpetrator and avert the crisis, surely you would be duty-bound to do it. As things are, the value of your switching remains small. It may seem, then, that agent-neutral value will be forgone even without anyone acting badly.

This conclusion is too quick, though, once we notice that the agent-neutral value of your action can be *intentionally enhanced*. It is easy to see how it could be enhanced by a moral monster, although that is not the only way. I could credibly threaten the hostage scenario, and thereby put you under a duty to move. My doing so would probably be morally wrong. I return to this case, and other moral qualms, later.[7] But there is another way for others to enhance the agent-neutral value of your act. Let's make a deal: if you will

would be produced if inequality-producing compensation were permitted, and otherwise would not be produced. But if such compensation is forbidden by justice, then some people might exercise options not to produce more value unless better paid, while it would be impermissible to offer them the extra pay. One way of producing more value—compensation—is morally precluded for the sake of the egalitarian distribution.

[7] See Section 6.

switch seats, then the airline will bend over backwards to guarantee everyone's connecting flights, many of which would otherwise be missed.[8] With this offer, the prospective agent-neutral value of your switching seats is higher, and so it might cross the threshold at which you would be obligated to perform, even though your burden is neither reduced nor compensated.

In a less silly example, suppose that you are morally permitted to refrain from putting in more hours as a doctor. This permission might be contingent on the limited amount of value that your extra doctoring could produce. If several others committed to extra doctoring conditionally on your joining with them, they could intentionally increase the value of your extra work, since your extra work would now bring it about that they all spend more hours doctoring. Under some circumstances, this might change the moral status of the extra work from optional to morally required.

Under the right conditions, there is a surprising kind of boot-strapping in a case like this. If my offer raises the value of your act enough, then you become *obligated to accept*. Furthermore, if you are likely to accept my offer, then the value of my making the offer becomes great enough that any option I might otherwise have had is cancelled and I am *obligated to make the offer*. Whereas it looked at first as though we were both permitted to refrain, it turns out that I am obligated to offer, you are obligated to accept and make your contribution, and then I am obligated to carry through and make my contribution as well. Prerogatives are admitted in both our cases, in the sense that we may give extra weight to agent-centred considerations in order to resist impartial moral requirements. But these prerogatives do not translate into moral options; we are bound, in these cases, to maximize agent-neutral value after all.[9]

There are familiar patterns of interaction that come to mind here. It is now commonplace for public radio fundraisers to announce that someone has offered to match any pledges within the next hour, perhaps only up to some specified dollar amount. These matching offers aim to motivate others not by compensating the burden of pledging (the free coffee mug does some of that), but by enhancing the agent-neutral value of a pledge. Whether or not this successfully motivates people, it may well change the status of a pledge from optional to obligatory. And if the matching offer is likely to be highly successful, it too may become obligatory.

---

[8] Suppose that, apart from this kind of deal, the airline's doing this would be morally optional.

[9] Terminology is tricky here. Kagan would say that when the threshold is met, the option or restriction is 'relaxed'. *The Limits of Morality* (New York: Oxford University Press, 1989), p. 5. It might be better not to call it an option in the general case, but only in the case where the threshold is not met. I settle on 'prerogative' as possibly a less misleading description of the general case. A prerogative generates an option when the threshold, if any, is not met. Constraints, I shall say, generate prohibitions when their thresholds are not met.

Call this a *leveraged enhancement*: by enhancing the value of your work, I leverage my ability to do good into a requirement for you to do good. I offer to contribute to the agent-neutral good conditionally on your doing so, with the aim that your option to refrain is cancelled by the value this adds to your so contributing. Leveraged enhancements are important generally for understanding the normative content of liberal morality, and specifically for understanding the problem of forgone value and its bearing on distributive justice.

The tension arises especially clearly if we assume that there is an obligation to promote agent-neutral value except where this is overridden by an agent-centred option or requirement to do otherwise. This sort of view has many adherents, and certainly it does not amount to assuming agent-neutral consequentialism with all its intuitively disturbing implications.[10] Still, this way of putting things suggests that any exceptions must be grounded in considerations with a sufficiently great weight of their own; otherwise the duty to promote the good would prevail. Kagan has put this strategy to ingenious use, concluding that the requisite weight for exceptions has not been demonstrated. This would support the conclusion that agent-neutral value must always be promoted, a position that is, as Kagan acknowledges, seriously at odds with vernacular views of the scope and stringency of moral requirements.[11] The tension I have described between liberal morality and distributive justice would be clear in that case, but it could exist in a lesser form even if morality were not so extreme. All that is necessary is that *sometimes* there is a duty to promote agent-neutral value so long as no agent-centred exception intervenes. Then, even if there are agent-centred exceptions, they might often have thresholds.[12] Those thresholds could often be met by leveraged enhancements. So, for example, suppose that Kagan is wrong and there is not even a *pro tanto* duty to promote just any agent-neutral value, and so the fact that you could improve matters by switching seats is no moral reason to do so at all.[13] Even so, if you could cure a disease or prevent a disaster by making some sacrifice, there might be a *pro tanto* reason to do it. Then, in that more urgent class of cases, the

---

[10] Prominent sympathizers include Thomas Nagel, 'War and Massacre', *Philosophy & Public Affairs* 1:2 (Winter 1972) pp. 123–44, at p. 128, and Samuel Scheffler, *The Rejection of Consequentialism* (Oxford: Oxford University Press, 1982), p. 20. Nozick, by contrast, explicitly avoids the idea that there are 'mandatory goals that must be pursued even within side constraints'. *Anarchy, State, and Utopia*, p. 29.

[11] Kagan, *The Limits of Morality*.

[12] 'Threshold' is Kagan's term (*The Limits of Morality*, p. 5). By 'agent-centred exceptions' I generally mean to include both agent-centred prerogatives and agent-centred restrictions. Restrictions can also have thresholds, and most of what I say about exceptions could cover both.

[13] Zena Childs raises concerns of this kind in 'Ordinary Morality and the Pursuit of the Good', *The Journal of Value Inquiry* 31 (1997), pp. 213–19.

complexities about agent-centred exceptions, their thresholds, and the ways the thresholds might be met naturally or artificially must be brought to bear. So the interest of leveraged enhancements is not limited to the controversial normative view that there is a *pro tanto* duty to promote agent-neutral value. As described here, though, it might still seem to depend on the view that there is such a thing as agent-neutral value, and that for some subset of such value there is a *pro tanto* duty to promote it. This, too, is disputed, but I shall not pursue this question further here, and I assume for the purposes of this chapter that it is correct.[14]

3. How Compensation can Produce Inequality (or Other Maldistribution)

I assumed that when someone claims a prerogative, say of self-interest, compensating them for their burdens might upset the just distribution. This is not obvious, but in the end I think it is correct. Here is why it is not obvious. If it is some burden that triggers the agent's prerogative not to do the agent-neutrally maximal act, compensation for this burden might simply restore the just distributive pattern rather than upset it. Consider egalitarianism. At first everyone has the same amount. Then you notice that you could do some work that would make us all better off, except that this would be burdensome to you. Liberal morality, suppose, says that this burden is sufficient to give you an option not to do the socially beneficial work. Finally, society might decide that it is worth it to compensate you for this burden in order to restore your duty to do the work. Since this is only compensation for the burden, you are merely being restored to an equal position, and the just distribution has not been upset. If, as this suggests, there is no threat of compensation-produced inequality, then there is no tension between liberal morality and egalitarianism in the first place, and the significance of leveraged enhancements is reduced.

Compensation can produce inequality, though, at least under some egalitarian views. It is important to distinguish between goods that are among those governed by the distributive principle—call these *normatively distributed goods*—and goods that are not—call these *normatively non-distributed goods*.[15]

---

[14] Philippa Foot raises powerful doubts about the idea of an agent-neutral value that gives morality its aim in 'Utilitarianism and the Virtues', *Mind* 94 (1985), pp. 196–209 (also reprinted in S. Scheffler. *Consequentialism and Its Critics* (Oxford: Oxford University Press, 1998).

[15] In these terms Sen's seminal question asks what is normatively distributed by the true egalitarian principle of justice. See 'Equality of What?', *The Tanner Lectures on Human Values* 1 (Cambridge: Cambridge University Press, 1980).

For example, an egalitarian theory might say that justice requires equal income, or equal welfare, or equal resources, etc.[16] In the first case income is normatively distributed, but welfare is not. If not all goods are normatively distributed, then some costs incurred by individuals might involve normatively non-distributed goods, while compensation involves distributed goods. In that case there could be exception-triggering burdens that do not disrupt the distribution from the standpoint of justice. Then, if these burdens were compensated with normatively distributed goods, the distribution would indeed be altered.

For a simple illustration of this distinction, consider an egalitarianism according to which justice requires equal income per adult per year. Annual income is the normatively distributed good. But this leaves entirely open what kinds of goods and burdens might trigger agent-centred prerogatives or restrictions. It is perfectly consistent with this simple egalitarianism to suppose that you are entitled to give extra weight to matters of your own welfare, even though your welfare is normatively non-distributed from the standpoint of justice. That is, if doing some extra work that would benefit us all, such as producing ingenious free educational software, would cost you the benefits of spending that time instead with family and friends, liberal morality can say that you may permissibly decline the productive work. Suppose you do. Then society faces a choice whether to remove your burden by giving you extra income, something it might be in society's interest to do if your software is very good. If we give you extra income to compensate for your welfare burden, the egalitarian distribution of income is upset. The welfare that you would lose if you did the work would not have upset the pattern, since justice, we are assuming, covers only income. Then, when we compensate your welfare burden with income, we upset the equal distribution.

So there is a genuine danger of compensation-produced inequality. Not all compensation will produce inequality, of course. There can be non-distributed burdens compensated with non-distributed goods, and distributed burdens compensated with distributed goods. But there can be normatively non-distributed burdens that trigger prerogatives—in our example, welfare losses—which could only be compensated with normatively distributed goods—in our case, income. And these are not far-fetched cases.

In the special case we might call *pure egalitarianism*, all benefits and burdens are normatively distributed equally, and no inequality would be produced

---

[16] For a good collection discussing a variety of contemporary egalitarian theories, see Clayton and Williams (eds), *The Ideal of Equality* (New York: Macmillan, 2000).

by compensation. The reason is that both burdens and compensation would be in the currency of distributive justice, cancelling each other out. The objection as I initially stated it seemed to presuppose a pure egalitarianism. But this idea is still ambiguous in several ways: is pure egalitarianism not even limited to benefits and burdens that are socially produced? Does it include, say, congenital disadvantages such as blindness? If it is limited to socially produced benefits and burdens, then there is still clear potential for compensation-produced inequality—where distributed goods are used to compensate losses of non-distributed goods. For a more pure form, suppose egalitarianism ranges over all benefits and burdens the distribution of which can be socially *affected*. Still, there may be burdens that cannot be socially affected and so do not affect the normative distribution, but that can still trigger exceptions. So compensation with distributed goods would produce inequality.

It is not clear, in any case, which are the burdens whose *distribution* cannot be socially affected. Certainly there are some that cannot be compensated. But are there burdens such that the welfare of others could not be reduced so as to produce approximate equality with the condition of the burdened? Autism cannot be remediated or compensated, but in a ghastly imaginary scenario, others could be brought to a state such that they were indifferent (*ex ante*) between that and being autistic. Pure egalitarianism in which all goods are normatively distributed is not incoherent, but it is difficult to see what there is to recommend it in the face of intuitive objections, at least in some cases, to levelling down.[17]

The example of income egalitarianism is conveniently simple. But distributive constraints can be violated by compensation under any distributive principle, egalitarian or not, that is impure—where not all benefits and burdens are normatively distributed. On those principles, agent-centred exceptions can be triggered by non-distributed goods, in cases where, for one reason or another, compensation can take the form only of distributed goods, thereby upsetting the just distribution. In these cases, the tension between liberal morality and distributive justice is intact, and the importance of leveraged enhancements, which cancel the agent's options without upsetting the distribution, remains.

---

[17] Despite my mention of the problem for egalitarianism of 'levelling down', my point here is not Parfit's in 'Equality or Priority?', *Lindley Lecture* (University of Kansas, 1991). His critique of egalitarianism is not limited to pure versions, while the point I'm making here is.

4. How Leveraged Enhancements Reduce the Tension between Liberal Morality and Distributive Justice

Suppose I am in a position to offer a leveraged enhancement of the value of some work by you. As we have seen, the extra value that a leveraged enhancement adds to both of our acts might cancel options for both of us, requiring us to maximize agent-neutral value, and at a higher level than was available even before the leveraged enhancement was considered. I cancel your option not by paying you for your trouble, which would threaten the just pattern, but by making your trouble more productive of agent-neutral value, which can still be justly distributed. Unlike compensation, the strategy of enhancement proceeds without upsetting the just distributive pattern.

One implication of this is that liberal morality's prerogative to give a preference of some weight to certain agent-centred considerations can be granted without necessarily giving rise to either maldistribution or forgone value. The reason is that the prerogative does not translate into an option to refrain from the extra contribution once the value of the contribution has been raised by a leveraged enhancement high enough to overcome the prerogative's threshold. Liberal morality includes prerogatives, but this does not guarantee options. Commonsense liberal morality admits this since, at least typically, it places limits or thresholds on the prerogatives it grants: if the agent-neutrally optimal act is enough better than the alternatives, then, at least for especially urgent classes of value, it becomes obligatory after all. Sometimes these thresholds are met naturally, as when aiding drowning babies or famine victims would have enormous value at only modest cost to the agent.[18] Leveraged enhancements, by contrast, are an example of how the agent-neutral value of someone's act can be intentionally raised so as to meet the threshold of their prerogative.

Thresholds can be met artificially as well as naturally. It is possible, and probably often obligatory, to enhance the value of someone's possible act so that their prerogative does not translate into an option to refrain. The tension

---

[18] So Singer's famous demanding normative conclusion in 'Famine, Affluence and Morality' is compatible with prerogatives (*Philosophy & Public Affairs* 1 (Spring 1972), pp. 229–43). They might be granted to be of some moral importance, but not comparable in weight to the great evils that exist and which could be reduced by our efforts. The threshold is just often met.

between liberal morality and distributive justice is reduced if the prerogatives are often prevented, by leveraged enhancements, from giving rise to options to act contrary to some *pro tanto* duty to promote the good.

It may be that for some agent-centred exceptions there is no threshold, and no amount of agent-neutral value could cancel the agent's moral option. For example, it may be that certain central personal commitments are always preserved or promoted in certain ways, no matter how much agent-neutral value is at stake.[19] I am not arguing either side of this case. Certainly, if *all* agent-centred exceptions are indefeasible, lacking any threshold at all, then the tension I have described between liberal morality and distributive justice cannot be reduced by noticing the possibility of leveraged enhancements. But many people think that morality admits many agent-centred exceptions with finite thresholds, even if some of them have no thresholds at all. Then leveraged enhancements will reduce the tension between liberal morality and distributive justice.

5. Leveraged Enhancements under Egalitarian Conditions

So far our examples have been on a small scale, concerning leveraging offers that one agent might make to another. Leveraged enhancements have a broader applicability at the level of social institutions as well—a level that is more central to egalitarian concerns.

Economically egalitarian social arrangements are widely charged with suppressing productivity by failing to provide the incentive of greater pay for greater work. Egalitarians sometimes reply that no such incentive would be needed in a fully just society where people's motives were not immorally partial.[20] This reply can be challenged from the perspective of liberal morality, in which there are permissible motives other than aiming at agent-neutral value. G. A. Cohen's egalitarianism grants some limited prerogative of self-interest, but then seems forced to admit a range of other partial motives as well.[21] Details

---

[19] Williams considers such a thing in his discussion of 'ground projects', in 'Persons, Character, and Morality', in Amelie Rorty (ed.), *The Identities of Persons* (Berkeley, CA: University of California Press, 1976).

[20] I thank Jerry Cohen for discussion of this point.

[21] See G. A. Cohen, 'Incentives, Inequality, and Community', *Tanner Lectures on Human Values*, vol. 13 (Salt Lake City, UT: University of Utah Press, 1992), pp. 302ff.; and also G. A. Cohen, *If You're An Egalitarian How Come You're So Rich?* (Cambridge, MA: Harvard University Press, 2000).

aside, liberal morality threatens to allow motives in which agent-neutral value must be forgone unless inequality is allowed.

Leveraged enhancements give egalitarians a better reply. Consider a Carens market (as I shall call it, after its inventor, Joseph Carens[22]): a highly imaginary arrangement in which people's motives are very different from those typical under capitalist economic arrangements, but in which equality is maintained consistently with many benefits of economic markets. All income is taxed at a rate of 100 per cent and redistributed so as to produce equality of income annually. Economic agents are assumed, however, to behave in the labour market much as they would under a standard wealth-maximizing motive since they are moved to that same extent by the aim of maximizing their pre-tax income—their own contribution to the pot that will be equally distributed. Higher skills, then, would demand higher pre-tax pay, and owners of firms would pay more for higher skills when they believed this would increase their own pre-tax income.

Carens himself later conceded that a morally sound arrangement could not demand unending devotion to the common good, and so maximization of pre-tax income could not be morally required.[23] In this concession to liberal morality, then, there are agent-centred exceptions from the demands of the common good. This raises the problem of forgone value, the agent-neutral value that cannot be obtained without inequality-producing compensation. The doctor who could be more productive by working longer hours may permissibly refrain in light of the burdens, and distributive justice disallows increasing his income so as to overcome his burdens. It is useful, then, to see how enhancements could induce the extra value without introducing the inequality that might accompany compensation.

In a Carens market the extra pre-tax pay that is commanded by a talented worker is never compensation for a burden, since pre-tax pay is all taxed away and redistributed equally. Everyone ends up with the same post-tax income regardless of how much pre-tax income their talents manage to command. *Extra pre-tax pay in a Carens market is nothing but a leveraged enhancement of the agent-neutral value of some possible work.*[24] The extra pay is aimed at increasing the agent-neutral value of extra work enough to render it obligatory. Consider this

---

[22] Carens, *Equality, Moral Incentives, and Markets* (Chicago, IL: University of Chicago Press, 1981).

[23] Carens, 'Rights and Duties in an Egalitarian Society', *Political Theory* 14:1 (1986), pp. 31–49.

[24] Actually, this is so only if the higher wages would not be paid unless I accepted the job. If it would go to someone or other in any case, then the offer does not enhance the agent-neutral value of my work at all and so is not an enhancement in the pertinent sense. Incidentally, Carens never mentions the potential of such enhancements to cancel the self-interest prerogative he grants, and so he is left with a problem of forgone value.

example, assuming that the market in labour is a Carens market. Suppose that in addition to other full-time work I could devise good educational software, but the time involved would mean that I could not also keep helping at my neighbourhood association. Suppose that this more local association triggers an agent-centred prerogative or obligation not to make the software. Even if the software job paid me something (in pre-tax wages), the overall contribution to the agent-neutral good might not yet be enough to cancel my option or duty not to work for the neighbourhood. In response to this option of mine, a software firm might offer me a handsome pre-tax wage. As always in a Carens market, since wages are redistributed equally anyway, this is not in any ordinary sense a significant compensation for the option-triggering burden. Rather, the higher pre-tax wage to me means slightly higher equal income for millions of people. The offer enhances the agent-neutral value of my making software, and may enhance it far enough to morally cancel my option to decline. Even so, equality of normatively distributed goods would be preserved. (Why would the software company offer me a higher wage? Perhaps they think my talents will allow their company to produce significantly more value—measured first as their revenue, and then as redistributed equal income—than would be produced without me.) The Carens market in labour illustrates how the device of leveraged enhancements can cancel genuine agent-centred exceptions at the level of institutions, and in a pervasively egalitarian context, ameliorating the problem of forgone value, and without resorting to inequality for incentive purposes.

Thomas Nagel observes that the motives prescribed by a Carens market are not very likely.[25] Still, the idea of a Carens market might yet cast doubt on Nagel's claim that 'individual choices and efforts and personal attachments which are themselves *unexceptionable* combine on a large scale and over time to produce effects that are beyond individual control and grossly unequal'.[26] Liberal morality grants that a certain element of partiality in motivation is unexceptionable, but allows that there will often be thresholds to the legitimate pursuit of partial motives. In the sort of Carens market described here the market will often offer enough pre-tax pay to reach that threshold, rendering the burdensome work obligatory all things considered. Even if real agents are not very likely to meet the resulting obligations, as Nagel observes, it would be wrong to conclude that the actual choices—resulting in 'gross inequality'—are 'unexceptionable'. If the thresholds of legitimate agent-centred exceptions have been met (by the leveraged enhancement of a conditional offer of higher post-tax income for all), then the continued refusal

---

[25] Nagel, *Equality and Partiality*, pp. 94, 128.   [26] *Ibid.*, p. 120.

to do the work, while perhaps predictable, can no longer be defended by appealing to liberal morality. Leveraged enhancements give liberal morality its (limited) due.

Before turning to three final issues, we might take stock. So far, the device of leveraged enhancements seems to have important normative implications of two broad kinds. First, liberal morality may not be as permissive as it seems. Not only are there often thresholds that limit the scope of permissible deviations from agent-neutral value, a feature that is already well known. In addition, the value of an agent-neutrally valuable act can sometimes be intentionally enhanced in order to push it over the threshold and render it obligatory. Furthermore, this kind of intentional enhancement might itself often be obligatory. These normative implications have interest even apart from questions about the design of social institutions, but there are also implications at a more institutional level. The conjunction of liberal morality with egalitarianism (and certain other conceptions of distributive justice in a set not specified here) yields a problem of forgone value—agent-neutral value that may not be produced because agents may permissibly refrain in light of certain burdens, and yet the burdens cannot be compensated without upsetting equality. Leveraged enhancements at an institutional level (as in a Carens market) could cancel these options and render the more productive work obligatory after all, consistent with equality.

In the second half of the chapter I consider two qualifications. First (Section 6), leveraged enhancements are sometimes morally questionable ways of manipulating others. Second (Section 7), while leveraged enhancements seem to increase liberal morality's stringency, they cause us to notice a countervailing phenomenon—leveraging in reverse—leaving the overall effect on stringency unsettled.[27]

6. Moral Manipulation

There is a dark side to leveraged enhancements. The idea of leveraged enhancements suggests that I could put you under new obligations simply by making it the case that certain possible actions of yours will have great agent-neutral value. But what if you were a very conscientious person and I had enormous resources, and I wanted nothing more than to lead you around

---

[27] There might be prerogatives to refrain from offering certain leveraged enhancements, so I doubt that they solve the problem of forgone value completely. I leave that issue aside for reasons of space.

by the nose. A clever way to do it would be to enhance the agent-neutral value of acts that it would be burdensome for you to perform, one after the other, steering you wherever I like, possibly even to your death. I might first make it known that if (and only if) you give $1000 to a fund for the starving, I shall give $100,000. Just as the ink dries on our respective checks I might add that I shall do the same each week, contingent on your giving your $1000. As you get poorer I might have to raise my enhancement, since $1000 gets increasingly burdensome to you the less you have, and so suppose I raise my contribution accordingly.

Also, recall the somewhat different case, passed over earlier, of inducing you to do some extra work by committing to a spree of murder and mayhem if you do not. This enormously enhances the agent-neutral value of your doing the work compared with your not doing it, not by promising a contribution, but by threatening to do great harm unless you make a certain contribution. Clearly, following through on the threat would be monstrously wrong. Whether making the commitment to follow through would be wrong is a separate question, since it may be perfectly clear that it will never have to be carried out.[28] A familiar case with this structure is a terrorist or a nation who threatens to kill many innocent people unless certain (so they think) valuable steps are taken by others. Even if the threat is morally wrong to make, it does not follow that such an immoral threat is incapable of creating obligations to do acts that were otherwise morally optional. On the other hand, terrorist threats do sometimes seem incapable of producing obligations to perform the target acts despite the gravity of the threatened harm. Leveraged enhancements raise similar questions.

What would seriously deflate the interest of leveraged enhancements is if they automatically raised the threshold of the targeted agent so as to maintain a prerogative. So, could it be that whenever the supposedly threshold-surpassing agent-neutral benefits of my possible action are due to a leveraged enhancement, the threshold is raised and I am restored to a state of moral option? This might be advocated specifically as a protection from the potential for manipulative leveraged enhancements. This is part of the more general question whether other agents have the power to arrange things so as to produce moral obligations we would not otherwise have had, a power that would allow a certain kind of moral manipulation. One small part of the answer seems obvious: the mere fact that the arrangement was produced precisely in

---

[28] Odious threats might bring about great good, or prevent enormous catastrophes such as nuclear attacks. See Gregory Kavka, 'Some Paradoxes of Deterrence', *The Journal of Philosophy* 75 (1978), pp. 285–302.

order to obligate someone does not generally and automatically prevent the obligation from arising. Babies abandoned on strangers' doorsteps are clear counter-examples to the general claim that obligations are never produced by such manipulative means.

It is a more difficult question whether obligations that are intentionally produced are merely weaker, more easily defeated, than they would otherwise be even though they sometimes succeed in being decisive nevertheless. For example I might have less obligation to help the baby abandoned on my doorstep than I would if it had been blown there by a storm. By less obligation, I mean an obligation that could be outweighed more easily by costs to me or other obligations or moral considerations. This can apparently be analytically treated as a rise in the targeted agent's threshold. I do not know whether such moral manipulation has this threshold-raising effect. But even if it does, still, if the leveraging offer is sweetened, it could then possibly outstrip this newly located threshold. Leaving the baby on the doorstep is moral manipulation, and also often immoral in itself, and yet the obligation will often be produced anyway given the stakes. Moreover, leveraged enhancements are even more likely to succeed than baby-leavings since they often operate without any threat to reduce any value of any kind relative to the *status quo*.

Moral manipulation by way of leveraged enhancements may or may not always be wrong, but whether it is or not in a particular case, it can still, at least sometimes, successfully change the targeted agent's act from optional to required. No full treatment of the ethics of leveraged enhancements is possible here, although I hope it is clear that they bear more thought.

7. Leveraging Down

The possibility of leveraged enhancements means that even when we have prerogatives, our option might be cancelled by someone's offer to leverage. Their doing so might even be morally required. The stringency of morality is heightened, then, in both of these ways: (1) we may find ourselves with duties to leverage others, along with the concomitant duty to carry through if the leveraging offer successfully induces the target action; (2) we may find many of the prerogatives we have, such as giving more weight to certain agent-centred considerations, to generate no options if others, by leveraged enhancement, have brought the value of the agent-neutrally best act over our prerogative's threshold. Indeed, it would now be an open question whether any moral options would remain if all morally required leveraging offers were made.

Just as leveraged enhancements have a dark side (see Section 6), they have a mirror image, and so the effects on the stringency of morality are not all in one direction. Suppose that you have an obligation to donate a certain amount to urgent charities such as famine relief. Suppose that this would have been optional if the agent-neutral value of your donation were not so great. In this case I could cancel your obligation by diminishing the value of your contributing. Suppose that because of my lower income, my contributing to that same cause is optional.[29] Suppose I was initially planning to contribute. Now I could say to you that if you contribute I will not, and so your contributing would have no net value at all. Under those circumstances, your contributing might now be optional. In this way I can leverage in reverse, and change your obligation into an option.[30]

Of course, this might be a morally troubling thing to do. Why would I go out of my way to neutralize the value of a contribution you might make unless I am simply malevolent? If my offer is morally wrong, this might cast doubt on whether it successfully cancels your obligation to contribute. It may be that morally you should contribute anyway despite the reduced or nonexistent agent-neutral value given your plans. Morality might include this feature specifically to pre-empt the possibility of reverse leveraging, just as it might include a duty not to give in to terroristic demands even when doing so would prevent many tragic deaths. I am not advocating or criticizing either of these moral ideas. The point is that it may seem as though reverse leveraging smells bad morally, leaving it unclear whether such a thing could really have the moral effect of cancelling obligations.

The moral smell can be improved if the leverager's reasons can be morally approved, as I think they can in a more complex example. Suppose my reason for cancelling your duty to contribute to an urgent charity is to bring it about that you are morally free to come to my daughter's graduation. This would be expensive for, and suppose you cannot afford both the graduation and the contribution to the needy. Unless I make my reverse leveraging offer, it would be wrong for you to come to the graduation instead of making the contribution given the great and urgent agent-neutral value of the latter, along with the fact that, suppose, you have no especially weighty moral relationship to my daughter. Nevertheless, I do, and I know that she would really like

---

[29] To avoid the possibility of just a smaller contribution, suppose the charity rejects donations below a certain minimum, an amount that is optional for me given my circumstances.

[30] Richard Arneson suggested this possibility to me. Thanks to him and to Thomas Hurka for useful discussion of this possibility.

you to be there. I may have an agent-centred prerogative or duty to get you to the graduation even though more agent-neutral value would be produced if you made the contribution instead. Presumably it would not be right for me to induce you by persuading you to do something wrong. But suppose I made it right. I could conditionally withhold my (optional) contribution as described (I won't if you will), thereby making it the case that your coming to the graduation instead of contributing is not wrong after all. My motive is to make my daughter happy, and I might well have a prerogative (or even a duty) to leverage you in reverse in this way. This suffices to show that leveraging in reverse is not necessarily malevolent or self-indulgent, but might often be morally acceptable or even required.

Since leveraging can go either forward or in reverse, it has at least partly countervailing effects on the stringency of morality. There is no reason to suppose they precisely balance out, nor to think that stringency is increased rather than reduced if all morally required leveraging offers are made. In one respect stringency is increased (compared to what it seemed to be before considering leveraging) without any countervailing factor, and that is the possibility of duties to leverage. This introduces a new category of duty and no new countervailing category of permission to refrain from putative duties. The effect of the leveraging is sometimes forward and sometimes reverse, but there might well be duties to engage in both kinds of leveraging. There is no way to tell from what has been said here whether the overall effect increases or reduces the stringency of morality's demands. This does not mean that the moral effects of leveraging might turn out to be negligible. It seems clear that they are bound to be of great moral importance, with pervasive effects on our moral duties and options, even if there is no clear answer to whether morality is as a result more stringent or less. Compare leveraging with another normative concept: rights. The introduction of rights into a normative framework that did not previously contain them does not obviously either increase or reduce morality's stringency either. There are rights to have others do or refrain from certain things at great cost to themselves, as there are rights to refrain from things that would otherwise be very costly. But the introduction of rights would still make an enormous normative difference. Whether or not the difference that leveraging makes is as great as rights, it could certainly make a great difference even if it sometimes created new duties and other times cancelled them.

In any case, the possibility of leveraging down is no challenge to my claim that leveraged enhancements will often be available as ways of cancelling agent-centred exceptions without introducing the distributive distortions that compensation would cause.

8. Conclusion

It remains only to be emphasized that leveraged enhancements do not depend for their interest on the connections to distributive justice that I have explored here. Whatever agent-centred exceptions we might have from the promotion of whatever morally relevant agent-neutral values there might be, these will often have thresholds. Therefore, whether we are required to promote agent-neutral value in these cases after all depends on whether the thresholds are met. Noticing this, we see that they can sometimes be met by the intentional offers of others, and sometimes these offers might even be required. The structure of our duties is importantly affected, and this is of some importance for normative moral theory.

In addition, and separably, where agent-centred prerogatives are invoked in order to avoid what would otherwise be duties to promote the good, leveraged enhancements can sometimes be used to bring these prerogatives over their thresholds, thus restoring duties to promote the good. In this way they are alternatives to compensation, which under some circumstances and on some views would upset distributive justice. Leveraged enhancements and their relatives, then, have a significant bearing on important questions in political philosophy as well as in moral philosophy more generally.

Bibliography

Adams, Don, 'Aquinas and Modern Consequentialism', *International Journal of Philosophical Studies* 12 (2004), pp. 395–417.

Anderson, Elizabeth, *Value in Ethics and Economics* (Cambridge, MA: Harvard University Press, 1993).

Annas, Julia, *An Introduction to Plato's Republic* (Oxford: Oxford University Press, 1981).
—— *The Morality of Happiness* (Oxford: Oxford University Press, 1993).

Anscombe, G. E. M., 'Modern Moral Philosophy', *Philosophy* 33 (1958), pp. 1–19; also in her *Ethics, Religion and Politics* (Oxford: Basil Blackwell, 1981), pp. 26–42.

Appiah, Kwame Anthony, 'Racisms', in *Anatomy of Racism*, ed. David Theo Goldberg (Minneapolis, MN: University of Minnesota Press, 1990), pp. 3–17.

Aquinas, St Thomas, *Summa Theologiae* [1266–73], transl. Fathers of the English Dominican Province (London: Burns, Oates and Washbourne, 1911).
—— *On Law, Morality, and Politics*, 2nd edn, trans. Richard J. Regan, ed. William P. Baumgarth and Richard J. Regan (Indianapolis, IN: Hackett, 2002).

Archard, David, 'Moral Partiality', *Midwest Studies in Philosophy* 20 (1995), pp. 129–41.

Aristotle, *Nicomachean Ethics* [325 bc], ed. T. Irwin (Indianapolis, IN: Hackett, 1985).

Arthur, W. Brian, *Increasing Returns and Path Dependency in the Economy* (Ann Arbor, MI: University of Michigan Press, 1994).

Austen, Jane [1775–1817], *The Complete Works*, in 7 vols (London: The Folio Society, 1996).

Baier, Kurt, *The Moral Point of View: A Rational Basis for Ethics*, abridged edn (New York: Random House, 1965).

Baron, Marcia, 'Impartiality and Friendship', *Ethics* 101 (1991), pp. 836–57.

Binmore, Ken, *Natural Justice* (Oxford: Oxford University Press, 2005).

Bloomfield, Paul, *Moral Reality* (Oxford: Oxford University Press, 2001).

Blum, Lawrence, *Friendship, Altruism, and Morality* (London: Routledge & Kegan Paul, 1980).

Bratman, Michael, *Intention, Plans, and Practical Reason* (Cambridge, MA: Harvard University Press, 1987).
—— 'Shared Cooperative Activity', *The Philosophical Review* 101 (1992), pp. 327–41.
—— 'Shared Intention', *Ethics* 104 (1993), pp. 97–113.
—— *Faces of Intention* (Cambridge: Cambridge University Press, 1999).
—— *Structures of Agency* (New York: Oxford University Press, 2007).

Brewer, Talbot, 'Two Kinds of Commitments (And Two Kinds of Social Groups)', *Philosophy and Phenomenological Research* 66 (2003), pp. 554–83.

Broad, C. D., 'Self and Others', in David Cheney (ed.), *Broad's Critical Essays in Moral Philosophy* (London: George Allen & Unwin, 1971).

Buss, Sarah, 'Respect for Persons', *Canadian Journal of Philosophy*, 29 (1999), pp. 517–50.

—— 'Value Autonomy and Respecting Persons: Manipulation, Seduction, and the Basis of Moral Constraints', *Ethics* 115 (2005), pp. 195–235.

Carens, Joseph, *Equality, Moral Incentives, and Markets* (Chicago, IL: University of Chicago Press, 1981).

—— 'Rights and Duties in an Egalitarian Society', *Political Theory* 14(1) February (1986), pp. 31–49.

Chappell, Tim (ed.), *The Problem of Moral Demandingness* (Basingstoke: Palgrave Macmillan, 2009).

Childs, Zena, 'Ordinary Morality and the Pursuit of the Good', *The Journal of Value Inquiry* 31 (1997), pp. 213–19.

Clayton, Matthew and Williams, Andrew (eds), *The Ideal of Equality* (New York: Macmillan 2000).

Cocking, Dean and Kennett, Jeanette, 'Friendship and the Self', *Ethics* 108 (1998), pp. 502–27.

Cohen, G. A., 'Incentives, Inequality, and Community', in *Tanner Lectures on Human Values*, vol. 13 (Salt Lake City, UT: University of Utah Press, 1992), pp. 261–329.

—— *If You're An Egalitarian, How Come You're So Rich?* (Cambridge, MA: Harvard University Press, 2000).

—— *Rescuing Justice And Equality* (Cambridge, MA: Harvard University Press, 2008).

Congreve, William, *The Mourning Bride* [1697] (Whitefish, MT: Kessinger Publishing, 2009).

Cottingham, John, 'Ethics and Impartiality', *Philosophical Studies* 43 (1983), pp. 83–99.

—— 'Partiality, Favouritism, and Morality, *The Philosophical Quarterly* 36 (1986), pp. 357–73.

—— 'The Ethics of Self-Concern', *Ethics* 101 (July 1991), pp. 798–817.

—— 'Partiality and the Virtues', in R. Crisp (ed.), *How Should One Live?* (Oxford: Oxford University Press, 1996), pp. 57–76.

—— 'Morality, Virtues and Consequences', in D. Oderberg and L. Laing (eds), *Human Lives* (London: Macmillan, 1997) pp. 128–43.

—— 'The Ethical Credentials of Partiality', *Proceedings of the Aristotelian Society* XCVIII (1997–8), pp. 1–21.

—— *Philosophy and the Good Life* (Cambridge: Cambridge University Press, 1998).

—— *On the Meaning of Life* (London: Routledge, 2003).

—— *The Spiritual Dimension* (Cambridge: Cambridge University Press, 2005).

—— 'Demandingness, Moral Development and Moral Philosophy', in T. Chappell (ed.), *The Problem of Moral Demandingness: New Philslophical Essays* (Basingstoke: Palgrave Macmillan, 2009), pp. 86–103.

Cullity, Garrett, *The Moral Demands of Affluence* (Oxford: Oxford University Press, 2004).

Dancy, Jonathan, *Ethics Without Principles* (Oxford: Oxford University Press, 2006).

Darwall, Stephen, 'Two Kinds of Respect', *Ethics* 88 (1977), pp. 36–49.

—— *Welfare and Rational Care* (Princeton, NJ: Princeton University Press, 2002).

Darwall, Stephen, 'Respect and the Second-Person Standpoint', *Proceedings and Addresses of the American Philosophical Association* 78 (2004), pp. 43–60.

—— *The Second-person Standpoint: Morality, Respect and Accountability* (Cambridge, MA: Harvard University Press, 2006).

—— 'Kant on Respect, Dignity, and the Duty of Respect', in *Kant's Virtue Ethics*, ed. Monika Betzler (Berlin: Walter de Gruyter, 2008), pp. 175–200.

Davis, Morton D., *Game Theory* (Mineola, NY: Dover, 1983).

Descartes, René, *Meditations* [*Meditationes de prima philosophia*, 1641], trans. in J. Cottingham, R. Stoothoff, and D. Murdoch, *The Philosophical Writings of Descartes*. vol. II (Cambridge: Cambridge University Press, 1995).

—— *Œuvres de Descartes*, ed. C. Adam and P. Tannery (12 vols, rev. edn, Paris: Vrin/CNRS, 1964–76).

—— *The Philosophical Writings of Descartes*, vols I and II, ed. J. Cottingham, R. Stoothoff, and D. Murdoch (Cambridge: Cambridge University Press, 1985).

Dickens, Charles, *Bleak House* [1852–53] (London: Penguin Classics, 1971).

Dworkin, Ronald, *Taking Rights Seriously* (London: Duckworth, 1977).

—— 'Rights as Trumps', in Jeremy Waldron (ed.), *Theories of Rights* (Oxford: Oxford University Press, 1984), pp. 153–67.

Estlund, David, 'Liberalism, Equality, and Fraternity in Cohen's Critique of Rawls'. *The Journal of Political Philosophy*, 6(8) (March 1998), pp. 99–112.

Euripides, *Medea* [431 bc], ed. John Harrison (Cambridge: Cambridge University Press, 1999).

Feinberg, Joel, *Social Philosophy* (Englewood Cliffs, NJ: Prentice-Hall, 1973).

Filmer, Robert, *Patriarcha* in Peter Laslett (ed.), *Patriarcha and Other Political Works* (Oxford: Blackwell, 1949).

Finnis, John, *Natural Law and Natural Rights* (Oxford: Oxford University Press, 1980).

—— *Aquinas—Moral, Political, and Legal Theory* (Oxford: Oxford University Press. 1998).

Flanagan, Owen and Adler, Jonathan, 'Impartiality and Particularity', *Social Research* 50 (1983), pp. 576–96.

Fleurbaey, Marc, Tungodden, Bertil, and Vallentyne, Peter, 'On the Possibility of Nonaggregative Priority for the Worst Off', *Social Philosophy and Policy* 26 (2009). pp. 258–85.

Foot, Philippa, 'Utilitarianism and the Virtues', *Mind* 94 (1985), pp. 196–209; reprinted in S. Scheffler, *Consequentialism and Its Critics* (Oxford: Oxford University Press 1988), pp. 224–42.

Frankfurt, Harry, *Necessity, Volition, and Love* (Cambridge: Cambridge University Press, 1999).

Fried, Charles, *An Anatomy of Values* (London: Harvard University Press, 1970).

Friedman, Marilyn, 'The Impracticality of Impartiality', *Journal of Philosophy* 86 (1989), pp. 645–56.

—— 'The Practice of Partiality', *Ethics* 101 (1991), pp. 818–35.

Garcia, Jorge, 'Racism and Racial Discourse', *The Philosophical Forum* 32 (2001). pp. 125–45.

Gaus, G. F., *Social Philosophy* (Armonk, NY: M.E. Sharpe, 1999).

—— *Contemporary Theories of Liberalism: Public Reason as a Post-Enlightenment Project* (London: Sage, 2003).

—— *On Philosophy, Politics and Economics* (Belmont, CA: Wadsworth, 2007).

—— 'Reasonable Utility Functions and Playing the Fair Way', *Critical Review of International and Social Philosophy* 11 (June 2008), pp. 215–34.

—— 'Recognized Rights as Devices of Public Reason', *Philosophical Perspectives: Ethics* 23 (2009), pp. 112–36.

Gauthier, David, *The Logic of Leviathan* (Oxford: Oxford University Press, 1969).

—— *Morals by Agreement* (Oxford: Oxford University Press, 1986).

Gert, Bernard, 'Hobbes's Psychology', in Tom Sorrell (ed.), *The Cambridge Companion to Hobbes* (Cambridge: Cambridge University Press, 1996), pp. 157–74.

—— *Morality* (New York: Oxford University Press, 1998).

—— 'Impartiality and Morality', typescript.

Gilbert, Margaret, *On Social Facts* (London; New York: Routledge, 1989).

—— 'Walking Together: a Paradigmatic Social Phenomenon', *Midwest Studies in Philosophy* 15 (1990), pp. 1–14.

—— *Living Together: Rationality, Sociality, and Obligation* (Lanham, MD: Rowman and Littlefield, 1996).

—— *Sociality and Responsibility: New Essays in Plural Subject Theory* (Lanham, MD: Rowman and Littlefield, 2000).

Giles, Jim, 'Maths Predict Chances of Divorce', *Nature@nature.com*, 14 February 2004. http://www.nature.com/news/2004/040209/pf/040209–18_pf.html

Gilligan, Carol, *In a Different Voice* (Cambridge, MA: Harvard University Press, 1982).

Gladwell, Malcolm, *Blink* (New York: Little, Brown, and Co., 2005).

Glasgow, Josh, 'Racism as Disrespect', unpublished.

Godwin, William, *Things As They Are; or The Adventures of Caleb Williams* [1794], ed. Maurice Hindle (London: Penguin Books, 1988).

—— *Enquiry Concerning Political Justice and its Influence on Modern Morals and Happiness* [1798], 3rd edn, ed. I. Kramnick (London: Penguin, 1985).

—— *Thoughts Occasioned by a Perusal of Dr Parr's Spital Sermon* [1801] (London: G. G. and J. Robinson, 1801).

Goldsmith, Oliver, *The Vicar of Wakefield* [1766], ed. Arthur Friedman and Robert L. Mack (Oxford: Oxford University Press, 2006).

Gomberg, Paul, 'Patriotism is Like Racism', *Ethics* 101 (1990), pp. 144–50.

Gottman, John, *et al.*, *The Mathematics of Marriage: Dynamic Nonlinear Models* (Cambridge, MA: MIT Press, 2002).

Hardin, Russell, *Indeterminacy and Society* (Princeton, NJ: Princeton University Press, 2003).

Heidegger, Martin, *Being and Time* [*Sein und Zeit*, 1927], trans. J. Macquarrie and E. Robinson (New York: Harper and Row, 1962).

Herman, Barbara, 'Integrity and Impartiality', *The Monist* 66 (1983), pp. 233–50.

Hobbes, Thomas, *Leviathan* [1660], ed. Michael Oakeshott (Oxford: Basil Blackwell, 1948).

Hooker, Brad, *Ideal Code, Real World: A Rule-consequentialist Theory of Morality* (Oxford: Oxford University Press, 2000).

—— 'Up and Down with Aggregation', *Social Philosophy and Policy* 26 (2009), pp. 126–47.

Hooker, Bishop Richard, *The Lawes of Ecclesiastical Politie* [1593], ed. Arthur Stephen McGrade as *The Laws of Ecclesiastical Polity, Preface, Bk. 1 & Bk. 7* (Cambridge: Cambridge University Press, 1989).

Hughes, Gerald J., *Aristotle on Ethics* (New York: Routledge, 2001).

Hume, David, *A Treatise of Human Nature* [1739–40], ed. David Fate Norton and Mary J. Norton (Oxford: Oxford University Press, 2000).

—— *Enquiries concerning Human Understanding and the Principles of Morals* [1751], ed. L. A. Selby-Bigge, with revisions by P. H. Nidditch (Oxford: Oxford University Press, 1975).

Hurka, Thomas, 'The Justification of National Partiality', in Robert McKim and Jeff McMahan, *The Morality of Nationalism* (Oxford: Oxford University Press, 1997), pp. 139–57.

—— *Virtue, Vice, and Value* (Oxford: Oxford University Press, 2001).

Hurley, Susan, 'Fairness and Beneficence', *Ethics* 113 (2003), pp. 841–64.

Hutcheson, Francis, *An Inquiry into the Original of Our Ideas of Beauty and Virtue*, 4th edn [1737] (London: Elibron Classics, Adamant Media, 2005).

Jeske, Diane, 'Friendship, Virtue, and Impartiality', *Philosophy and Phenomenological Research* LVII (1997), pp. 51–72.

John Paul II (Wojtyla, Karol), *Rise, Let Us Be On Our Way* [*Wstancie, Chodzmy!*] (London: Cape, 2004).

Jollimore, Troy, 'Friendship Without Partiality?' *Ratio* 13 (2000), pp. 69–82.

Kagan, Shelly, *The Limits of Morality* (New York: Oxford University Press, 1989).

Kant, Immanuel, *Kant's gesammelte Schriften*, Akademie edition (Berlin: Reimer/De Gruyter, 1900–).

—— *Foundations of the Metaphysics of Morals* [*Grundlegung zur Metaphysik der Sitten*, 1785] ed. and trans. Lewis White Beck (Indianapolis, IN: Bobbs-Merrill, 1959).

—— *Metaphysics of Morals* [1797], in Kant, *Practical Philosophy*, trans. and ed. Mary J. Gregor, intro. by Allen Wood (Cambridge: Cambridge University Press, 1996).

—— *The Critique of Practical Reason* [1788], in *Practical Philosophy*, ed. and trans. Mary Gregor (Cambridge, MA: Cambridge University Press, 1998).

Kavka, Gregory, 'Some Paradoxes of Deterrence', *The Journal of Philosophy* 75 (1978), pp. 285–302.

Kekes, John, 'Morality and Impartiality', *American Philosophical Quarterly* 18 (1981), pp. 295–303.

Keller, Simon, 'Welfare and the Achievement of Goals', *Philosophical Studies* 121 (2004), pp. 27–41.

—— 'Making Nonsense of Loyalty to Country', in Boudewijn de Bruin and Christopher S. Zurn (eds), *New Waves in Political Philosophy* (Basingstoke: Palgrave Macmillan, 2009), pp. 87–104.

Kennett, Jeanette and Cocking, Dean, 'Friendship and the Self', *Ethics* 108 (1998), pp. 502–27.

Kierkegaard, Søren, *Diary of the Seducer* [1843], trans. Gerd Aage Gillhoff (London: Continuum Press, 2006).

Kolodny, Niko, 'Love as Valuing a Relationship', *Philosophical Review* 112 (2003), pp. 135–89.

—— 'Which Relationships Justify Partiality? Parents and Children', *Philosophy & Public Affairs* 38 (2010), pp. 37–75.

—— 'Partiality and the Contours of the Moral', unpublished.

Korsgaard, Christine, 'The Reasons We Can Share', *Social Philosophy and Policy* 10 (1993), pp. 24–51.

—— *The Sources of Normativity* (Cambridge: Cambridge University Press, 1996).

—— 'Realism and Constructivism in Twentieth-Century Moral Philosophy', in her *The Constitution of Agency: Essays on Practical Reason and Moral Psychology* (Oxford: Oxford University Press, 2008), pp. 302–26.

Kramnick, Isaac, *William Godwin: Enquiry Concerning Political Justice* (London: Penguin, 1985).

Kundera, Milan, 'What is a Novelist?' *The New Yorker* (9 October 2006), pp. 40–5.

Kvanvig, Jonathan L., 'Divine Hiddenness: What Is the Problem?', in D. Howard-Snyder and Paul K. Moser (eds), *Divine Hiddenness: New Essays* (Cambridge: Cambridge University Press, 2002), pp. 149–63.

Lamb, Charles and Mary, *Letters of Charles and Mary Lamb, I, 1796–1820*, ed. E. V. Lucas (London: Methuen, 1904).

Locke, Don, *A Fantasy of Reason: The Life and Thought of William Godwin* (London: Routledge and Kegan Paul, 1980).

Locke, John, *Second Treatise of Government* [1690], in *Two Treatises of Government*, ed. W. S. Carpenter (London: Everyman's Library, 1924).

Long, A. A. and Sedley, D. N., *The Hellenistic Philosophers* (Cambridge: Cambridge University Press, 1987).

Luce, R. Duncan and Raiffa, Howard, *Games and Decisions* (New York: Wiley, 1957).

McCabe, M. M., 'The Stoic Sage in the Original Position', typescript.

McInerny, Ralph, 'Ethics', in Norman Kretzmann and Eleonore Stump (eds), *The Cambridge Companion to Aquinas* (Cambridge: Cambridge University Press, 1993), pp. 196–216.

MacIntyre, Alasdair, 'Is Patriotism a Virtue?', *Lindley Lecture* (University of Kansas, 1984).

McLennen, Edward F., *Rationality and Dynamic Choice* (Cambridge: Cambridge University Press, 1990).

McNamara, Robert, *Annual Meeting of the World Bank, IFC/IDA* (1976).

—— *World Development Report* (Washington, DC: World Bank, 1978).

Marshal, Peter H., *William Godwin* (London: Yale University Press, 1984).

Mead, G. H., *Works of George Herbert Mead* (Chicago, IL: University of Chicago Press, 1934).

Mencius, *Mencius*, trans. D. C. Lau (London: Penguin Classics, 1970).

Mill, John Stuart, *On Liberty* [1859], in *The Collected Works of John Stuart Mill*, series ed. J. M. Robson (Toronto: University of Toronto Press, 1977).

—— *Utilitarianism* [1861], in Mary Warnock (ed.), *Utilitarianism* (London: Fontana Press, 1962).

—— *Collected Works*, series ed. John M. Robson, 33 vols (London: Routledge, 1963–91).

Miller, David, *Principles of Social Justice* (Cambridge, MA: Harvard University Press, 1999).

Moore, G. E., *Principia Ethica* (Cambridge: Cambridge University Press, 1903).

Mulgan, Tim, 'How Should Impartialists Think about God?', typescript.

Murdoch, Iris, *The Sovereignty of Good* (London: Routledge & Kegan Paul, 1970).

—— 'The Sublime and the Good', in *Existentialists and Mystics*, ed. Peter Conrad (New York: Penguin Books, 1999), pp. 205–20.

Murphy, Liam, *Moral Demands in Nonideal Theory* (New York: Oxford University Press, 2000).

Nagel, Thomas, 'War and Massacre', *Philosophy & Public Affairs* 1(2) (Winter 1972), pp. 123–44; reprinted in *Consequentialism and Its Critics*, ed. Samuel Scheffler (Oxford University Press, 1988), pp. 51–73.

—— *The Possibility of Altruism* (Princeton, NJ: Princeton University Press, 1978).

—— *The View from Nowhere* (New York: Oxford University Press, 1986).

—— *Equality and Partiality* (Oxford: Oxford University Press, 1991).

Nehamas, Alexander, *The Art of Living: Socratic Reflections from Plato to Foucault* (Berkeley, CA: University of California Press, 1998).

Nicole, Pierre, *De la charité et de l'amour propre* [1675] (excerpted in J. B. Schneewind (ed.), *Moral Philosophy from Montaigne to Kant* (Cambridge: Cambridge University Press, 1990), Vol. II, pp. 370ff.).

Nietzsche, Friedrich, *Beyond Good and Evil* [*Jenseits von Gut und Böse*, 1886], trans. W. Kaufmann (New York: Random House, 1966).

Noddings, Nel, *Caring: A Feminine Approach to Ethics and Moral Education* (Berkeley, CA: University of California Press, 1984).

Nozick, Robert, *Anarchy, State, and Utopia* (New York: Basic Books, 1974).

Oldenquist, Andrew, 'Loyalties', *Journal of Philosophy* 79 (1982), pp. 173–93.

Parfit, Derek, *Reasons and Persons* (Oxford: Oxford University Press, 1984; repr. 1987).

—— 'Equality or Priority?', *Lindley Lecture* (University of Kansas, 1991).

—— 'Equality and Priority', *Ratio* 10 (1997), pp. 202–21.

—— *On What Matters* (Oxford: Oxford University Press, forthcoming).

Pascal, Blaise, *Pensées* [1670], ed. L. Lafuma (Paris: Seuil, 1962).

Philp, Mark, 'William Godwin' [2009], *Stanford Encyclopaedia of Philosophy*, http://plato.stanford.edu/.

Plato, *Apology* [360 bc], trans. Hugh Tredennick, in Edith Hamilton and Huntington Cairns (eds), *The Collected Dialogues of Plato* (Princeton, NJ: Princeton University Press, 1963).

——— *Crito* [360 bc], trans. Hugh Tredennick, in Edith Hamilton and Huntington Cairns (eds), *The Collected Dialogues of Plato* (Princeton, NJ: Princeton University Press, 1963).

——— *Protagoras* [380 bc]; in *Protagoras and Meno*, trans. W. K. C. Guthrie (Harmondsworth, Middlesex: Penguin Classics, 1956).

——— *Republic* [375 bc], trans. Desmond Lee (London: Penguin, 1987).

Postema, Gerald, 'Morality in the First Person Plural', *Law and Philosophy* 14 (1995), pp. 35–64.

Pritchard, H. A., 'Does Moral Philosophy Rest on a Mistake?', in his *Moral Obligation* (Oxford: Oxford University Press, 1949).

Protagoras, *Die Fragmente der Vorsokratiker*, ed. H. A. Diels, rev. Walther Kranz (Berlin, 1952).

Raiffa, Howard and Luce, R. Duncan, *Games and Decisions* (New York: Wiley, 1957).

Railton, Peter, 'Alienation, Consequentialism, and the Demands of Morality', *Philosophy and Public Affairs* 13 (1984), pp. 134–71.

Raphael, D. D., *The Impartial Spectator: Adam Smith's Moral Philosophy* (Oxford: Oxford University Press, 2007).

Rawls, John, 'Justice as Fairness' [1958], in Samuel Freeman (ed.), *John Rawls: Collected Papers* (Cambridge, MA: Harvard University Press, 1999), pp. 47–72.

——— 'Distributive Justice' [1967], in Samuel Freeman (ed.), *John Rawls: Collected Papers* (Cambridge, MA. Harvard University Press, 1999), pp. 130–53.

——— *A Theory of Justice* (Cambridge, MA: Harvard University Press, 1971; rev. edn 1999).

——— 'Kantian Constructivism in Moral Theory', *Journal of Philosophy* 77 (1980), pp. 515–72.

——— *Political Liberalism*, paperback edn (New York: Columbia University Press, 1996).

Raz, Joseph, *The Morality of Freedom* (Oxford: Oxford University Press, 1986).

——— *Value, Respect, and Attachment* (Cambridge: Cambridge University Press, 2001).

——— 'The Myth of Instrumental Rationality', *Journal of Ethics and Social Philosophy* 1 (2005), pp. 2–28.

——— 'Darwall on Rational Care', *Utilitas* 18 (2006), pp. 400–14.

Reiman, Jeffrey, *Justice and Modern Moral Philosophy* (New Haven, CT: Yale University Press, 1990).

Rhonheimer, Martin, 'Sins Against Justice (IIa IIae, qq. 59–78)', trans. Frederick G. Lawrence, in Stephen J. Pope (ed.), *The Ethics of Aquinas* (Georgetown, Washington, DC: Georgetown University Press, 2002), pp. 287–303.

Rokeach, Milton, *The Nature of Human Values* (New York: The Free Press, 1973).

——— 'From Individual to Institutional Values,' in his *Understanding Values* (London: Collier Macmillan, 1979), pp. 47–70.

Ross, W. D., *The Right and the Good* (Oxford: Oxford University Press, 1930).

Savage, L. J., 'The Theory of Statistical Decision', *Journal of the American Statistical Association*, 46 (March 1951), pp. 55–67.

Scanlon, T. M., *What We Owe to Each Other* (Cambridge MA: Belknap Press of the Harvard University Press, 1998).

—— *Moral Dimensions: Permissibility, Meaning, Blame* (Cambridge, MA: Harvard University Press, 2008).

Scheffler, Samuel, *The Rejection of Consequentialism* (Oxford: Oxford University Press, 1982).

—— 'Relationships and Responsibilities', *Philosophy & Public Affairs* 26 (1997), pp. 189–209, reprinted in his *Boundaries and Allegiances* (Oxford: Oxford University Press, 2001), pp. 97–110.

—— 'Conceptions of Cosmopolitanism', *Utilitas* 11 (1999), pp. 255–76, reprinted in his *Boundaries and Allegiances*, pp. 111–30.

—— *Boundaries and Allegiances* (Oxford: Oxford University Press, 2001).

—— 'Projects, Relationships, and Reasons', in *Reason and Value: Themes from the Moral Philosophy of Joseph Raz*, ed. R. Jay Wallace, Philip Pettit, Samuel Scheffler, and Michael Smith (Oxford: Oxford University Press, 2004), pp. 247–69.

—— *Equality and Tradition* (New York: Oxford University Press, 2010).

Schellenberg, J. L., *Divine Hiddenness and Human Reason* (Ithaca, NY: Cornell University Press, 1993).

Schneewind, J. B. (ed.), *Moral Philosophy from Montaigne to Kant* (Cambridge: Cambridge University Press, 2003).

Second Vatican Council, *Gaudium et spes* [1965], Second Vatican Council Document.

Sedley, D. N. and Long, A. A., *The Hellenistic Philosophers* (Cambridge: Cambridge University Press, 1987).

Sen, Amartya, 'Equality of What?', *The Tanner Lectures on Human Values* 1 (Cambridge: Cambridge University Press 1980), pp. 353–69.

Shafer-Landau, Russ, *Moral Realism* (Oxford: Oxford University Press, 2003).

Shelby, Tommie, 'Is Racism in the "Heart"?' *Journal of Social Philosophy* 33 (2002), pp. 411–20.

—— 'Ideology, Racism, and Critical Social Theory', *The Philosophical Forum* 34 (2003), pp. 153–88.

—— *We Who Are Dark: Philosophical Foundations of Black Solidarity* (Cambridge: Harvard University Press, 2005).

Sidgwick, Henry, *The Methods of Ethics*, 7th edn [1907] (Chicago, IL: University of Chicago Press, 1962).

Singer, Peter, 'Famine, Affluence and Morality', *Philosophy & Public Affairs* 1 (Spring 1972), pp. 229–43.

—— *Practical Ethics* (Cambridge: Cambridge University Press, 1979).

Skyrms, Brian, *Evolution of the Social Contract* (Cambridge: Cambridge University Press, 1996).

—— and Vanderschraaf, Peter, 'Learning to Take Turns,' *Erkenntis* 59 (2003), pp. 311–46.

Smart, J. J. C. and Williams, Bernard, *Utilitarianism: For and Against* (Cambridge: Cambridge University Press, 1973).

Smith, Adam, *The Theory of Moral Sentiments*, 6th edn [1790], ed. D. D. Raphael and A. L. MacFie (Oxford: Oxford University Press, 1976).

—— *The Theory of Moral Sentiments* [1759], ed. D. D. Raphael and A. L. MacFie (Indianapolis, IN: Liberty Classics, 1982).

Stoppard, Tom, *Rosencrantz and Guildenstern are Dead* (London: Faber & Faber, 1967).

Strawson, P. F., 'Social Morality and Individual Ideal', *Philosophy* 36 (January 1961), pp. 1–17.

—— 'Freedom and Resentment', in *Studies in the Philosophy of Thought and Action* (London: Oxford University Press, 1968).

Stroud, Sarah, 'Epistemic Partiality in Friendship'. *Ethics* 116 (2006), pp. 498–524.

—— 'La partialité par les projets', *Les ateliers de l'éthique* 3 (2008), pp. 41–51.

Thompson, Michael, 'What is it to Wrong Somebody? A Puzzle about Justice', in *Reason and Value: Themes from the Moral Philosophy of Joseph Raz*, ed. R. J. Wallace, Philip Pettit, Samuel Scheffler, and Michael Smith (Oxford: Oxford University Press, 2006), pp. 333–84.

Unger, Peter, *Living High and Letting Die: Our Illusion of Innocence* (New York: Oxford University Press, 1996).

Vanderschraaf, Peter and Skyrms, Brian, 'Learning to Take Turns,' *Erkenntis* 59 (2003), pp. 311–46.

Vega-Rodondo, Fernando, *Economics and the Theory of Games* (Cambridge: Cambridge University Press, 2003).

Velleman, David, 'Love as a Moral Emotion', *Ethics* 109 (1999), pp. 338–74.

Vogt, Katja, 'Freundschaft, Unparteilichkeit und Feindschaft', *Deutsche Zeitschrift für Philosophie* 40 (2001), pp. 517–32.

Wallace, R. Jay, *Responsibility and the Moral Sentiments* (Cambridge, MA: Harvard University Press, 1994).

—— 'The Deontic Structure of Morality', unpublished draft, 3 December 2005.

Watson, Gary, 'Responsibility and the Limits of Evil: Variations on a Strawsonian Theme', in *Responsibility, Character, and the Emotions: New Essays in Moral Psychology*, ed. F. D. Schoeman (Cambridge: Cambridge University Press, 1987), pp. 256–86.

Wellman, Christopher Heath, 'Relational Facts in Liberal Political Theory: Is There Magic in the Pronoun "My"?' *Ethics* 110 (2000), pp. 537–62.

Wiggins, David, 'Truth, Invention, and the Meaning of Life', in *Needs, Values, Truth, Second Edition* (Oxford: Blackwell, 1991), pp. 87–137.

Wilde, Oscar, *The Happy Prince and Other Stories* [1888] (London: Penguin Classics, 2007).

Williams, Andrew and Clayton, Matthew (eds), *The Ideal of Equality* (New York: Macmillan, 2000).

Williams, Bernard, 'Persons, Character, and Morality', in Amelie Rorty (ed.), *The Identities of Persons* (Berkeley, CA: University of California Press, 1976), pp. 197–216;

also in Williams, *Moral Luck* (Cambridge: Cambridge University Press, 1981), pp. 1–19.

Williams, Bernard, 'Internal and External Reasons', in Ross Harrison (ed.), *Rational Action* (Cambridge: Cambridge University Press, 1980), pp. 17–28; reprinted in Williams, *Moral Luck* (Cambridge: Cambridge University Press, 1981), pp. 101–13.

—— *Moral Luck* (Cambridge: Cambridge University Press, 1981).

—— *Ethics and the Limits of Philosophy* (London: Fontana Press, 1985).

—— 'The Human Prejudice', in his *Philosophy as a Humanistic Discipline*, ed. A.W. Moore (Princeton, NJ: Princeton University Press, 2006), ch. 16.

Williams, Bernard and Smart, J. J. C., *Utilitarianism For and Against* (Cambridge: Cambridge University Press, 1973).

Wojtyla, Karol (John Paul II), *Rise, Let Us Be On Our Way* [*Wstancie, Chodzmy!*] (London: Cape, 2004).

Wolff, Robert Paul, *Understanding Rawls* (Princeton, NJ: Princeton University Press, 1977).

Wolf, Susan, 'Morality and Partiality', *Philosophical Perspectives* 6 (1992), pp. 243–59.

Yack, Bernard, *The Problems of a Political Animal—Community, Justice, and Conflict in Aristotelian Political Thought* (Berkeley, CA: University of California Press, 1993).

Zangwill, Nick, 'Against Analytic Moral Functionalism', *Ratio* 13 (2000), pp. 275–86.

Index

DISCARDED
CONCORDIA UNIV. LIBRARY

CONCORDIA UNIVERSITY LIBRARIES
MONTREAL